ISBN 978-1-5283-3668-0
PIBN 10914663

1 MONTH OF
FREE
READING

at
www.ForgottenBooks.com

By purchasing this book you are eligible for one month membership to ForgottenBooks.com, giving you unlimited access to our entire collection of over 1,000,000 titles via our web site and mobile apps.

To claim your free month visit:
www.forgottenbooks.com/free914663

English
Français
Deutsche
Italiano
Español
Português

www.forgottenbooks.com

Mythology Photography **Fiction**
Fishing Christianity **Art** Cooking
Essays Buddhism Freemasonry
Medicine **Biology** Music **Ancient**
Egypt Evolution Carpentry Physics
Dance Geology **Mathematics** Fitness
Shakespeare **Folklore** Yoga Marketing
Confidence Immortality Biographies
Poetry **Psychology** Witchcraft
Electronics Chemistry History **Law**
Accounting **Philosophy** Anthropology
Alchemy Drama Quantum Mechanics
Atheism Sexual Health **Ancient History**
Entrepreneurship Languages Sport
Paleontology Needlework Islam
Metaphysics Investment Archaeology
Parenting Statistics Criminology
Motivational

CORRECTIONAL AND PENAL TREATMENT

BY BURDETTE G. LEWIS

PART IV
OF THE CLEVELAND FOUNDATION SURVEY OF
CRIMINAL JUSTICE IN CLEVELAND

CORRECTIONAL AND PENAL
TREATMENT

THE CLEVELAND FOUNDATION

1202 Swetland Building, Cleveland, Ohio

COMMITTEE

J. D. Williamson, Chairman
Thomas G. Fitzsimons
Malcolm L. McBride
W. H. Prescott
Belle Sherwin

Leonard P. Ayres, Secretary
James R. Garfield, Counsel

———

Raymond Moley, Director

———

THE SURVEY OF CRIMINAL JUSTICE

Roscoe Pound
Felix Frankfurter } Directors

Amos Burt Thompson, Chairman of the
Advisory Committee

CORRECTIONAL AND PENAL TREATMENT

BY

BURDETTE G. LEWIS

STATE COMMISSIONER OF INSTITUTIONS AND AGENCIES IN NEW JERSEY

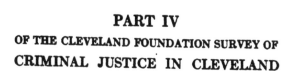

PART IV

OF THE CLEVELAND FOUNDATION SURVEY OF

CRIMINAL JUSTICE IN CLEVELAND

Copyright, 1921, by
The Cleveland Foundation

FOREWORD

THIS is one of eight sections of the report of the Cleveland Foundation Survey of Criminal Justice in Cleveland. The survey was directed and the reports edited by Roscoe Pound and Felix Frankfurter. Sections which have been published are:

The Criminal Courts, by Reginald Heber Smith and Herbert B. Ehrmann
Prosecution, by Alfred Bettman
Police Administration, by Raymond B. Fosdick

Other sections to be published are:

Medical Science and Criminal Justice, by Dr. Herman M. Adler
Newspapers and Criminal Justice, by M. K. Wisehart
Legal Education in Cleveland, by Albert M. Kales
Criminal Justice in the American City, a Summary, by Roscoe Pound

The sections are being published first in separate form, each bound in paper. About November 10 the report will be available in a single volume, cloth bound. Orders for separate sections or the bound volume may be left with book-stores or with the Cleveland Foundation, 1202 Swetland Building.

Copyright, 1921, by
The Cleveland Foundation

FOREWORD

THIS is one of eight sections of the report of the Cleveland Foundation Survey of Criminal Justice in Cleveland. The survey was directed and the reports edited by Roscoe Pound and Felix Frankfurter. Sections which have been published are:

The Criminal Courts, by Reginald Heber Smith and Herbert B. Ehrmann
Prosecution, by Alfred Bettman
Police Administration, by Raymond B. Fosdick

Other sections to be published are:

Medical Science and Criminal Justice, by Dr. Herman M. Adler
Newspapers and Criminal Justice, by M. K. Wisehart
Legal Education in Cleveland, by Albert M. Kales
Criminal Justice in the American City, a Summary, by Roscoe Pound

The sections are being published first in separate form, each bound in paper. About November 10 the report will be available in a single volume, cloth bound. Orders for separate sections or the bound volume may be left with book-stores or with the Cleveland Foundation, 1202 Swetland Building.

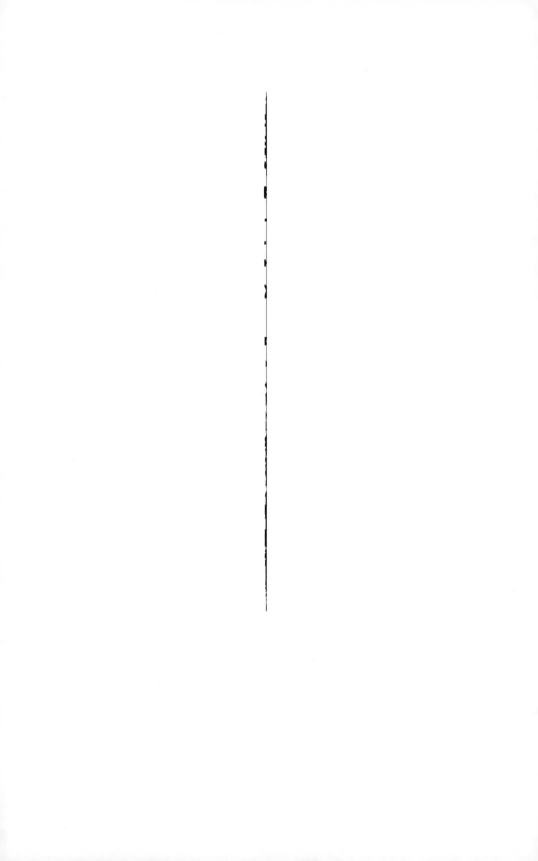

PREFATORY NOTE

THIS branch of the survey was made with the assistance of Calvin Derrick, superintendent of the State Home for Boys, at Jamesburg, New Jersey, and of Dr. Edgar A. Doll, psychologist and chief of the Division of Education and Classification of the State Department of Institutions and Agencies of New Jersey. The detailed studies of the Juvenile Court, the probation system, the Warrensville Workhouse, the Boys' Farm, and the Girls' School, were made by Mr. Derrick in accordance with a plan outlined by the chief of the division, after personal visits to these institutions, to the city infirmary, the tuberculosis sanatorium, county and city jails, the city hospital, the Cleveland State Hospital for the Insane, the Lakeside Hospital, the offices of the State Board of Administration at Columbus, and after conferences with Governor Harry L. Davis, members of the State Board of Administration, and well-known social workers and government officials in Cleveland. Dr. Doll conferred with the various school officials, juvenile court officials, educational officials of the city, and with the director of the Bureau of Juvenile Research at Columbus, to arrange a plan of coöperation between these agencies. I am deeply indebted to these gentlemen for their assistance.

Through the courtesy of the architect an opportunity was afforded to see the final plans for the city hospital and the city psychopathic hospital, and to discuss their details at length. It has also been possible to study the detailed plans for the proposed new court-house, county building, and county jail, and to have access to primary sources of information which have aided materially in the study of this proposed new building.

I wish also to thank Dudley S. Blossom, Director of Public Welfare, Charles B. Ryan, of the Bureau of Municipal Research, C. E. Gehlke, and Miss Helen Chew, of the Cleveland Foundation, for the valuable assistance they have rendered. I wish to acknowledge my indebtedness to Miss Agnes L. Mulrey, my secretary, and Miss Anna M. Culliton, of my staff.

Four public institutions in Cleveland typify four different ideas of the way offenders and unfortunates should be treated. These are:

1. The City Jail.
2. The Warrensville Workhouse.
3. The Boys' Farm at Hudson.
4. The Tuberculosis Sanatorium.

Notwithstanding the fact that the city and the county jails, which are of about the same type, are old, and the other institutions enumerated are comparatively new, these two and each of the others are significant as typifying the respective points of view of large groups of people rather than as examples of prevailing views at the time they were erected. The old city and county jails are satisfactory to those who look upon offenders as "the scum of the earth." Such places are tolerated by others who are in doubt as to where to draw the line and who are willing to condemn brutality, but feel, nevertheless, that the way to purify the soul is to mortify the flesh. Added to these is the army of citizens who take no interest in the offender unless they are aroused to action temporarily by scandal or a brutal murder. Only then do they demand reforms, sometimes in the direction of leniency and sometimes of severity.

The Warrensville Workhouse, marking a revolution in the treatment of the offender in Cleveland, is a product of an aroused public whose conscience revolted when its imagination pictured for a time the injustice and sheer futility of the jails in the city. In breaking away from the old system Cleveland was regarded justly as a pioneer. Visitors came from all over this country, and even from abroad, to see the great 2,000-acre Warrensville estate and to study its beautiful institutional buildings.

It is now evident that this revolution ran true to form and exhausted itself in demarking broad general boundary lines and in combat on behalf of principles of treatment, then bitterly fought over, but now accepted in welfare fields generally as ordinary and essential. Like all revolutions, this one ignored fundamental details.

The director of the institutions at that time, the leader in the movement, was, like all pioneers, a dreamer. He demanded that the outside of the House of Correction should be beautiful and that the interior should be bright, cheerful, and sanitary. In securing these results he depended upon the architect, who, like many of the architects of that day, was a picture-maker. He produced a beautiful exterior, but in order to do so adopted a design for the building, a lay-out for the interior and provision for equipment, which seriously interferes with modern administration of the institution. If the buildings were remodeled, its administration could be vastly improved, but the fundamental errors in design cannot be overcome.

This revolution, before it ran its course, produced not only this institution, but also a new charter of city government, a fundamental reorganization upon paper. Unfortunately, however, it burned itself out before it got down to the brass tacks of administration, so that Cleveland departments of government today are paper federations, not strong cohesive administrative organizations.

The Boys' Farm belongs to the thrifty period of the city's development, and is an example of what care and prudence may do. It is expressive of the points of view that the spirit is everything and that the flesh amounts to little or nothing; that Mark Hopkins on one end of a log and a boy on the other make a public school. There is a touch of the Germanic in the plain buildings, which are always spotlessly clean, in the reclamation and fullest use of materials, and in the concentration upon individual care and treatment of the boys. The school is primitive in many respects, its equipment is most meager, but taken all in all it is an inspiration, a promise of American life.

The Tuberculosis Sanatorium typifies the modern spirit in its broad characteristics and in every department. It represents a perfect union of the beautiful with the practical down to the smallest detail. This splendid institution was also a product of the revolution which produced the Workhouse and the City Infirmary, but physicians, social workers, and administrators filled in the details of the picture in the spirit of modern realism.

It is this spirit which must permeate the courts, the public institutions, the private welfare agencies, and the homes if the people of Cleveland are to achieve lasting results in the administration of justice. Beauty, spirit, and perfection of detail must be brought into harmony with bold, forceful action, guided by that triad of modern progress, common sense, scientific understanding, and effective sympathy.

BURDETTE G. LEWIS

TABLE OF CONTENTS

LIST OF TABLES

LIST OF DIAGRAMS

LIST OF ILLUSTRATIONS

CORRECTIONAL AND PENAL TREATMENT

CHAPTER I

PENAL INSTITUTIONS FOR ADULTS

THE DEPARTMENT OF PUBLIC WELFARE

THE Department of Public Welfare of the city of Cleveland is divided for administrative purposes into four subdepartments—the Division of Health, the Division of Charities and Correction, the Division of Employment, and the City Immigration Bureau. In the Division of Health are the following bureaus, each under the control of a chief: Communicable diseases, child hygiene, public nurses, food and drug inspection, chief chemist, and laboratories and sanitation. The last has two persons in charge. In the Division of Charities and Correction are the following agencies: Bureau of Outdoor Relief, city hospital, tuberculosis sanatorium, city infirmary, workhouse, parole office, the boys' home, and the girls' home.

The charter provisions give the Director of Public Welfare wide powers. They read in part as follows:

"The Director of Public Welfare shall manage and control all charitable, correctional, and reformatory institutions and agencies belonging to the city; the use of all recreational facilities of the city, including parks, playgrounds, public gymnasium, public bath houses, bathing beaches, and social centers.[1] He shall have charge of the inspection and supervision of all public amusements and entertainments. He shall enforce all laws, ordinances, and regulations relative to the preservation and promotion of the public health, the prevention and restriction of disease, the prevention, abatement, and suppression of nuisances, and the sanitary inspection and supervision of the production, transportation, storage, and sale of foods and food-stuffs. He shall cause a complete and accurate system of vital statistics to be kept. In time of epidemic he may enforce such quarantine and isolation regulations as are appropriate to the emergency. He shall have the supervision of the free employment office. The Commissioner of Charities and Correction shall be the deputy officer of public welfare.

---

[1] The director's power to supervise parks, etc., has been withdrawn.

"The Commissioner of the Division of Health shall be the health officer of the city and shall, under the direction and control of the Director of Public Welfare, enforce all ordinances and laws relating to health, and shall perform all duties and have all the powers provided by general law relative to the public health, to be exercised in municipalities by health officers; provided that regulations affecting the public health, additional to those established by general law for the violation of which penalties are imposed, shall be enacted by the council and enforced as provided herein.

"The Commissioner of the Division of Employment shall have charge of the free employment office established to assist persons in securing employment. He shall extend such information and assistance to immigrants and strangers and perform such duties in the collection of labor statistics and information relative to labor conditions in the city as may be required by ordinance."

A study of the organization and work of the present director's office shows clearly that there has never been developed any machinery or plan of work which would permit the director to exercise adequate control over the various divisions. The department is, in fact, an example of the failure of statutory enactment alone to effect a considerable change. It is a paper federation of bureaus, divisions, departments, and institutions without administrative cohesion.

The sincerity and good purpose of the director of the department are unquestioned. He has never stood in the way of any good work; he has accepted cheerfully aid given him. The new city hospital and the new psychopathic hospital now under construction in his department show clearly the director's desire to carry out the recommendations of the Hospital and Health Survey. The changes he has directed to be made at Warrensville City Infirmary are indicative of the same desire.

Within the Division of Charities and Correction the director exercises some control over the workhouse because of his active interest in the parole of prisoners. He has changed the officers and appointed an administrative board, besides making certain structural changes in the girls' home. But his supervision over the city infirmary, the Bureau of Outdoor Relief, and the boys' home is limited to occasional visits and to haphazard consideration of their work. Moreover, his appointment of advisory boards for the girls' home, for the city hospital, and for the employment bureau has had little significance, because he has never followed up their work. The boards were never given specific tasks and no effort has been made to keep up their interest. He has apparently even left the chiefs of divisions and superintendents free either to accept or to reject his suggestions, as suited their fancy.

We do not mean to make excuses for the director's failure to meet his major opportunities, but it would be unjust to let him appear as a "scape-goat" for the perfectly apparent indifference of a whole city and the impotence of so many of the heads of welfare agencies and societies. Moreover, the people have been willing to accept the high civic standing of the director as a substitute for adequate appropriations and a real welfare program for the city.

Recommendations

1. The people of Cleveland should be made to realize that the Department of Public Welfare, combining, as it does, a Health Department with a Division of Charities and Correction, offers an unusual opportunity to demonstrate a great economy in municipal service under the supervision of a single director.

2. The Director of Public Welfare should exercise direct control over all the work of the department in such a manner that general policies are formulated under his supervision, and every employee of the department feels responsible to him.

3. The director should have an assistant, or deputy director, who should, in accordance with the charter, supervise the correctional institutions.

4. The director should have the kind of secretary who can supervise and coördinate the work of the institutions with the employment bureau, the Bureau of Outdoor Relief, and the parole department.

5. The director should see to it that the health commissioner coöperates under the director's supervision with other divisions, institutions, and public schools of the city, with the other hospitals in the city, with the Western Reserve University Medical School, and with all the social agencies upon a well-thought-out public welfare and health program for the city, which would make the institutions diagnostic, treatment, and preventive health centers.

THE CITY JAIL AND CENTRAL POLICE HEADQUARTERS

The city jail occupies the same building as police headquarters, Rooms 1 and 2 of the Municipal Court, and the offices of the adult probation officers. The jail is under the general jurisdiction of the Division of Police. The entire municipal building is in a dilapidated and uncared-for condition. Obviously, the jail has been allowed to suffer more than other parts of the building. It is a dark, dingy place. This is on account of the type of construction by which the limited amount of light from the outside finds entrance only on two sides of the building. The dingy appearance is accentuated by rusty iron work, filthy old iron toilets, and dirty, blackened walls. Rats and vermin live on easy terms with the inmates of the jail. We were assured by officers in charge that a continual campaign is waged unsuccessfully against vermin, but when one considers the method used in the fight, one must conclude that its endlessness is inevitable.

The jail is almost entirely devoid of equipment or furnishings, except those supplied when the building was built. Each cell contains an iron toilet and a plank, 20 inches wide, extending the length of the cell, which is used for a bed. Not even a blanket is furnished the prisoners. The stock of dishes used for feeding the prisoners consists entirely of cups.

On the second floor is a small room, about 8 by 12 by 14 feet, that has been set aside as a "hospital" "in case one of the girls gets sick." This "hospital ward" is outfitted with a single bed and a small wash-stand. There is no toilet or running water or other convenience.

Near the hospital room is the "bull pen"—a bare room, about 10 by 15 feet, adjacent to the municipal court-rooms, where prisoners are detained awaiting their turn before the judge. It is often necessary to put from 30 to 50 men in this room, and at one time 80 persons were crowded into it.

The population of the jail on Sunday, May 1, consisted of seven women and about 50 men. These were found segregated into three groups. All of the women were placed together in one ward, on the sides of which were cells opening either on the ward or on an open space. None of these cells had doors. The prisoners ranged in age from twenty to thirty. In one ward on the first floor there were 11 men, and in another ward on the second floor about 30. There appeared to be no grading or segregation except according to sex and except as the cases had or had not been disposed of by the court.

The city jail is used for the detention of prisoners charged with violations of ordinances and other minor offenses. The period of detention varies from ten or twelve hours to three or four days. The longer stay happens only in cases where the municipal judge, at the hearing, "continues" the case. If a prisoner is bound over for the grand jury, he is transferred at once to the county jail.

The prisoners are served no food at public expense during the first twenty-four hours of their commitment. If they have funds of their own, they may purchase food at a nearby restaurant. After twenty-four hours the city furnishes a sandwich and a cup of coffee, morning and evening. Prisoners are allowed to use the public telephone to communicate with friends, family, or counsel for the arrangement of bail or for other matters pertaining to their cases. There are no facilities in the jail except a lavatory in the corridor.

[4]

Talking with some of the prisoners brought out stories, afterward checked up, of the careless and indifferent manner in which prisoners are handled in this wretched place. Two extreme cases are presented here, not because they are typical of the way prisoners are treated, but in order to show what may happen under the present system.

A man arrested by the Cleveland police on May 12 at 5.45 P. M., near Euclid Beach, was taken to the central police station and held for investigation under no court charge. He was released May 19 at 6.30 P. M. He claims he was never booked on any charge, but was told he was suspected of having committed murders and other crimes in Detroit and Boston. Detroit, Boston, and Toledo detectives came to Cleveland and stated they were unable to identify him as the man connected with the crimes. During the time the prisoner was at central station he was confined in the jail. Bread, salt, and water were supplied by jail officials, but the prisoner was compelled to spend his own money to buy other food. Almost all his money was spent for food and cigarettes for himself and others. The jail was very crowded, and he was forced to sleep four nights on the cement floor with nothing under him. He had no covering and no pillow. During the other nights he slept on the board bed in the cell, without mattress, covering, or pillow. He did not remove his clothing during the entire time he was in jail. He was not provided with a towel. Because of his arrest the prisoner lost a good position as chauffeur, and at the time of the investigation he was without work and money. When released he was ill and was told to see a doctor. The doctor found he had tonsillitis and bronchitis in a severe form, which the prisoner says he caught because of the manner in which he was handled at the city jail.

The prisoner's wife stated that she was arrested at home on May 12 at 10.30 P. M., and taken to central police station, where she was held for investigation until May 17 at 11.30 A. M. No charge was made against her. She was told she was held for investigation in connection with her husband, who was suspected of being connected with murders in Detroit and Boston. During the time the woman was in jail she did not remove her clothing; she had no towel and was compelled to sleep on a board bench or bed without mattress, covering, or pillow. On May 16 she was placed in the "hospital cell" on account of her weakened condition. Here she had a bed with a mattress, a covering, and a pillow. Jail officials supplied her with bread, salt, and water, but she had to send out for other food. One night the jail was so crowded she had to share her board bed with another woman.

The only record to be found in the jail proper was the jailer's docket.

This contained the name of the prisoner and the charge only. Each prisoner's name and charge are entered when the prisoner is brought in; the name is scratched off when the prisoner is released from jail. In the police office are more complete records, dealing with the facts of the complaint, the name of the officer making the arrest, and the name and address of the prisoner.

Recommendations

This structure should be abandoned, as it is wholly inadequate from every standpoint. Until then the following recommendations should be followed:

1. The interior of the jail and other parts of the building should be cleaned and kept clean.

2. Prisoners should be provided with blankets, adequate and sanitary cots, bedding, toilet, and bathing facilities.

3. Prisoners should be supplied wholesome food at the expense of the city; luxuries they should be required to purchase at their own expense, but the officer in charge should see to it that no prisoner is required to pay exorbitant prices for any food.

4. The hospital room should have complete equipment.

5. There should be more careful segregation of prisoners.

6. An adequate record system should be installed, which would permit the superior officers of the department to ascertain just how prisoners are treated.

THE WARRENSVILLE WORKHOUSE

The Correction Farm at Warrensville, where the workhouse, the city infirmary, the tuberculosis hospital, and the girls' home are situated, is about 12 miles from Cleveland. The workhouse building, a comparatively new, two-story structure, well lighted and ventilated, is in the form of a square, enclosing completely a large yard which is used by the prisoners. The institution is built on the dormitory plan, and has only a few cells on the second floor of one section of the building. Each cell accommodates a number of prisoners. The dormitories themselves are well lighted and ventilated, but the dormitory plan and the form of the structure defeat the very purpose for which such an institution is intended. The prisoners are thrown together more or less indiscriminately, except when at work, and that is seldom. This structure and the city infirmary represent the period when architects were intent on the details of picture making rather than the purposes for which a building is to be used.

In addition to the dormitories there are a small, poorly equipped hos-

[6]

pital, an excellent kitchen, splendid dining-rooms, a fairly good laundry, and shops.

The superintendent is assisted by a chief clerk, a stenographer, and about 30 officers, exclusive of night-watchmen and engineers. The inmates are used as assistants to the officers and in some cases are in charge of subdepartments. The officers are paid $60 a month, which, in view of the location of the institution, seems small.

The superintendent, C. J. Burns, is, in our opinion, wholly unfitted for the position he occupies, and if retained, should be assigned to parts of the work which do not call for so much training, experience, and personality. In our judgment it is not "in him" to be a good institutional superintendent, and he makes a mistake in trying to be one. It is no disgrace for a man not able to do one kind of work to acknowledge it and to undertake work he is well fitted to perform.

The census of the institution varies between 400 and 800; 480 is a fair average. The commitments vary between 4,000 and 6,000 a year, about 700 of whom are women. The women's section, with a capacity of 150, had a daily average population of 52 in 1919, and during the past year and a half has had a still smaller number of inmates. The inmates represent all grades of offenders, from petty short-term delinquents to prisoners charged with serious crimes, or habitual offenders charged with ordinary offenses, for which they are permitted improperly to serve in this institution. There were at the time of the investigation about 40 Federal prisoners, few of whom were charged with serious crimes. Most of them were violators of the prohibition law.

In order to determine the general characteristics of the male population, the army Alpha Group Test was applied by the surveyors to one out of every five of a considerable number of the so-called petty offenders and to a considerable group of the so-called more serious offenders. Contrary to expectations, the results of these tests showed a higher level of intelligence and adaptability than was expected. In fact, the intelligence level of the population compared more favorably with that of reformatories and prisons for so-called serious offenders than is usual in the case of workhouse inmates.

Because of the prevailing idleness and the resulting demoralization as well as the general lack of plan and purpose which characterize the management, discipline cannot be said to be good, although outward appearances might convince one of the contrary. There is no general plan under which the institution is administered. Each officer is a power unto himself. He may place a man in a punishment cell and report the matter to the superintendent, or he may take a man from a cell and report to the superintendent afterward. No written report of any kind is required, either as to the complaint against the prisoner or as to the method used in punishing him. There is no organized method of getting prisoners' complaints or officers' charges before the superintendent for consideration, nor is there any general plan of review of the disciplinary work of the institution. The fact that a man is assigned to a bed, that he is known throughout the institution by the bed he occupies, and that the officer in charge is supposed to remember the appearance of the man and to see that he gets into the right bed is sufficient commentary upon the administrative and disciplinary practices of this institution.

The superintendent assured us that he visits the punishment cells daily and talks with every man and knows everything that is going on about the institution. He stated that he was able to give the punishment record and individual history of every man. However, when asked for the punishment record and history of one Sloan, an inmate who had died, the officer who had punished Sloan a short time before had to be sent for to give from memory whatever details he could. There was no record in the office of the alleged facts related.

During one of our visits to the institution 15 or 16 men arrived under sentence and we observed the process of reception. The officer in charge handed the clerk the commitments of the group of prisoners being received in the anteroom to the bath-house. After the men had entered the room the prisoners who thought they were "lousy" were asked to step up, whereupon two negroes came forward. They were taken into the bath-house, divested of their clothing, and required to stand under the showers. Afterward new clothing was distributed to them and they were assigned to their "beds."

All underclothing of these two men was placed in a receptacle to be burned, and the outer clothing, after being superficially examined for lice, was packed away in boxes with moth-balls. The officer in charge said close watch was kept on the new men, and if lice were discovered, the men were sent to the barber-shop to have their hair clipped and "anquintin" applied. As to the presence of vermin in the dormitories, the attitude seemed to be that, although effort was made to get rid of them, their complete avoidance was considered practically impossible in such an institution. The procedure outlined covers the reception of prisoners at the workhouse, except for a rough classification which separates Federal from other prisoners and men with long from men with short sentences.

The hospital is in charge of a visiting physician, who comes to the institution daily from the city infirmary. Every man in the institution is permitted to go to the hospital whenever he wishes. It is not necessary for him to have a permit, nor is any written record kept of such visits except in the office of the hospital. An interne keeps a very good record of the men who visit the hospital and indicates the diagnoses by simply stating the complaint: for example, "John Jones, sore throat." The record does not specify the treatment nor the length of time under treatment unless the man is a bed patient; then the daily chart record is depended upon to show how long he is in bed and the other facts supposed to be recorded on the chart.

The modern and rather expensive woodworking plant is evidence that those who planned this institution failed to realize how impossible it is to employ short-term offenders in an industry such as this, which requires skill, previous training, and considerable specialized experience. The plant is idle because men cannot be found to operate it. Before prohibition, an occasional experienced cabinetmaker, furniture worker, or carpenter was sent to the institution for intoxication or petty assault, but since prohibition has come, commitments of this type have stopped.

A few men were found at work in the broom shop, which has fair equipment, but the work is carried on in an aimless, listless manner, and little is accomplished. Women have been taken out of the laundry and given ironing only, because, according to the superintendent, the Federal prisoners were found to be particularly good in the laundry, and it was considered safer to have them here than working outside the buildings. In view of the fact that laundry work is traditionally women's work, this plan seems to us a very poor one.

During our survey many men were seen pretending to be busy cleaning dormitories and making beds. The superintendent explained that in order to keep as many men as possible busy, one group of men cleaned one-half of the dormitories in the morning and rested in the afternoon, while the half which had been resting in the morning cleaned the remainder in the afternoon. It was perfectly apparent that this division of labor was not sufficient to keep the men really occupied.

Some of the men, whom the superintendent feels he can trust, are engaged about the farm and in the dairy. The general manual labor about the institutions situated on this tract is performed by the prisoners. Our visit to the horse and dairy barn showed clearly that these buildings are kept in good condition and are well supervised.

We discussed with the superintendent the possibility of more outside work for prisoners, suggesting road work. We described how Major Lewis Lawes, as superintendent of New York City Reformatory, had

[9]

taken 500 unclassified young reformatory inmates to the country, where they had lived in a cantonment-like institution and had continued to live and work there for four years, without walls, bars, locks, or guns. These young men were much more difficult to handle than Cleveland workhouse prisoners, and yet during this time there were but 40 attempts at escape a year, with a yearly average of only five successful escapes. To this account the superintendent looked at the surveyor incredulously and said nothing.

During a discussion of the treatment of drug addicts, the investigator stated that in his experience manual labor in the open air was one of the best restoratives for drug addicts. The superintendent replied that this was utterly impossible with the addicts which came to him, as they were so emaciated they would die if sent out to work. Pointing to an inmate lying in bed, upon whose face the death pallor had already stolen, the superintendent said, "Would you require this man to work with a pick and shovel?" and seemed to think that the discussion was closed.

During the three months of January, February, and March, 1920, there were 39 escapes, and in July, August, and September of the same year 58, or a total of 97 for six months of that year. That there should be so large a number of escapes from this institution in so short a time is proof enough of the inability of the superintendent to manage the institution as it should be managed.

A modern reception service should be installed, so that on arrival at the institution every inmate should go through an adequate prescribed routine. The record of his arrival should be entered in the proper record books. All clothing in every case should be removed and immediately sterilized and washed, or, if necessary, burned. After a bath and an initial physical examination, in order to discover the presence of any disease or vermin, the prisoner should be furnished a clean institutional uniform, including under and outer clothing, stockings, and shoes. His finger-print identification record should then be taken and filed. The man should remain in quarantine at least two weeks, which is the time required for the incubation of any ordinary disease. During this time he should be given the Army Group Test and a psychiatric examination, if the psychological test or observation indicates this to be necessary. He should also be interviewed by the officers responsible for school work and other work, and a written record made of the interviews. All these records should then be placed in the hands of the superintendent of the institution, who as soon as possible should have a personal interview with the man. Care should be taken to assign each man to the kind of work he is fitted to do, and if the prisoner has not had a common school education or cannot read or write the English language, he should be sent to school for part of the day.

A careful record should be kept of his conduct, effort, and performance during his stay through the adoption of a credit marking system, which can be used to clear up disputes concerning his record of conduct and performance at the end of each week.

Where so many men are received and discharged during a month, it is advisable to have a finger-print record of every man before discharge, to be compared with the print taken after conviction and at the time the prisoner is received at the institution. This is the system adopted in New York to prevent men from hiring some one else to serve their terms. A comparison of the finger-print taken immediately after conviction with the one taken upon arrival at the institution and before discharge prevents these substitutions. Under the present system it is possible for John Jones to make a bargain with Henry Smith to permit Jones to answer for Henry Smith when Smith's name is called to be discharged. This swapping of identities may account for the rumors, for which there was no time for investigation, that persons sentenced to the workhouse for considerable periods are seen upon the streets of Cleveland in a very short time. At any rate, the adoption of this identification comparison ended such a scandal in New York.

When the clearing-house and probation investigations are completed, copies of all the reports should be sent with his commitment papers, so that the institutional authorities may have all information as soon as the man arrives. This avoids duplicating investigations and checks up inaccuracies of statement which the prisoner is frequently willing to make after all the reports have been checked up and his confidence has been won.

Recommendations

The summary of our recommendations for this institution is:

1. A man of strong personality, thoroughly equipped for this type of correctional work, should be employed as superintendent.

2. The inmate population should be studied to determine the aptitudes and the mental and physical ability of the men, and these should be utilized as a basis for determining what work is to be found for the prisoners to perform.

3. The Director of Public Welfare should employ a specially equipped person to establish a system of employment for inmates of the workhouse.

4. The dormitories should be changed into single rooms, so as to put an end to the present mingling of prisoners.

5. The city Superintendent of Schools should be requested to work

out a system of education for the workhouse and to supply teachers to carry on the work.

6. Modern reception, classification, credit marking, and administrative systems should be established.

7. A modern system of identification should be made the basis of administration and parole work.

THE COUNTY JAIL

The county jail, under the jurisdiction of the sheriff of Cuyahoga County, is an old-fashioned, insanitary, and inadequate institution. It has 136 cells—120 for men and 16 for women. Of the men's cells, 115 are in use, and one padded cell is used occasionally, since refractory prisoners are placed in a strait-jacket in a side room provided for the purpose. The cells in the men's section are in a block four tiers high, and instead of being placed back to back, according to the conventional Auburn plan, have gallery fronts facing the outside walls of the building. These walls are fitted with doors facing the outside windows. The backs of the cells face a center court about 12 feet wide. This center court is roofed over by stone flagging, which serves as a flooring for the second tier of cells and forms a continuous gallery for the same tier. There are four large openings guarded by iron rails to this flooring, from which guards can view the prisoners exercising in the court. The openings also help to ventilate the lower tier of cells and the lower court, which is known as the "bull pen." Prisoners mingle indiscriminately in the "bull pen" during exercise periods, except in the case of murderers or dangerous agitators.

Each cell is about seven feet wide and eight feet long, except on one side, which is about 10 feet wide. The front of the cell is constructed of latticed iron bars. Each cell contains two cots covered with clean bedding, an old black insanitary toilet, and running water.

The so-called women's prison is in a section separate and apart from the men's prison. The cells are arranged in a block four tiers high, with four cells to the tier, all of which face an open court.

Each prisoner is provided one towel and a piece of soap. On the day of our inspection some of these towels were dirty. The toilets were very dirty and corroded. No toilet paper was provided. The cells were not clean, and the corridors were indeed very dirty. The deputy guard in charge of the prison stated that the prisoners were bathed once a week. There were four shower-baths in a fair condition in a separate room of the building.

From a sanitary standpoint the most serious condition in the prison is the antiquated plumbing, which cannot be made adequate or safe except by installing a new system. Feeding prisoners in their cells is another drawback, as it permits prisoners to hide food in their cells, which attracts all sorts of vermin.

The kitchen is in the basement. The kitchen equipment is provided by the sheriff, who is allowed 45 cents a day to pay for food and cover the cost of the food service. The kitchen equipment consists of one medium-sized kitchen range, one copper boiler in fair condition, one copper urn in good condition, and one small ice-box.

The food served on the day of inspection was clean, of good quality, and well served when one considers that the prison was never constructed to permit the easy transfer of food from the kitchen in the basement to the various cells. The diet, however, is monotonous. Breakfast consists of bread and coffee; supper, of coffee and bread. There is some variation in the dinner; for example, on Fridays there are pea soup with potatoes, bread, and coffee; on Thursdays boiled corned beef and cabbage, bread, and coffee; on Wednesdays and Saturdays, mutton or pork, beans, bread, and coffee; on Tuesdays, pork or mutton, bread, and coffee; and on Mondays boiled beef or pork, bread, and coffee.

The padded cell is only occasionally resorted to, as more refractory prisoners are sent to the psychopathic ward of the city hospital, or occasionally to the State Hospital for the Insane, which is not far away. One room was improvised to serve as a hospital, and a doctor is supposed to visit the prisoners daily. Serious cases are sent to other hospitals.

Visitors are admitted to the cell block and guarding is restricted to drawing a screen at the end of the "bull pen" to separate visitors from prisoners. This is a dangerous practice, and should be ended at once, as wide experience has proved conclusively that such arrangements are no safeguard against the smuggling in of all sorts of contraband articles, such as knives, razors, pistols, saws, and drugs. The only safe method of receiving visitors in such institutions is to have separate quarters in a section of the building where one officer can watch a single prisoner and his or her visitors continuously during the whole period of the visit. If there is more than one prisoner to watch at a time, the guard is helpless.

In the jail proper there are 24 employees, five of whom are on night duty. These officers go to court with cases. The deputy in charge explained that on an average four of the officers were out of the prison daily, taking cases to the penitentiary at Columbus and to other institutions. The officers receive a monthly salary without board or maintenance. Until the prison has a better trained and higher type of guard or other employee, it will continue to do unsatisfactory work. Some of the men are undoubtedly faithful, but nearly all of them have had insufficient training. It is extremely important that prisoners brought to a detention prison for trial should be in the hands only of the most capable, conscientious, high-minded, and responsible employees.

Recommendations

1. The present jail should be abandoned as soon as possible, but while in use it should be kept decidedly cleaner and the administration improved at once.

2. The kitchen should be equipped with a roaster, to permit the roasting of meats: boiled beef and stews become too monotonous.

3. The walls should be painted and the windows kept clean.

4. Every man should be required to keep his towel clean.

5. The cells should be kept clean and free from vermin, and in particular the toilet bowls should be cleaned and kept in that condition.

6. A sufficient salary should be paid to permit the employment of guards who understand the responsibilities of their position, and whose language is less, rather than more, profane than that of the prisoners under their charge.

7. A simple but adequate record system should be installed in the office, so that a continuous check may be kept upon the movement of prisoners.

8. Prisoners should be sent to the psychopathic ward of the city hospital and should not be placed in strait-jackets in the prison or kept in a padded cell, except upon rare occasions, where there is some real reason for confining them in the prison.

9. There should be better classification of the prisoners, so that there be less intermingling than there is at present.

CHAPTER II

CORRECTIONAL AGENCIES FOR MINORS

THE JUVENILE COURT

CLEVELAND has gained in population, according to the United States census, at the rate of 40.3 per cent. in the last ten years. During the thirteen years from 1907 to 1920 the number of delinquent boys brought into the Juvenile Court of Cleveland rose from 984 in 1907 to 2,524 "official" cases in 1920, a gain of 1,540 cases, or 156 per cent. If to this number of delinquent boys "officially" brought into court there be added the 1,724 boys "unofficially" in court in 1920, the increase in delinquent boys in 1920 over the number in 1907 is 3,264, or over 331 per cent. In other words, the number of delinquent boys brought into the Juvenile Court is increasing from three to eight times as fast as the population. The report on "Delinquency and Spare Time" by Henry W. Thurston, which was part of the Cleveland Recreation Survey, directed attention to the necessity of considering the conditions under which Cleveland children are growing up as an essential to grappling with the problem of juvenile delinquency. The growth of delinquency is no criticism of the Juvenile Court: it simply shows the problem the court has been facing.

According to the report of the chief probation officer for the year 1920, the total number of cases handled by the judge and attachés of the court was 6,540, summarized as follows:

OFFICIAL CASES:
```
        Delinquent boys....:................................    2,524
        Delinquent girls.........................................      584
        Neglected cases (involving 638 children)..............      326
        Dependency cases (involving 714 children)...........      341
        Consent to marry..................................       13
                                                              _____
            Total official cases...........................................3,788

UNOFFICIAL CASES:
        Boys.............................................    1,724
        Girls............................................      187
ADULTS:
        Male.............................................      760
        Female...........................................       81
                                                              _____
            Total unofficial cases....................................2,752
                                                              _____
        GRAND TOTAL FOR YEAR 1920...............................6,540
```

About 600 juveniles are upon probation at a time. To look after these, as well as the neglected and dependent children, the court has a staff of four men and 12 women probation officers. Some investigation is made of all "official" cases, and an attempt is made through the "Confidential Exchange" of the Associated Charities to make use of the particular organization which has some knowledge of the child or the family. Although full records have been obtained through the exchange in some cases, in the majority the records are incomplete and in many consist only of the probation officer's reports. These investigations are supplemented by mental examinations in the discretion of Miss Marion Wilcox, who is the connecting link between the courts and the clearing-house in case investigations.

All the information obtained is placed before the judge in the original form, without compilation or interpretation, except as supplemented by the probation officer who made the investigation and who is always present at the court hearing of the case. The judge sometimes reads the original reports, but more frequently relies upon the verbal statements and recommendation of the probation officer.

As most of the court hearings are usually held during two or three days a week, the number of cases on the docket frequently aggregates 70, and occasionally more. The records of the verbal statements of the probation officer are those contained in the shorthand notes of the hearing which are later transcribed and added to the records, with the notation describing the disposition of the case.

It is evident that the staff is too small. There should be two additional clerk-stenographers and two additional typists, besides four additional probation officers, to handle "official" cases. There should also be five additional field investigators for "unofficial" cases. The additional clerk-stenographers and typists would relieve investigators of the necessity of spending so much time compiling reports and would permit these officers to furnish much fuller and more detailed reports than are furnished by them at present. In any event, the new "control blank," which is a marked improvement over the old card form, should provide on its face for the scoring of homes and neighborhood environment by the probation officer, in accordance with well-known standardized requirements, as well as three or four word summary of the mental examination. Attached to this "control blank" should be a summary of the facts in the case, headed by a recommendation, after discussion of the case in the probation officers' staff meeting and after approval by the chief probation officer or his first assistant. All the papers in the case should be attached to the summary and should go before the judge, as at present, for his consideration.

If the suggestions contained therein were followed, the court would be less severely handicapped than at present, and the number of re-appearances of delinquent boys in court, who are finally committed to institutions, would be less than is indicated by the summary, in Table 1, from the 1920 report of the chief probation officer.

TABLE 1.—COMMITMENTS OF BOYS

City Farm School, Hudson, Ohio....................................... 93
Boys' Industrial School, Lancaster, Ohio............................... 245
Ohio State Reformatory, Mansfield, Ohio.............................. 24

Number of commitments	City Farm School	Boys' Industrial School	Ohio State Reformatory
First	29	55	6
Second	40	71	3
Third	13	61	4
Fourth	7	40	3
Fifth	3	8	4
Sixth	..	5	3
Seventh	1	2	..
Eighth	..	2	1
Ninth	..	1	..
	93	245	24

One of the greatest weaknesses of the Juvenile Court is the fact that it is housed in the old criminal courts building, which, with all its sordid associations, is not a proper place for a juvenile court. If the court were in a building adjacent to the detention home or in a school building, its effectiveness and its power for good would be vastly increased. The Juvenile Court quarters should not be included in the proposed new county criminal courts building and county jail.

In order to carry out this idea of separation it might be better to organize the Juvenile Court somewhat as it is in the city of Cincinnati, as part of the Court of Common Pleas. In that event the court would handle insolvency and other domestic relations matters not connected with the actual trial, or handling of children's cases in quarters in the new court building, and all children's court matters and dependency work in quarters associated with the schools or with the Juvenile Detention Home.

This last suggestion is offered with some reluctance for the reason that, as juvenile courts are only in process of development, it would

3

seem wise that they should develop in accordance with local conditions. In Cleveland the coöperation of the court with the schools indicates the greater importance at present of continuing in this direction, rather than transferring the court from insolvency jurisdiction to Common Pleas jurisdiction.

Our study of the Juvenile Court in Cleveland has been limited chiefly to a consideration of its activities from the social point of view. In its final implications the court is one of the greatest agencies upon which Cleveland must depend for the healthy development of its child life.

Moreover, the interest displayed by Judge George S. Addams in the work of the various organizations in the Welfare Federation and other social agencies indicates that these organizations are getting benefit from his wide experience in dealing with the children of the city. The particular interest of the judge in the boys at Hudson Farm is most helpful, and increases the effectiveness of that hopeful place to a marked degree. Furthermore, this kindly judge, by reason of the breadth of his interests and desires and his sensible and colorful outlook upon life, brings to bear upon each case the point of view which tends to gloss over the petty and unimportant and to concentrate upon the larger and more significant issues. The children of Cleveland know that the Juvenile Court is no "snubbing" post, and that Judge Addams is neither a species of lion tamer nor a narrow-minded purist.

In order to cope with the situation the court and its attachés should be actively participating in a continuous survey of conditions of child life in the city, and should not limit themselves to the consideration of delinquent and dependent children alone. The court cannot deal adequately with such children unless it is a clearing-house of the city's child life.

Great emphasis is placed upon the fact that the probation office "clears" through the Associated Charities clearing-house every morning at 10. But at the present time the clearing-house is little more than a record office to indicate which agencies are at work on a case. The court is rather poorly served, as a clearing-house out of touch with actual cases means little or no effort to "clear" cases upon the basis of information submitted for the purpose of assigning specific agencies to each case for definite work upon it. The Probation Department, better than any other agency, could see to it that all this work is vitalized.

The clearing-house of the Associated Charities is a great constructive achievement, but even if it were vitalized by continuous close contact with "flesh and blood" rather than "paper" cases, it would still be unable to furnish for the use of the Juvenile Court an adequate moving picture of the social life of the city, especially as it affects children.

[18]

The all-important clearing-house of Cleveland child life is the Department of Education. Unfortunately, it is not as serviceable to the Juvenile Court as it might be. It is not attempting to do all it should, and its available forces for attacking the various problems of childhood are too much scattered. They cannot function properly for school purposes, and they present an aspect of confusion to the judge and to the attachés of the Juvenile Court. This is particularly unfortunate, for the opportunities for coöperation are very great, and the various workers within the school system and the other associations appear eager to respond to Judge Addams' desire for coöperation.

Leonard P. Ayres pointed out, in the School Survey of Cleveland, that the health work of the city school system was retarded because the Director of School Health Work was responsible to the Director of Schools for health work in the schools and to the city Superintendent of Schools for education in public health. This same overlapping is present in other divisions of school work. Miss Claire Walters, psychologist for the boys' school, makes most of the examinations of children in the Juvenile Court, and after September 1 will have charge of all school children appearing in court. She is also the agent of the School Department of Attendance, and is under the direct supervision of the Assistant Superintendent of Schools, Frank G. Pickell.

Dr. Bertha Luckey is Director of the School Psychological Clinic, which is under the direction of Assistant Superintendent of Schools Eldridge. Dr. Luckey's principal work is the examination of school children referred to her by the teachers, to determine whether they should be assigned to special classes. There are three assistant examiners. This department makes no routine examination of delinquents, but occasionally cases are referred to it by the Department of Attendance or by the Juvenile Court.

Dr. Luckey has also applied intelligence tests to nearly 5,000 children in the first grade. Dr. W. W. Thiesen, Director of the School Department of Reference and Research, has also applied these tests in the course of his studies of school problems, using the children of the sixth grade, who are preparing for junior high school. Thus Dr. Thiesen and Dr. Luckey are both giving group intelligence tests, but from a somewhat different standpoint.

Special education in the schools also lacks coördination. Assistant Superintendent Pickell has charge of special education of delinquents in the boys' school, the Juvenile Court Detention Home, the boys' farm at Hudson, and the girls' school at Warrensville. Assistant Superintendent Albert C. Eldredge has charge of this work as it relates to mental defectives, and H. D. Bixby as it relates to sense defectives, speech correction, and orthopedic class work.

Special education, psychological measurement, the medical and psychiatric work of the schools should be coördinated under one assistant superintendent of schools, who should work in the closest coöperation with the Juvenile Court and the Associated Charities Clearing-house. If for any reason medical and special educational work cannot be placed under one person, special education and psychological measurement should be so combined and a psychiatric division should coördinate the school medical work, the special educational work in the schools, and the psychiatric work of the Juvenile Court. In this way the records of physical, mental, and dental examinations in the school department would be available for use in the Department of Special Education and in the Juvenile Court.

If Cleveland were to coördinate special education and psychological measurement, as Detroit has done, and were to add psychiatric examination, child delinquency and the various social maladjustments of children which are reflected in the children's court would be greatly reduced. In Detroit, Professor Charles S. Barry, of the University of Michigan, with the aid of a corps of assistants, has examined within the past year over 4,000 children with Binet tests. The results of these examinations are extremely important. They have shown that when children are classified according to general intelligence, all types of children progress more rapidly. They have also demonstrated the need for differentiating courses of study for different types of ability, and have greatly stimulated teachers to take into account the individuality of their pupils. Various agencies in Detroit have shown eagerness to avail themselves of the information obtained by the psychological clinic, and the examinations have been used not only in placing dependent children, but also by the judge of the Juvenile Court.

To those who say that it is not the business of a juvenile court to have close relations with educational work, let it be said that the function of the juvenile court, as of the school system, is to serve the children, and since the children will profit most through the closest coöperation of the court and the schools, these two great agencies must consider the welfare of the children and not the legal or customary divisions of court and school work. Coöperation may be secured by careful planning and supervision without any overlapping of administrative functions. In fact, duplication of investigations, examinations, and reports may be avoided in this way.

The significance of numerous basic needs, such as the provision of simple but comprehensive records of work done and of facts ascertained, is not appreciated. Altogether too much depends upon Chief Probation Officer Thomas L. Lewis and his assistants to "remember" details. This applies both to court work alone and to its coöperation with other agencies.

Too much of the chief probation officer's time is devoted to the consideration of individual cases. The position of chief probation officer in the Juvenile Court is one which calls primarily for a trained executive. He should have a capable assistant to supervise the record system, and this assistant should see to it—(1) That a modern control card or sheet is made out for every complaint, a copy of which should follow the assignment of the case from the court to the detention home, to the Probation Department, to the institution or agency; (2) that an adequate official file is kept of each case which should be the public official record, containing such things as the certificates and official citations and statements; and (3) a probation or court record file containing all other records pertaining to each case, with a first-page summary containing the essential information up to date. The official file should be open for public inspection; the probation and court record file should be confidential but not secret. It should also be the duty of this assistant to see that all complaints are properly entered, assigned for investigation either to a probation officer or to some agency through the clearing-house, or to both a probation officer and an agency, that the facts of record are correctly copied into the form used by the probation officer and by the clearing-house and that the reports come back promptly, as at present too much time elapses between complaints and assignments and between assignments and reports of investigation.

The chief probation officer, relieved of details by such organization of his work, could devote his time to initiating conferences with school officials, private agencies, different divisions of the city Department of Public Welfare, and officials of the various State and county institutions, upon whose coöperation the success of his work depends to a degree yet unrealized. It is not necessary to cite records to show that many "background" facts are not getting the consideration their importance warrants. The chief probation officer should have time to devise ways and means of remedying this situation without duplication of effort and at the lowest total cost. At the present time no information from the probation office accompanies or follows any commitment to any institution. Information acquired by the clearing-house is used only by the Juvenile Court and the clearing-house, and finally there is a complete breakdown of the follow-up system in both probation from the court and parole from the various institutions. After leaving the institution a case too frequently is lost track of until it is again brought to attention through delinquency. As a result, from 25 per cent. to 30 per cent. of the work done is lost.

Investigations

According to the chief probation officer's report for 1919 there were 3,338 "unofficial" cases, as follows: boys, 2,137; girls, 298; male adults, 721; female adults, 106; letters of warning, 79. In 1920 there were 2,752 cases, divided as follows: boys, 1,724; girls, 187; male adults, 760; female adults, 81. It is altogether admirable for the Probation Department to adjust as many cases as possible without bringing the child into court or before the judge in formal fashion, but it is a somewhat unwise procedure in Cleveland, where there is an inadequate record and follow-up system to inform the court of the details of unofficial cases in particular. Under present conditions the judge is hardly in a position to know enough of the pertinent facts with respect to any particular unofficial case. In fact, no one but the chief probation officer himself could, from a study of the records, determine what has been done. Every such case should be carefully registered in the clearing-house and no final decision should be made without the specific concurrence of the judge entered upon the unofficial records of the court.

We are not impressed by those who urge that a juvenile court judge should pass upon the details of each case, for that would mean he would be his own chief probation officer. We are, however, strongly of the opinion that it is the duty of the chief probation officer to furnish to the judge a complete summary of each case, and that the judge, in writing or upon the minutes of court, should direct the chief probation officer in making final disposition of so-called "unofficial" cases.

There should be as careful a record of essential details in "unofficial" cases as there is in "official" cases. Apparently this is overlooked by the officials of the court, for Mr. Lewis, the chief probation officer, receives all complaints. A complainant gives his story verbally to Mr. Lewis, who then decides whether:

(a) To handle the case himself, or

(b) To have an affidavit prepared and filed covering the subject matter of the complaint, or

(c) To have the case investigated by a probation officer.

A study of cases shows that not enough care is used in jotting down, in report form, all the facts for future investigation. It is obviously wrong practice to have the investigation of 2,500 to 3,500 "unofficial" cases per year depend at vital points upon the ability of the chief probation officer to remember important details. The methods used lead the probation officer to decide upon a line of action, either without investigation or with only partial investigation. Few cases can be handled wisely without thorough knowledge of the child himself, the facts concerning his family life, the attitude of the parents and all the environmental conditions, yet in this Probation Department many scores of cases are handled by people who depend upon their own ability to "size up" the situation through personal interviews and without reports from social workers, a psychiatrist, or a probation officer.

General Criticism

The obvious weaknesses of a system which places too much emphasis upon the conduct of children and too little upon the responsibility of parents are present here. There are, of course, commendable attempts to avoid punishing the child for the offenses of parents. Evidently the court officials aim to protect the child from such mistakes, but often the traditional practices which are accepted as a basis for action lead to undesirable results. It could not be otherwise where there are too few home and field investigations. It is also the natural result where the attempt is made to guide parents and children by telling them in effect, "Do so and so and you will be punished," when the emphasis should be in effect, "You must do so and so for the good of your children."

Cleveland has vested in its Juvenile Court jurisdiction over dependent children, delinquent children, and widows' pensions. Strictly speaking, dependency and widows' pensions are not proper subjects for juvenile court administration, which carries over too many traditional practices from courts for adults. It is doubtful if probation officers will do as efficient child placement work as some of the other organizations, although there is no inherent reason why they cannot be trained to perform placement work properly. The various agencies coöperating through the Associated Charities Clearing-house, the Division of Outdoor Relief of the Public Welfare Department of the city, the various hospitals under the jurisdiction of or coöperating with the city Health Department, are also vitally concerned. The best organization for Cleveland would probably be one in which the Probation Department could call upon the Associated Charities clearing-house, upon the school and upon the Division of Outdoor Relief for investigation and information. In that case the Welfare Federation might organize a child welfare bureau to function partly in response to specific requests of the Juvenile Court Probation Department, partly on its own initiative, and partly in response to requests from other sources. If $25,000 in private funds were available to pay and equip an executive for such a clearing-house investigation committee, the latter could secure the active coöperation of the newspapers, as well as of reluctant or busy officials and private persons, who could see the great advantages flowing from the intensive development of this work.

Judge Addams, who has been a conscientious and able public official, should not fail to have all cases examined either by a skilled psychiatrist or clinical psychologist, if possible, or, if not, by the Bureau of Juvenile Research in Columbus. The ability of the judge and the chief probation officer to "size up a case" with skill is not disputed, and this ability undoubtedly increases with experience, but Cleveland cannot afford to depend upon that ability, however great, as a substitute for a more comprehensive study of its delinquent children. Judge Addams can also help develop still further the remarkable child welfare clinics of the public schools by using them more frequently.

We question the adequacy of Mr. Lewis as chief probation officer as we have envisaged that office. Mr. Lewis has many good qualities, but he lacks those qualifications which are essential to the greatest success of probation work in the Juvenile Court of the future. The greatest chance for the success of this court in Cleveland is through the development of the widest coöperation with the schools, where its success has already been notable. The chief probation officer should be a man of the best training, specifically for work with children. Not only should he be acquainted with educational and public health methods, but he should have a rank and salary equal to those of an assistant superintendent of schools. Such a man would be in a position to secure a maximum of coöperation with the schools.

Summary of Recommendations

In summary form, our recommendations are:

1. The budget of the court should be increased $22,000 a year, to permit an increase of the judge's annual salary to $8,000, of the chief probation officer's salary to $5,000, and to allow the employment of nine additional officers, two additional clerk stenographers, and two additional typists, and to pay whatever additional expenses this improved service requires.

2. A highly trained and experienced person should be employed as chief probation officer, to have rank equivalent to that of an assistant

superintendent of schools, who should be able to secure the maximum coöperation with the schools and all public and private agencies in the city. The duties of the chief probation officer of the Juvenile Court should become wholly executive.

3. A more effective record system should be established. There should be a complete interchange of records between the Juvenile Court and the public schools, the Associated Charities clearing-house, the Detention Home, the various institutions to which children are committed by the Juvenile Court and the Division of Outdoor Relief of the Department of Public Welfare.

4. In order to increase their own effectiveness and coöperation with other agencies, the Board of Education and the Superintendent of Schools should place all functions with respect to special education under the supervision of one assistant superintendent of schools.

5. The health work of the schools should include consideration of mental hygiene. A capable psychiatrist should be placed, if possible, in the Division of Special Education as part of an organization composed of workers in the various fields, or at the head of such a group to make psychiatric as contrasted with psychological measurements of school children, or, if this is not possible, he should be the special representative of the head of schools and the liaison between the Division of Special Education, the school dispensaries, and the Juvenile Court. Psychological measurements in that event should be made in the Division of Special Education. There should be a mental and physical examination of every child brought to the attention of the Juvenile Court or its Probation Department, and an extensive interchange of records of examinations among all the agencies interested before the case comes up in court for formal action.

6. If the functions of probation and parole in the Juvenile Court be not separated, a sufficient number of probation officers should be employed at once to permit effective parole work, not now performed at all, for children released upon parole from the various institutions. The history of every case, as far as it is known to the probation officer, should accompany or follow the commitment papers of every case committed to an institution. It should be the business of the probation officer to summarize the clearing-house information, with the information concerning medical, psychological, and psychiatric examinations and the child's school record.

7. In order to increase the effectiveness of the work for dependent children and pension work a joint investigation bureau should be estab-

lished with a paid secretary, capable of coöperating with all public and private agencies.

8. The Children's Court should be removed entirely from the criminal courts building and quartered either in a new building adjacent to the Detention Home or in a public school building.

9. If it becomes advisable to change the Children's Court from Insolvency Court jurisdiction to Common Pleas Court jurisdiction, the work for children should be kept separate and apart from work for adults and domestic relations work not directly affecting children, so that the latter need not be brought in personal contact with the sordid details of such cases.

10. Judge Addams should exert his own influence and the prestige of the court to the furtherance of the fullest coöperation with the public schools, in particular, and with the other public and private agencies of the city.

THE DETENTION HOME

The Cleveland Detention Home is, unfortunately, located at a considerable distance from the Juvenile Court, thus greatly impairing its usefulness to the court and to the Probation Department. It consists of a remodeled mansion, used for offices and staff residence, and a fire-proof extension which is thoroughly modern, except for the provision of dormitories instead of private rooms. The county has recently acquired an adjoining property, thus providing space for a fairly good playground. It was intended, at the time of the original purchase, to convert the residence into a home for dependent children under the care of the Juvenile Court, but this plan was given up because the building could not, within reasonable expense, be made fire-proof, and, therefore, under the provisions of the city ordinances, it could not be used for housing children. There is sufficient room on the combined plots owned by the county to house the probation office and Juvenile Court and still leave the same amount of playground space that is now being used. Such an arrangement, from an administrative viewpoint, would be highly desirable, though the present location of the Detention Home is not as central as would be desirable for a probation office and Juvenile Court.

The excellent new building, which has two stories and a basement, has a roof designed for use as a playground. The second floor, which is used exclusively for boys, contains officers' quarters, two dormitories, five cells, a dining-room, pantry, playroom, and toilet facilities. The first floor, laid out in much the same manner, is used exclusively for girls. In the basement are located the kitchen, laundry, storehouse, a room about 23 by 86½ feet used as a gymnasium, and shower-baths.

The basement also has a reception room for new arrivals. The building is clean and sanitary throughout.

The Detention Home staff consists of a superintendent, Miss Laura A. Marlow, appointed by the Juvenile judge; a girls' matron and boys' master; a housekeeper, two cooks, a laundress, a man acting as engineer and fireman, a bookkeeper, a nurse, and a teacher. There are also one or two relief officers and a night-watchman.

Children under eighteen may be sent to the Detention Home either by the probation officer or the Juvenile judge. The police and truant officers may also turn over to the Detention Home children under eighteen to be detained until they can be produced in court. The number of boys varies considerably from day to day. There are rarely less than 50 or more than 90, though there have been at times over 100. When newcomers arrive, they are carefully bathed, their heads are treated with a solution of larkspur, or washed with coal oil, their clothing fumigated and put away for future use, and fresh clothing is given them. Practically no information, except the name, age, home address, and charge, is received with the new arrival. A physical examination is given by a non-resident physician.

The home has no adequate means of segregation. There are two dormitories for boys and two for girls, and when these are not overcrowded, it is possible to segregate the younger from the older children.

The only facilities for school purposes consist of one small room where six or eight of the younger girls receive instruction, under a teacher appointed by Assistant Superintendent Pickell, of the Educational Department of the city. Boys are given instruction in the Boys' School, a block and a half from the home, which is under the jurisdiction of Mr. Pickell. The boys who attend this school are taken back and forth morning and afternoon by a relief officer from the Detention Home.

Children may be detained in the Detention Home from a few hours to several months. When a child is to be released, a written order from the court is presented to the superintendent by the individual into whose custody the child is given. The superintendent has no knowledge of the conditions of release or of what becomes of the child afterward.

The greatest criticism to be offered in the boys' department is the utter lack of suitable employment. Under the supervision of the two officers in charge, a matron-housekeeper and a male officer, the work of keeping the place in order is done by the boys themselves. There is a total lack of indoor recreational facilities and a failure to take advantage of such outdoor facilities as a good playground on the roof. This failure to use the roof was explained by the officer in charge as due to past misbehavior on the part of two boys who had been allowed to play there. During our visit there were about 30 boys playing noisily in the playroom. The officer commanded quiet and then lined the boys up, and, turning to the investigator, said that he would now tell him about the boys. The following questions were then asked:

Officer: What is your name?

Boy: John Smith.

Officer: How many times have you been here?

Boy: Three times.

Officer: What are you here for this time?

Boy: Stealing.

Officer: Did you ever go to Lancaster?

Boy: Yes.

Officer: You broke parole from Lancaster, didn't you?

Boy: Yes.

Officer: And then you stole and had to come back here?

Boy: (In a crestfallen manner) Yes.

The officer then passed to four other boys with similar questions. Much the same answers were given in each case. The officer then said that boy No. 2 was a very bad boy and could be depended upon to lie and to steal if he had the chance. The investigator interrupted this brutal interchange by talking directly with the boys.

There is practically no oversight of the boys' dormitories at night. A watchman, whose bedroom is nearby, visits the dormitories once an hour "to ring up." There is nothing to prevent the grossest kind of immorality, and although the officer in charge admitted that he was aware of the existence of this problem, the night-watchman is still the only reliance against it.

The Girls' Department is under much better supervision than the Boys' Department, except that there is some lack of supervision in the dormitories and not enough work or directed recreation. The laundry furnishes employment for older girls. There is a resident school teacher for the Girls' Department, but only girls under fourteen, of whom there are few, are required to attend school. The girls are sometimes allowed to play on the roof. It should be possible to provide them with many simpler and more beneficial occupations.

The medical examinations made by the visiting doctors from Fairview Park Hospital are not always adequate or timely. Sometimes the doctors have barely begun work when the telephone orders them to return to the hospital for some emergency. This situation could perhaps be remedied if the visiting staff of the hospital could be induced to become responsible for the work at the Detention Home, and an interne were provided who should be held responsible for the ordinary medical work at the Detention Home, subject to the general direction of the visiting staff.

Coöperation with the schools should be encouraged. The present plan of conducting practically all school work in the home deprives the children of a chance to go to school in a regular school building, and of the opportunity to secure training in industrial classes. It also reduces the school work to the level of perfunctoriness into which detention schools degenerate, since the management cannot offer to a teacher the inducements which can be offered by a school system whose work with delinquents is conducted not in a detention home, but in a school building.

Recommendations

1. The recent plan of coöperation with the boys' school should have been extended instead of being abandoned.

2. A better program for both work and play should be provided for the boys' department. The Cleveland school system offers excellent suggestions for use along these lines.

3. It is altogether wrong and indefensible that from 30 to 50 boys should be kept in small quarters in comparative idleness, some few of them for periods of several months.

4. Although the man who was supervisor of the boys' department during the spring has many excellent qualities, his entire lack of understanding of the problems connected with his institution nullifies his effectiveness, and unless this can be changed, there should be a change of supervisors.

5. Criticism may well be made of the present salary scale ($60 a month), which is hardly enough to secure the services of a really competent person.

THE BOYS' SCHOOL

Cleveland maintains a special school for truant, delinquent, and incorrigible boys, known as the Boys' School. It is a part of the public school system and is under the direct supervision of Assistant Superintendent Pickell, of the Department of Education, who personally approves all admissions. Applications to Mr. Pickell are made through the Department of Attendance after all attempts at adjustment by family appeal and school transfer have failed. No routine mental examinations are made before admission, although a fairly good social study is conducted. The officer or teacher recommending admission may apply to the psychological clinic for special examination, but this is seldom done. It is admitted by Mr. Pickell that a certain amount of odium is attached to the compulsory attendance of children in this school, which is known locally as "the bad boys' school."

Mental examinations are conducted principally by Miss Claire Walters, of Mr. Pickell's division. So far as could be learned, these results are used only for the classification of the feeble-minded boys in the school. A general classification of all boys on the basis of intelligence is not undertaken.

As already stated, there is close coöperation between this school, the Detention Home, and the Juvenile Court. The work of the school is divided into three parts—regular grade work carried on as special class instruction, manual training and handicraft work, and the Department of Psychological Examination and Placement.

The regular grade and special class work presents no features that are not found in other similar class-room work. Teachers in charge of special classes are not employing modern methods of teaching this type of child. It has been found that there is practically no direct bearing of the psychological examinations upon class-room work. The work is mechanical, and the only clear advantage it has is that of relieving the grades in the regular public schools of certain backward children.

In one particular at least the vocational and manual training work in the Boys' School is above the average. This is the printing department. This department is in charge of a man who, besides being a master printer, is a devoted student of boy life, as well as a capable teacher with initiative and ingenuity. All these traits are reflected in the quality of work being done in the pressroom.

The course of study for this work has been adapted to the various requirements of vocational education with unusual understanding: one part correlates history, another geography, a third arithmetic, and so on.

The class in handicrafts, which is also under capable direction, includes basketry, weaving, knitting, and the like. The kind of work turned out is far above the average usually found in similar classes elsewhere. It should be pointed out, however, that this work is performed by boys who are practically normal. Nevertheless, the secret of success in these two departments is undoubtedly the fact that those in charge are working in the closest and most harmonious relation with the Division of Psychological Measurement and Placement.

The woodworking department is not up to the average manual training work found in grade schools, although some of the objects are fairly well made. The work seems commonplace, because the instructor lacks freshness and resource. Only the most obvious lines of work are being followed and the most obvious and commonplace opinions expressed about the work by the teacher. This department presents an ideal opportunity for incorporating some of the principles of free-hand and mechanical drawing, as well as for teaching some of the simpler truths of geometry, but nothing of this kind is done. On the whole, it seems that the most vital features of manual training work are being ignored.

The Department of Psychology and Placement is under Miss Walters' directions. Fundamentally, this department exists for the purpose of studying, adjusting, and replacing the truant, backward, and delinquent children sent from the public schools to the Boys' School. Its purpose is the application of mechanical tests for the purpose of discovering, according to Terman's Revision, the mental age of children with reference to its effectiveness. We quote the following from the Cleveland Hospital and Health Survey:

"The important relationships of juvenile delinquent boys to mental diseases and other disorders of the mental system are well understood, and many efforts are made to secure psychiatric and psychological examinations that will throw light on this subject in individual cases. Miss Claire Walters, who is attached to the Boys' School, makes 'intelligence tests.' At her suggestion the services of the psychiatrist attached to the Probate Court were employed. At the Boys' School and Detention Home children were observed while their cases were pending or while awaiting placement, but, of course, *this observation was not made by those trained to detect the most significant alterations in behavior*" (p. 480).

There are many evidences of the fact that much thought has been given to the question of measurement, and that the intention of the founders was clearly to establish contact with all bureaus, courts, and institutions which could profitably be related to this work, but the work has not thus developed, indicating the need for a change in administrative control, which we have previously recommended.

Recommendations

1. The school is one of the most potent constructive agencies for the prevention of delinquency in the State, and its principles should be extended throughout the city.

2. At the present time manual education is not being offered in the public schools below the junior high school, except incidentally or through special classes for defectives.

3. Judge Addams of the Juvenile Court should be encouraged to continue committing boys to this school, since by doing so he is setting

an example in coöperation between correction agencies and the school system.

4. Boys should not be committed to this school except after mental examinations, supplementing social investigation.

5. It is easily conceivable that readjustments in the ordinary public schools might be made on the basis of some such examinations without the need for admission to this school.

6. Feeble-minded delinquents could then be adjusted directly through the Department of Special Classes in the city school system.

7. These examinations could be made by Miss Walters, as at present, or more properly through a mental clinic, comprising a capable psychiatrist as well as a clinical psychologist, whose assistant Miss Walters should be.

8. The administration of the school should be based on scientific principles and on a scientific classification of the boys in all lines. The printing division and handicraft work are examples of a good beginning. Probably a better and more comprehensive examining system and course of study could be worked out, adapted to the particular needs of each child. The school might well adapt many of the methods developed by the extraordinary Moraine Park Private School in Dayton, Ohio.

9. When schools for delinquents and truants have set the example, it will then be necessary for the city to extend to all schools proper classification and differentiation in education based upon actual experience in Cleveland. When this is done, delinquency growing out of truancy and lack of interest in studies or failure to keep up in school will in all probability be drastically checked.

THE CLEVELAND BOYS' FARM AT HUDSON

The Cleveland Boys' Farm, opened in 1903, is about 35 miles from the city. As indicated by its name, it is a city farm colony institution. There are eight frame cottages, a power plant, greenhouse, school-house, barns, shops, laundry, and central kitchen. The population usually averages about 140 boys, who range in age from ten to eighteen years. The staff consists of the superintendent, eight cottage fathers and eight matrons, a principal of the school, a farmer, an engineer, and a general utility man. The general training offered by the institution consists of farming, gardening, housework, with limited opportunities for a few students in mechanical work, and good opportunities for prevocational and vocational work. While the equipment for manual work is limited, this handicap is somewhat compensated for by the small numbers to be taught and the intimate relationship existing between instructors and pupils.

Boys are committed to this institution nominally by the Juvenile Court, but in practice by virtue of a "gentlemen's agreement" between the court and superintendent. The superintendent, John A. Eisenhauer, personally visits the Detention Home at Cleveland and selects the candidates for the farm. As a result he is able to carry out a well-graded classification system along the cottage lines. This promotes more constructive efforts with the boys.

When the superintendent visits the Detention Home in the city with a view to selecting candidates for his institution, he gets some facts with respect to their history from the matron of the home, but practically nothing in record form. When a boy arrives at the farm he is accompanied by a commitment paper; beyond this there are no facts or other information available to the superintendent. The latter may visit the Boys' (Truant) School and learn from Miss Walters something of the mental traits and personal characteristics of each boy. This is furnished verbally in most cases and not, as a rule, in written form, except when a psychological report is necessary. The probation office and the Juvenile Court supply information only by special request.

In order to determine the intelligence level of the population as a whole, Dr. Herman M. Adler's assistant, E. K. Wickman, administered group intelligence tests to all the boys of the school, 121 in number, except 14 who were engaged about the farm. The ages of the boys examined vary from eight to fifteen years. The results for 118 are classified below.[1]

The results in the cases of three boys were omitted because of doubtful information concerning chronological ages. The results as a whole are computed in mental ages according to the mental age norms of the

[1] TABLE 2.—INTELLIGENCE SURVEY OF CLEVELAND BOYS' FARM

Intelligence quotient	Below 9	9	10	11	12	13	14	15	Total	Per cent.
40-49	..	..	..	..	..	..	..	2	2	1.7
50-59	..	..	..	..	3	2	2	..	7	5.9
60-69	..	..	2	5	2	2	2	2	15	12.7
70-79	..	..	8	6	1	2	7	1	25	21.2
80-89	..	2	3	2	2	2	2	4	17	14.4
90 and over	1	4	3	5	6	14	9	10	52	44.1
Total	..	..	..	..	..	..	..	..	118	100.0

Delta 2 Scale of Hagerty's Intelligence Examination, and these in turn are reduced to approximate intelligence quotients. We believe the results give a general estimate of the intelligence of the boys.

It appears that 44 per cent. of the boys have adequate intelligence; 14 per cent. are somewhat backward, and 40 per cent. are retarded or somewhat inferior. The definitely inferior number about 24 boys out of a total of 118. The results as a whole indicate that the greater proportion of the boys are of average or above average mental development and able to do regular school work, but it is also clear that the institution is confronted with a problem of education and training subnormal children, since out of 118, 25 are retarded in their mental development and 24 are inferior mentally.

The educational work of the institution is under the general supervision of Assistant Superintendent Pickell, of the Cleveland Department of Education. In addition to general training the superintendent himself gives personal thought and oversight to character building and training in ethics. The discipline is the same as that usually found in institutions of this type. Corporal punishment is permitted and can be administered only in the presence of and with the consent of the superintendent. Nothing severe is countenanced. Usually punishments consist of deprivation of privileges, extra work, short rations, or prolonged stay in the institution.

Paroles and discharges are arranged chiefly over the telephone by the probation officer or the judge of the Juvenile Court. It is almost always a verbal arrangement. The superintendent's duty begins and ends with the boy in the institution. There is no follow-up or parole work whatsoever, either by the institution or the Juvenile Court Probation Department.

This is the most hopeful of Cleveland's penal institutions, not because of its buildings or equipment, but because of the intelligent leadership of the superintendent and his assistants. It is the best example of intelligent thrift we have seen in the institutional life of Cleveland. There are, however, serious administrative defects:

The administrative plan of the institution is faulty. Its superintendent is appointed by the Director of Public Welfare, but the latter has had no further active responsibility in the matter. The Juvenile Court is concerned with commitments and recalls, and is supposed in a vague way to have further supervising powers, but as a matter of fact does not exercise them. The Probation Department acts as agent for the court in placing and releasing boys from the institution, but is otherwise unconcerned; hence the superintendent is responsible to no one, and succeeds because its present head is both capable and conscientious.

It has no adequate knowledge of the social and mental histories of its wards.

It keeps only the usual school work record of its inmates and a record of infractions and bad conduct, but no system of recording progress.

It furnishes no supervision, directly or indirectly, of boys on parole, nor does it receive any information concerning their progress or failure while on parole.

Recommendations

1. The Director of Public Welfare should appoint a representative group of citizens to act as an advisory board for this institution; an administrative code should be worked out, setting forth the duties and responsibilities of such an advisory board, its relation to the Department of Public Welfare, the Juvenile Court, and the probation office, and providing for a proper reception and classification system for inmates, a system of records, and an adequate parole plan. These should be in thorough accord with the spirit, purposes, and work of the Juvenile Court, the Detention Home, the Juvenile Probation Department, and the Department of Public Welfare.

2. A regular plan should be formulated for the exchange of information to the end that this institution shall receive the fullest possible family and individual history of all inmates from the Associated Charities clearing-house.

3. There should be one final and supreme supervisory authority exercised over the institution. If for any reason it be deemed advisable for the Juvenile Court to continue any manner of supervision over this institution, a clearer demarkation should be made between executive and judicial functions, so that this important experiment of administrative and judicial coöperation be allowed to develop normally. All school and other productive work of the institution should be coördinated through mental and industrial tests. There should be the fullest development of the medical service.

THE GIRLS' HOME AT WARRENSVILLE

The Girls' Home at Warrensville consists of a single wooden structure containing two stories, an attic, and a basement, with a capacity of 39. This capacity is usually exceeded. Recent alterations have provided four bath-tubs, two showers, six toilets and lavatories, well-lighted and ventilated dormitories, a dining-room and kitchen on the first floor, a school-room, and a living-room. The building is a virtual fire-trap. The boilers and furnace are in the basement, and the clearance between the top of the furnace pipe and the ceiling is about one foot. A small heater for hot water is attached to the plant. The connection between this heater and the smokestack has a clearance of 15 or 16 inches from the ceiling, which consists of floor beams and flooring for the rooms above. There is no asbestos or other covering for these pipes, nor is there any metal, asbestos, or other protection for the ceiling above the pipes.

The institution is administered without any thought-out plan. It is neither a home, a school, a correctional institution, nor a recreational center, but a little of each. At the time of the survey the new appointees had been in charge less than two weeks, but the administrative faults were by no means entirely the fault of the present management.

Such records as come to the institution are kept in bureau drawers. There is no accounting system worthy of the name. Receipts and memoranda of past transactions have been kept on miscellaneous slips of paper. It is impossible, by consulting the records, to find out anything about the institution. There seems to be an almost total lack of appreciation of the problems connected with the attempt to train and guide the type of girl committed to its charge.

As the building was undergoing extensive repairs a group of plumbers and carpenters, inmates of the workhouse at Warrensville, were about. While visiting the kitchen, which is located in the basement, the investigator found five girls and one old man there. It was explained that the old man was an errand boy who spent most of his time in the kitchen, because the girls gave him good things to eat. Leading out of the kitchen through a passage free of doors is the boiler room, under the care of two girls, aged sixteen and seventeen. These girls fire the boiler, carry the ashes, and generally take care of the janitorial work in that part of the basement. The boiler room opens into a large basement room which had been used by the workmen. The girls' toilet is in the boiler room and is unprotected, even by a screen. The workmen have had free access through this passage either to the boiler room or to the kitchen, and the girls have had free access to the basement where the workmen are. It is our conclusion that two women can hardly keep careful watch over five or six young inmates of the workhouse and 34 inmate girls of the institution.

The training consists of housework and school work. The housework is simply cooking, cleaning, making beds, and the like. No attempt is made to teach the girls the arts of cooking and homemaking. The investigators who visited the home are all of the opinion that the housework is poorly performed. The girls themselves appear to be careless in general appearance and manner. Everything about the place speaks either of neglect or ignorance or both. Recently an advisory board, appointed by the Director of Public Welfare, has been making improvements. It is to be hoped that the new superintendent will bring the administration of the home up to the level of the boys' farm and that the city will furnish equipment which the school so much needs.

The course of study provided for these delinquent girls contains several periods a week of algebra, geometry, and art; one period a week for French, hygiene, and vocational guidance. These subjects are obviously unsuited to the institution, and the superintendent should organize the school upon a proper basis.

Recommendations

1. A thoroughly experienced woman should be put in charge at once.

2. Methods of good business administration should be adopted, such as the use of proper filing cases and a store-room for supplies. A good system of accounting should be installed.

3. Algebra, geometry, and art should be eliminated and an appropriate curriculum be substituted in which household art, physiology, hygiene, dressmaking, millinery, and kitchen gardening are emphasized.

4. A matron should be engaged for all-night duty, and additional officers employed for day duty in the school. These officers should not be sent out to make field investigations, but should remain at the institution to care for and instruct the girls.

5. The windows of the cellar and the first floor should be made secure against intrusion from without. Girls should be permitted to go to the tuberculosis sanatorium to work only when accompanied by a responsible and capable woman officer of the Girls' School.

6. The present building should be moved to a proper location as soon as possible, and upon the new site one additional modern cottage should be erected to accommodate the girls who cannot be sent there now.

CHAPTER III

PROBATION

T HE city of Cleveland employs probation officers in the Municipal and Cuyahoga County employs them in the Juvenile Court. Probation work in Common Pleas Court is supposed to be performed by parole officers attached to the State Reformatory at Mansfield and the penitentiary in Columbus. While a detailed study of the work of the State Parole Department did not fall within the scope of this survey, it is obvious that the small staff of officers attached to these two State institutions is overwhelmed with parole work and can give little time to probation work in the various counties. The Common Pleas judges in Cleveland have for a long time recognized that they cannot depend upon the parole officers of the State to conduct the painstaking investigations which the modern probation system requires. As a consequence, these judges are attempting to settle cases in advance through the imposition of sentences or by change of disposition. No matter how well intentioned the judge, the fact that he changes his dispositions so frequently in itself has a tendency to lower respect for the courts as impartial tribunals, for to the ordinary criminal a favorable change of disposition means that the court or some officer has been "seen." This attitude of offenders must be appreciated in planning a proper correctional system for Cleveland.

Municipal Court judges observe this tendency of the Common Pleas courts and have pushed it to absurd extremes. The number of cases municipal judges have to handle, the speed required, and all of the conditions surrounding the courts are productive of results which are unworthy of Cleveland. Other branches of this survey have observed in detail how cases are handled. We have confined ourselves to a study of the results of their work as these are reflected in the disposition of cases sent to the Warrensville workhouse. A portion of the results of this study are summarized in Tables 3 and 4 and graphic comparisons of the figures in the tables are presented in Diagrams 1 and 2, the former illustrating material in Table 3 and the latter the material in Table 4.

This analysis indicates clearly that Cleveland courts are attempting to perform not only the services of a court, but also those of a well-

TABLE 3.—ANALYSIS OF SENTENCES TERMINATED DURING THE MONTHS OF JANUARY, FEBRUARY, AND MARCH, 1920, CLASSIFIED BY THE KIND OF SENTENCE IMPOSED BY THE COURT

Kind of sentence	Labor	Labor and costs	Expiration and costs	Paroles	Court orders	Escapes	Still in	Misc.	Totals	
									Number	Per cent.
Time, fine, and costs	33	66	107	68	17	22	1	8	322	51.4
Time and fine	..	..	..	..	23	4	..	2	29	4.6
Time and costs	61	37	63	17	8	11	..	2	199	31.8
Time only	10	..	..	1	2	..	..	..	13	2.1
Fine and costs	24	23	..	3	1	2	..	..	53	8.5
Fine only	..	..	..	..	1	..	..	..	1	0.2
Costs only	4	2	..	2	1	..	..	..	9	1.4
Totals Number	132	128	170	91	53	39	1	12	626	100.0
Totals Per cent.	21.1	20.4	27.2	14.5	8.5	6.2	0.2	1.9	..	

TABLE 4.—ANALYSIS OF SENTENCES TERMINATED DURING THE MONTHS OF JULY, AUGUST, AND SEPTEMBER, 1920, CLASSIFIED BY THE KIND OF SENTENCE IMPOSED BY THE COURT

Kind of sentence	Labor	Labor and costs	Expiration and costs	Paroles	Court orders	Escapes	Still in	Misc.	Totals	
									Number	Per cent.
Time, fine, and costs	51	125	126	57	26	47	2	6	440	63.2
Time and fine	..	..	..	..	17	5	2	..	24	3.4
Time and costs	24	17	49	10	17	5	2	2	126	18.1
Time only	1	..	..	..	1	..	..	..	2	0.3
Fine and costs	22	60	..	1	5	1	..	..	89	12.8
Fine only	..	..	..	..	..	..	..	..	..	..
Costs only	9	4	..	..	1	..	..	1	15	2.2
Totals Number	107	206	175	68	67	58	6	9	696	100.0
Totals Per cent.	15.4	29.6	25.1	9.8	9.6	8.3	0.9	7.3	..	

conducted correctional system. The frequency with which fines are resorted to, the relatively large number of sentences terminated by court order, and the kind and length of sentences imposed indicate that the municipal courts have made dispositions of cases which, under all circumstances prevailing, place a serious check upon the development of a modern correctional system. This is brought out even more strikingly by Tables 5 and 6, which indicate the quotient of the fine plus costs

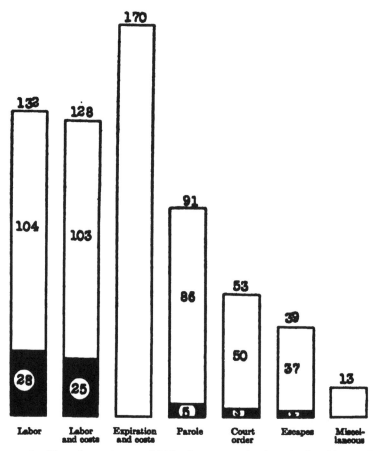

Diagram 1.—How the sentences of 626 prisoners received at the Workhouse during January, February, and March, 1920, were terminated. The black portions of the columns represent sentences which consisted only of fines and costs

divided by 60 cents per day, which is the common rate utilized for computing fines into days where prisoners do not pay their fines.

These tables show that 258, or 40.12 per cent., of these cases expired in sixty days or less, and that practically 293, or 46.80 per cent., expired in six months or less. These analyses, and the other studies made during the course of this survey, indicate the crying need for a thoroughly

modern and efficient city probation department. It is our conclusion
that judges of municipal courts could further the development of such

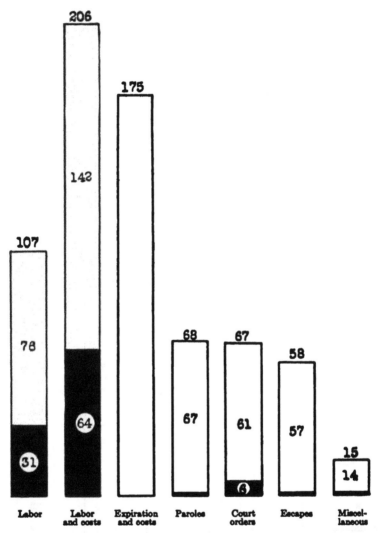

Diagram 2.—How the sentences of 696 prisoners received at the Workhouse during
July, August, and September, 1920, were terminated. The black portions of the
columns represent sentences which consisted only of fines and costs.

a modern department by refusing to impose sentence without adequate
information and demanding that the city provide a probation system
which would furnish them with information to be utilized in making

disposition of cases. The fact that the present probation system is inadequate, that the officers are much overworked, and that a cry of false

TABLE 5.—ANALYSIS OF SENTENCES IN 258 CASES, EXPIRING DURING THE MONTHS OF JANUARY, FEBRUARY, AND MARCH, 1920, BY LENGTH OF SENTENCE AND BY THE MANNER IN WHICH THE SENTENCE WAS TERMINATED

Manner of termination of sentence	1-9 days	10-19 days	20-29 days	30-39 days	40-49 days	50-59 days	Total 1-59 days	Per cent. of 626 cases
Labor	2	13	14	51	11	6	97	0.15
Labor and costs	..	6	5	26	12	11	60	0.10
Expiration and costs	..	4	1	39	14	8	66	0.11
Paroles	..	1	..	7	5	1	14	0.02
Court orders	..	2	1	5	2	..	10	0.02
Escapes	..	1	..	7	..	1	9	0.01
Still in	..	..	..	..	..	..	..	..
Miscellaneous	..	..	..	2	..	..	2	0.01
Total prisoners	2	27	21	137	44	27	258	0.41

TABLE 6.—ANALYSIS OF SENTENCES IN 293 CASES, EXPIRING DURING THE MONTHS OF JANUARY, FEBRUARY, AND MARCH, 1920, BY LENGTH OF SENTENCE AND BY THE MANNER IN WHICH SENTENCE WAS TERMINATED

Manner of termination of sentence	60-69 days	70-79 days	80-89 days	90-99 days	100-124 days	125-149 days	150-174 days	175-199 days	Totals Days	Per cent. of 626 cases
Labor	4	23	2	2	1	2	..	1	35	0.06
Labor and costs	3	22	7	8	16	4	3	2	65	0.10
Expiration and costs	11	17	20	10	25	12	4	1	100	0.16
Paroles	1	15	8	3	12	4	4	2	49	0.08
Court orders	..	3	3	1	5	1	..	1	14	0.02
Escapes	..	9	4	3	1	2	4	..	23	0.04
Still in	..	..	..	..	..	..	..	..	..	..
Miscellaneous	..	4	1	..	2	..	..	..	7	0.01
Total cases	19	93	45	27	62	25	15	7	293	0.47

economy is now insistent ought not discourage judges and citizens generally in pressing for this much-needed reorganization of Municipal Court work.

The probation system of Cleveland Municipal Courts has two distinct branches—probation for adult men and probation for adult women. Technically, probation for both men and women is under the supervision of the chief probation officer, James Metlicka. As a matter of fact, Mr. Metlicka has charge only of male adult probation. Mrs. Antoinette Callaghan regards herself as chief of the Woman's Probation Department, holds herself wholly independent of Mr. Metlicka, and conducts her branch of the work as an entirely separate unit.[1]

The physical conditions under which this department is carried on constitute a serious handicap to effective work. It is housed in a small room adjoining Municipal Court-room No. 1, and accommodates Mr. Metlicka and his two assistants.

When observed on May 2 and 3, the office was continually crowded. Three probation officers were attempting to carry on investigation work with individuals, receive reports, collect money, make out receipts, and at the same time keep track of the court-room. They were actually receiving prisoners placed on probation by the court. As a further aggravation, each probation officer must be his own clerk, as no clerk or typist is provided. The record work is crude and unsatisfactory. The records are of little value. The filing system could hardly be called a system, and the entire volume of work is done under a strain which makes good work impossible.

The chief probation officer collects from $3,000 to $5,000 a month from probationers. Until a short time ago large amounts of this money were carried on his person, as he banked money but once or twice a week. His accounts are audited but once a year. Mr. Metlicka could not tell the surveyor how many people were on probation. He said the number fluctuated rapidly, and since he had neither clerk nor stenographer, it was impossible to keep this and many other vital matters up to date. He referred to past reports as the only source of information on such points.

Examination of the files of the department show that its work is confined to the investigation of police reports and cases requested by the judge, prosecutor, or police, which are reported upon generally by one of the two assistants. The reports are written in pencil on different kinds of stationery, and filed generally, if at all, in this form. Reports

---

[1] Mr. Metlicka complains that Mrs. Callaghan will not coöperate. Mrs. Callaghan complains that Mr. Metlicka's records, procedure, and general handling of the office make coöperation impossible, but Mr. Metlicka has been able to coöperate with the Women's Protective Association and the latter has been able to coöperate with him.

to judges or to the police department are, as a rule, in verbal form. There are no stenographic or other notes. There is a small report card, which becomes a part of the permanent file, and some, but not all, of the facts obtained by investigation are placed upon this card.

Obviously, the adult probation work is lacking in efficiency. It is clear that there is no real administrative ability back of the work; that the court gives no decisive direction or oversight; that the chief probation officer is without a constructive plan, but makes an effort day by day to meet the problems of that day. In view of the absurd conditions under which he undertakes so vast a work, the wonder is that he does anything at all. We are of the opinion that the chief responsibility for this condition must rest upon the Chief Justice of the Municipal Court, who has power to appoint additional help, to cause a reorganization of the work, and to provide better quarters.

Mrs. Callaghan labors under practically the same handicaps that confront Mr. Metlicka. She has two associates—one a college graduate and the other, a young colored woman, who has had considerable experience in the Colored Y.W.C.A.

Mrs. Callaghan has a definite organization, a definite plan of work, a consistent and fairly well-kept record of what she has done and is doing, a fair system of reports, and a follow-up system which, while not adequate, is as well thought out and as well administered as lack of facilities will permit. She stated frankly that she had little occasion to call upon Mr. Metlicka's division, because there was rarely anything in common in the cases under consideration. She said that whenever she called upon Mr. Metlicka she found him ready to coöperate. On the other hand, we found that she makes use of the Children's Bureau of the Welfare Federation, of the work performed by Miss Walters in the Boys' School, and frequently calls upon the latter for mental tests of probationers.

The Women's Protective Association maintains an office which opens into Municipal Court-room No. 2. The Association's work in the Municipal Court is non-official. It tries to be of assistance to both divisions of the Probation Department, and is willing to furnish field investigations and assist even in clerical work. It is difficult to believe, however, that its work can be effective unless a harmonious working basis is established between the official Probation Department and the Association. If this organization could be used officially, perhaps under the direction of the Chief Justice of the Municipal Court, its coöperation might make the probation office effective, for the Association not only has trained workers and a competent administrator at its head, but also a well-organized plan of work, essentials which the official Probation Department lacks.

A modern Probation Department, serving as an aid to the court in conducting impartial inquiries and as a potent agency for effecting the rehabilitation of offenders, has long since passed the experimental stages and is now a primary essential of every community. In considering alternative plans for the development of an effective probationary system in lieu of the present inadequacies, we have inquired particularly whether better results could be obtained if probation work in the Common Pleas Courts were left in the hands of the State Board of Administration and the probation work of Municipal Courts were placed either under the control of the Board of Administration or were permitted to remain under the jurisdiction of the city government. In this connection consideration has been given to possible modern developments which might flow from coöperation of the Parole and Probation Departments of the new State Department of Public Welfare and its Bureau of Juvenile Research, particularly if that Bureau were expanded into a psychopathic clearing-house, classification and research institution for adults as well as juveniles.

After a full inquiry, with the opportunities to consider the problem with the Governor of the State and the various State officials, the investigator reached the conclusion that the desired policy is to be found in the so-called Gorrell Bill. The chief feature of this bill, as amended, is its provision that probation work should be carried on under the jurisdiction and supervision of the various county courts. This provision, if enacted, will permit the courts in Cuyahoga and other counties to conduct their own probation work subject to the inspection and supervision of the State Board of Administration or its successor, the Department of Public Welfare. We are of the opinion that the enactment of this law would lead to extensive developments in various counties in accordance with their ability or desire to develop probation work, and that these developments or experiments in probation work would lead to helpful rivalry between the counties in developing this necessary division of judicial administration. It is our belief that the results obtained by such competition would more than outweigh any disadvantages that might flow from lack of common probation standards. At any rate, the legislature could authorize the State Department of Public Welfare so to exercise regulatory supervision over the work of the various counties as to prevent unwholesome rivalry or unwise experiments.

This raises the question of the manner in which a proper investigation staff is to be developed, and the number of persons required for such work. A capable and resourceful chief probation officer, an office manager, two chiefs of field investigation, 20 parole officers, eight clerks and stenographers should be employed at once to begin the work. Such a staff should be increased gradually until the number of probation officers reaches at least 56. The recommended immediate staff is smaller by 14 than that provided for the Parole Commission of New York, which handles about 5,000 cases per year, under a system which might well serve as experience for consideration in developing a real Probation Department for Cleveland and Cuyahoga County.

After considering the situation in Ohio, we are convinced that it is not advisable from any point of view to hold back the development of probation in Cleveland pending the possible extension of the work in the State Bureau of Juvenile Research. The people of Cleveland should develop in their school system, in the psychopathic and city hospitals, in the various other hospitals, the Normal School, the Western Reserve University Medical School, and in the Health Department, mental and other diagnostic services which would insure the most careful examination of every individual handled by the courts, whether ultimately placed on probation or sentenced to an institution. The fullest development of this service would work a revolution in court, probation, and institutional activities.[1] The city has the opportunity to provide, in its contemplated new court-house, office building, and jail, adequate quarters for an examining staff of physicians, psychiatrists, psychologists, probation officers, and other necessary attachés of a modern probation system. Ordinary cases could be examined in the new building at a minimum cost, while more difficult cases could be sent to the city and psychopathic hospitals, now under construction.

RECOMMENDATIONS

1. The courts should stop trying to make final disposition of so many cases and reduce the number of changes in dispositions.

2. A capable chief probation officer and 20 adult probation officers

---

[1] The investigator has given considerable attention to the identification system in operation in Cleveland. The work appears to be thoroughly reliable and within its limits competent, but the scope is too limited, because of the studied opposition of habitual criminals and of the unthinking opposition of the occasional citizen who, for some reason or another, associates finger-prints with crime. This opposition is not well founded, for the reason that finger-print identification has been applied throughout the army, is utilized by many banks and private corporations and by public bodies in this and other countries, and is the least objectionable identification record yet devised.

should be employed at once. An adequate office should be provided for the department, and a capable follow-up record system and field investigation system should be adopted. The chief probation officer should be the liaison officer between the Municipal Courts and the other official and non-official organizations capable of assisting the courts in determining all the facts of the personal, family, social, educational, and industrial histories of prisoners.

3. The courts in the various counties of the State should be authorized to organize their own probation departments.

4. The Common Pleas and the Municipal Courts should join with other public and private agencies in establishing proper diagnostic and treatment centers in the public schools, the city's new general psychopathic hospital, the various hospitals, the School of Education, the Western Reserve University Medical School, the Health Department, and the large industries of Cleveland.

5. If the two courts are combined on their criminal side, as recommended in the section of this Survey devoted to the criminal courts, the chief probation officer of the Juvenile Court should become chief probation officer of the combined city and county criminal court.

CHAPTER IV

PAROLES, COMMUTATIONS, AND PARDONS

THE Ohio General Code vests the managers of the workhouses with considerable discretion in discharging and paroling inmates committed thereto.[1]

In the city of Cleveland the Director of Public Welfare, the parole

---

[1] Sections 4133, 4134, 4135, 4136, and 4137 of the code granting the authority to release, re-arrest, and return inmates of the workhouse, read as follows:

"Discharge and record thereof. An officer vested by statute with authority to manage a workhouse, may discharge, for good and sufficient cause, a person committed thereto. A record of all such discharges shall be kept and reported to the council, in the annual report of the officer, with a brief statement of the reasons therefor.

"Parole of inmates. Such officer also may establish rules and regulations under which, and specify the conditions on which, a prisoner may be allowed to go upon parole outside of buildings and enclosures. While on parole such person shall remain in the legal custody and under the control of the officer, and subject at any time to be taken back within the enclosure of the institution. Full power to enforce the rules, regulations, and conditions, and to retake and reimprison any convict so upon parole, is hereby conferred upon such officer, whose written order shall be sufficient warrant for all officers named therein to authorize them to return to actual custody any conditionally released or paroled prisoner. All such officers shall execute such order the same as ordinary criminal process.

"Violation of parole. Such officer may employ or authorize any person or persons to see that the conditions of a parole are not violated, and in case of violation to return to the workhouse any prisoner so violating his parole, and the time between the violation of the conditions of such parole, or conditional release by whatever name, as entered by order of the officer on the records of the workhouse, and the reimprisonment or return of the prisoner, shall not be counted as any part or portion of time served under his sentence.

"Return of paroled to custody. Any prisoner at large upon parole who fails to return to the actual custody of the workhouse as specified as one of the conditions of his parole, or commits a fresh crime and is convicted thereof, shall be, on the order of the officer, treated as an escaped prisoner and subject to the penalties named in Sec. 12840. But no parole shall be granted by any such officer without previous notice thereof to the trial judge.

"Officers to have police powers. The superintendent, assistant superintendent, and each guard of the workhouse shall have such powers of policeman as may be necessary for the proper performance of the duties of his position."

officer of the department, and the superintendent of the workhouse jointly exercise the powers conferred by law upon the director alone.

ADMINISTRATION

The parole officer prepares the records of prisoners whose cases are under consideration for parole. The so-called records are in reality the results of his own and the director's personal investigations, as no information about cases is furnished by the courts or the probation officers save what appears upon the commitment papers. The director hence puts in a great deal of time upon the investigation and consideration of individual cases.

Under the existing arrangement, extensive consideration of cases is largely labor lost, for the workhouse keeps practically no records. When a man presents himself for consideration, information concerning him is furnished verbally by the superintendent of the workhouse. If the superintendent's recommendation is favorable and the man has a letter from a friend or an alleged former employer or an alleged relation, his chances of parole are good. If he is paroled, he is merely turned out of the institution and allowed to look after himself without supervision, unless there is an unremitted fine to look after or some adjustment with respect to children, in which case the parole officer looks after the case. Many men who spend the winter at the workhouse at the city's expense are released when the ice goes out with the hope that they may get jobs on the lake during the navigation season. Under prevailing conditions adequate and necessary supervision of men on parole is impossible.

Director Blossom and Parole Officer Miller are conscientious and use good judgment in handling cases, but the whole system of parole is so crude and undeveloped as to be wholly inadequate. Under existing conditions, where there is no record system either in the institutions or in the central office, a single parole officer should not be required to handle more than 50 cases. If an adequate system of institutional and parole records were installed, such as we are filing with the Survey Committee as a part of this report, a single parole officer should be able to handle 100 cases.

If the courts did not attempt to handle the cases by the form of sentence imposed, by the great number of changes in dispositions and the number of recalls, the pressure exercised by the prisoners would doubtless have forced a better parole system long ago, but, although the judges are admittedly without adequate information concerning the prisoners, they are apparently content not only to guess and guess again, but also to change their guesses frequently in particular cases, as statistics collected in the course of this survey clearly show. In this connection we confine ourselves to a study of the manner in which 626 and 696 prisoners previously sentenced to the workhouse were released therefrom during January, February, and March, 1920, and during July, August, and September, 1920, respectively.

TABLE 7.—SUMMARY OF THE MANNER IN WHICH 626 AND 696 PRISONERS WERE RELEASED FROM THE WORKHOUSE DURING STATED PERIODS IN 1920

Manner of release	January, February, and March, 1920	Percentage of 626	July, August, and September, 1920	Percentage of 696
Labor	132	21.1	107	15.4
Labor and costs	128	20.4	206	29.6
Expiration and costs	170	27.2	175	25.1
Paroles	91	14.5	68	9.8
Court orders	53	8.5	67	9.6
Escapes	39	6.2	58	8.3
Still in	1	0.2	6	0.9
Miscellaneous	12	1.9	9	1.3
Total	626	100.0	696	100.0

Table 7 shows the great preponderance of court action and the relative infrequency of parole department action in bringing about the release of prisoners at the workhouse.

Space does not permit detailed analysis here of the data[1] summarized in Table 7 and also in Tables 2 and 6 inclusive.[2] From the material at hand the conclusion may be drawn that judges, in sentencing prisoners to the workhouse, are seriously overworking fines and do not give sufficient attention to the factors which determine whether prisoners are fit to return to the community as law-abiding citizens. The courts in Cleveland, like the courts all over the country, are confining their action too closely to the determination of innocence or guilt, and have not only lost sight of the equally significant consideration of preparing prisoners for return to society, but also, in attempting to determine in advance how long prisoners shall remain in correctional institutions and the manner of their release, have so hampered and restricted the institutions that the latter have not been able to function adequately. Courts, pro-

---

[1] The detailed analysis is contained in 10 statistical tables which, because of the limitation of space, are filed with the Cleveland Foundation, where they may be consulted by those interested.

[2] See Chapter V.

bation officers, institutions, and parole departments all have their parts to play, but they must not be allowed to function in isolation. The laws, no less than the mental habits governing the work in Cleveland, should be so modified that these agencies can and will function together.

The insistent claim as to the proneness of prisoners on parole from State institutions to commit serious crimes led us to try to determine the truth or falsity of these charges. As there was not sufficient time at our disposal to complete such a study, and preliminary investigation indicated that there were not enough cases to demonstrate beyond doubt that the charges were true, we applied to Warden P. E. Thomas, of the penitentiary at Columbus, and were furnished by him with an analysis of the number of cases received at the penitentiary during the years 1918, 1919, and 1920. The percentage of parole violators among those received for each of the years is reported as follows:

1918................................... 5.6 per cent.
1919................................... 4.9 per cent.
1920................................... 4.4 per cent.

Warden Thomas states that his figures for the eight years from 1913 to 1921 show only 196, or 4.15 per cent., of 4,713 prisoners serving indeterminate sentences, previously paroled from the penitentiary, who were returned parole violators. Also that about 18 per cent. of the total population of the penitentiary at the present time previously served terms in the State Reformatory at Mansfield. If we are to accept these figures at their face value, the charges against the system in Ohio are clearly disproved, for the percentage of violators is phenomenally low. Only a most careful investigation would show clearly why the percentage is so low. It is necessary to determine whether released prisoners have gone to other States, whether they have been clever enough to use others as "cat's-paws," or whether the police in the various Ohio cities and the parole work of the penitentiary have allowed a number to operate with immunity. These would be fruitful lines of inquiry, and until they have been followed, the parole system is entitled to considerable benefit of the doubt.

In order to bring about the most efficient court, probation, institutional, and parole work, we recommend that a law be enacted somewhat similar to the New York legislation (Chapter 579 of the laws of 1915 of the State of New York, as amended by Chapter 287 of the laws of 1916),[1] pursuant to which offenders of various classes, if twice con-

---

[1] Copies of these statutes were attached to this report but were omitted because of lack of space. They are on file at the office of the Cleveland Foundation.

victed of any one of a number of offenses within twenty-four months or three times previously within any period, if sentenced to imprisonment in any institution, must be given an indeterminate sentence not to exceed two years, which may be terminated by the parole commission at any time. Another section of this law provides that judges imposing sentence to imprisonment in a workhouse similar to the one at Warrensville shall be members of the parole board which determines the time a prisoner is to remain in the workhouse and his eligibility for parole. The law also gives judges sentencing prisoners to the penitentiary absolute veto power over the parole commission's release on parole. Such a method depends for its success not only upon the care exercised by judges, but also upon the use of an infallible system of identification which, as we have already set forth, must become the corner-stone of any efficient correction system.

The recent enactment of the so-called Norwood Bill[1] complicates the situation in Ohio. This law attempts to strike at the reported evil of too frequent paroles by penitentiary authorities by requiring the courts to fix, within the limit prescribed by law, a minimum period of duration of all sentences in all felony cases, except in the case of treason and murder in the first degree.

The objections to this measure we set forth in a memorandum to Governor Davis, who refused to approve the bill, which, however, became law without his signature.[2] The objections as given in the letter were:

1. It will produce confusion and serious inequalities because of the individual differences in minimum sentences which will be imposed in the various courts.

2. It will lead to the imposition of short sentences in some courts for offenses committed by frequent offenders, who will become sullen agitators and disturbers in the penitentiary if the Board of Clemency or the Board of Parole, its probable successor, imposes the usual requirement of a longer stay within the prison enclosure before such a repeater is allowed to go out upon parole.

3. It is not the best way in which to achieve the results the introducer and many of its supporters evidently had in mind as necessary and important.

4. It will seriously hamper, if not prevent, the progressive development of the proper administration of the penitentiary and of the parole law, since the whole tendency of its administration will be to place emphasis upon penalties imposed by the various judges alleged to be necessary to fit the crime and to

---

[1] See Appendix.

[2] A substitute bill was submitted as a part of this report, but was omitted because of lack of space. It is on file at the office of the Cleveland Foundation.

push into the background questions of reformation and restoration of the prisoner as a law-abiding citizen.

We recommend in its place the enactment of a law similar to Chapter 579, of the laws of the State of New York for the year 1915, pursuant to which the court sentences the prisoner to the penitentiary for the statutory maximum but with no minimum. Within ninety days after the prisoner is received at the penitentiary the results of a full study of all the information the court had at the time the prisoner was sentenced and of all information the parole board and the penitentiary officials are able to secure in addition, are embodied in a classification report which is forwarded to the judicial officer presiding in the court where sentence was imposed, with a recommendation of what minimum requirement shall be imposed upon the prisoner as a condition of his parole. If the judicial officer presiding approves the recommendation, he affixes his signature to the report. If he disapproves, he so states in writing, and if he so desires, he indicates in writing upon the face of the report in the space provided what minimum requirement he thinks should be imposed. In any event, after this return is received by the parole commission, it notifies the prisoner what the minimum requirement shall be and both it and the prisoner know that the prisoner cannot go out upon parole until the judicial officer presiding in the court in which sentence was imposed gives his approval thereto in writing.

The principal arguments in favor of this law may be summarized as follows:

1. It breaks down the Chinese wall between the courts and the penitentiary, and forces reasonable coöperation between these two most important correctional forces.

2. It avoids the imposition of minimum sentences by different judges which produce bitterness and lack of respect for the courts in the minds of the very persons who are in most need of gaining more respect for courts and the law—the prisoners themselves.

3. It places a reasonable check upon any undue leniency of ministerial officials and in most cases will give their work judicial sanction.

4. It provides a channel through which the judicial authorities may exercise proper control over punishment and become officially and vitally interested in administration and the rehabilitation of the prisoner.

5. It allows the judicial officer to express his judgment as to minimum requirements, not when the prisoner is sentenced when conditions are abnormal and only some of the facts about the prisoner and his crime are known, but after a much more complete investigation of the prisoner's record and environment has been made and after much more is known about the peculiar and particular characteristics of the prisoner himself.

For five years such a law has been in successful operation in New York city, and there is now a likelihood that its provisions will be made applicable to State prisons. It is looked upon with favor by judges and penologists generally.

We, therefore, urge the repeal of the Norwood Bill.

It must be expected that the Norwood law will largely increase the demands for executive clemency and conditional pardons in order to overcome the inequalities of the minimum sentence imposed by the judges in the various courts of the State. In some States the judges in one section place on probation a man who steals chickens, while in another section of the same State such a man is sentenced to imprisonment from two to eight years. Demands for executive clemency and conditional pardons mean not only a vast increase in the work of the Governor's office, but also develop a tendency to break away from the present system, which vests in the Board of Clemency rather than the chief executive officer of the State the duty of determining whether a man shall be released on parole or recommended to the Governor for executive clemency or pardon. This development is particularly unfortunate, as the executive clemency and pardon should be reserved for obvious miscarriage of justice or in recognition of unusual conduct during imprisonment.

We have been furnished with a tabulation of pardons and commutations granted by the Governors of Ohio in 1915–1916 and 1917–1918, which indicate that the present tendency in Ohio already is for the Governor to exercise functions which should be reserved for consideration of the Pardon and Parole Department of the State government. The too free exercise of the pardon and commutation powers of the Governor is open to criticism because it seriously interferes with the proper functioning of corrective agencies.

Table 8 shows the pardons and commutations granted in the years 1915 to 1918 inclusive.

In 1915 and 1916 life sentences were reduced to terms varying from one year and two months to thirty years; and indeterminate sentences of one to fifteen and twenty years were changed to terms carrying from one month to twelve years. During 1917 and 1918 life sentences were reduced to terms varying from nine months to nineteen years and indeterminate sentences of one to twenty and thirty years were reduced to terms varying from twenty days to fourteen years.

It may be that the Governor, recognizing the imperfections of the Ohio Indeterminate Sentence Law, was attempting to right obvious injustices, but free use of the power of the Governor is not the best remedy for such conditions. A Governor of a State is too busy to attend to these matters and may easily be imposed upon. This is indicated by

[54]

TABLE 8.—PARDONS AND COMMUTATIONS BY THE GOVERNOR OF OHIO, 1915 TO 1918

Offense	1915–1916		1917–1918	
	Pardons	Commutations	Pardons	Commutations
Murder, first degree	3	6	5	7
Murder, second degree	13	18	26	7
Homicide	..	..	1	..
Manslaughter	5	1	3	1
Shooting to kill	4	3	3	1
Shooting to wound	1	..	..	..
Cutting to kill	1	..	1	1
Cutting to wound	..	..	1	..
Assault to kill	2	2	6	..
Maiming	1	..	..	1
Rape	3	5	6	2
Assault to rape	3	1	..	..
Having carnal knowledge of insane women	..	..	1	..
Abortion	1	1	..	..
Incest	..	1	..	..
Burglary of inhabited dwelling	2	3	5	6
Burglary	11	7	3	..
Burglary and larceny	6	2	5	5
Grand larceny	6	2	7	3
Robbery	1	4	6	..
Robbery and operating motor vehicle without owner's consent	..	..	1	..
Safe-blowing	1	..	..	..
Pocketpicking	1	3	3	2
Theft of automobile	1	..	2	1
Horse-stealing	..	1	1	..
Having burglar tools in possession	..	1	..	..
Receiving stolen goods	..	1	2	..
Forgery	5	3	6	..
Embezzlement	6	3	5	3
Extortion	2	..	..	..
False pretenses	1	..	1	..
Blackmail	..	..	1	..
Carrying concealed weapons	1	2	2	1
Attempt to dynamite cars	1	..	..	..
Arson	5	1	..	..
Burning building with intent to prejudice insurer	..	..	1	..
Non-support	5	1	9	2
Bigamy	..	..	1	..
Perjury	1	1	1	..
Unlawful transportation of female for purpose of prostitution	..	..	1	..
Contributing to juvenile delinquency	..	..	1	..
Aiding prisoner to escape	..	..	1	..
Sub-total	93	73	118	43
Total	166		161	

the typical causes for pardons and commutations assigned in the applications submitted to the Governor or stated by the Governor in taking action. Among these were the following:

> Recommended by county officials and reputable citizens
> Recommended by prison officials
> Recommended by trial judge and prosecuting attorney
> Good prison record
> Desire to join relatives in another State
> Imminent danger of death
> Long term and good prison record
> Because of doubt as to guilt
> Strong evidence of reform and repentance
> Lack of mental responsibility
> Weak circumstantial evidence
> Poor health and good conduct in prison
> Worthy of a pardon in honor of a holiday
> Ignorance of our American laws

A serious objection to the wide use of executive clemency is the encouragement it gives to disreputable lawyers to "bleed" relatives and friends of prisoners by making promises of pardon which they hope to secure.

RECOMMENDATIONS

The summary of recommendations is as follows:

1. The Department of Public Welfare in Cleveland should have an appropriation for an adequate parole system.

2. The Norwood Bill, enacted by the 1921 session of the Ohio Legislature, should be repealed.

3. A law similar to the Indeterminate Sentence and Parole Law of New York, known as Chapter 579, Laws of 1915, as amended by Chapter 287 of the Laws of 1916, should be adopted so that the courts and institutional authorities may coöperate to the greatest advantage.

4. The governor should not exercise the pardon, parole, and commutation powers vested in him by the State constitution, except to right obvious wrongs where there is no other legal remedy, or in the event of any unusual conduct. All other cases should be passed upon first by the Division of Pardons and Paroles, and should go to the governor only upon the recommendation of that division.

CHAPTER V

THE PROPOSED NEW CRIMINAL COURT, COUNTY JAIL, AND POLICE HEADQUARTERS BUILDING

CLEVELAND'S postponement of the erection of a new building or buildings to house criminal courts, insolvency and juvenile courts, police headquarters, and city and county detention prisons has brought one compensation: namely, that of being now in a position to build in accordance with the most modern plans and at a great reduction in cost. As a result of extensive public discussions and reports, the people of Cleveland are now in a better position to pass intelligently upon proposed plans and to determine the most practicable administrative and building programs.

Any solution of the problem is conditioned to a certain extent by what has already been done. The city plan committee of the Chamber of Commerce, under date of January 26, 1921, expressed the opinion that all business offices of the city and county should be removed from the present civil courts building and that building used exclusively for the courts; and that the criminal court should be housed in a more imposing building than that which would be necessary for the county treasurer and other county offices, or the police department, detention rooms, police headquarters, and the like. The committee was further of the opinion that the latter should be housed in a completely utilitarian type of building. The suggestion was made that the site to the west and north of the court-house be left for the office services of the county, the departments of the treasury, auditor, recorder, engineer, and the like, for in this way excavation already begun on the present site need not be entirely lost.

While many of the suggestions of the Chamber of Commerce committee are worthy of serious consideration, they do not seem to give sufficient attention to the desirability of placing police headquarters, county and city jails, the various criminal courts, prosecutors' offices, jury-rooms, witness-rooms, and probation offices in the same building. Time and energy spent in making transfers and in providing a staff of officers for courts, jails, and other offices housed in separate buildings will then be saved, besides the cost of maintaining separate identification and other record systems for courts, prosecutors, police, city, county, and State institutions. Opportunity for this complete and necessary record system ought not to be lost through a system of building construction and housing which would make it prohibitive.

In making this change Cleveland would be taking another step forward in eliminating evil conditions which result from sentencing prisoners to terms in the county jail. City and county jails should be used exclusively as detention prisons; terms should be served in the city, county, and State institutions provided for that purpose.

If we are to disregard for the moment the cell blocks for the jails, and if the requirements of the Group Plan Commission limit the architect, as is claimed, we are of the opinion that the latter has made an acceptable layout of rooms and offices. However, the requirements of the Group Plan Commission are such as to preclude any possibility of combining a modern jail with the remainder of this building, as a modern jail cannot be planned except in a building where the cells are in wings permitting plenty of light and air, proper classification of prisoners, and proper courts for exercise in the open air.

The building commission should not be stampeded into accepting an architectural design which limits the possibility of thoroughly modern and up-to-date criminal administration. If the commission were to yield this point, it would repeat the mistakes made in designing the Warrensville workhouse and the city infirmary at Warrensville.

There is danger that the commission may swing to the opposite extreme, for there are some who believe that the courts should be housed in a building of classic design, and that anything is good enough for a jail and almost anything good enough for a police headquarters. This is an erroneous viewpoint, for the reason that poor design and bad taste lower the whole tone of administration and thus indirectly increase the cost of administration. This has been demonstrated in public institutions in the East, as well as the fact that the office building type of construction can be used to advantage in public buildings.

The whole tendency in modern office building construction is to build four walls, provide elevators, stairways, fire-escapes, and proper corridors, and arrange the remainder of the interior as tenants desire. There is no difficulty in constructing a modern hotel in devoting two stories or a part of the building to a theater, dining-room, or banquet hall.

We are, therefore, of the opinion that unless the Group Plan Commission can change its réquirements, as reported, so as to permit a

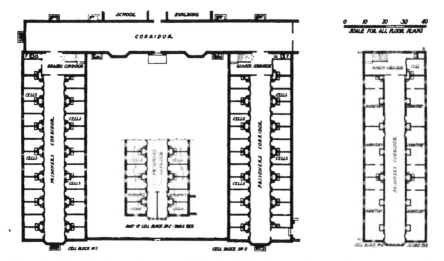

Fig. 1.—Typical floor plans of cell blocks, Westchester County Penitentiary and Workhouse, White Plains, N. Y.   Alfred Hopkins, architect

Fig. 2.—General view, Westchester County Penitentiary and Workhouse.   Alfred Hopkins, architect

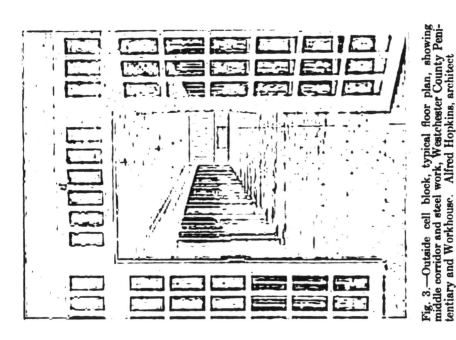

Fig. 3.—Outside cell block, typical floor plan, showing middle corridor and steel work, Westchester County Penitentiary and Workhouse. Alfred Hopkins, architect

Fig. 4.—Typical cell, Westchester County Penitentiary and Workhouse, showing equipment and outside window. Alfred Hopkins, architect

higher building with three wings containing three cell blocks which might extend either toward the lake or toward the present Civil Courts Building, it is advisable to build a structure of office building type to contain the criminal court, prosecutor's office, police headquarters, and county and city jails upon the site on the public square now occupied by the county jail and old court-house. This site is more favorably situated with regard to transportation and population to be served than that on the Mall. It would not be difficult to wreck the buildings on the old court-house and county jail site if temporary quarters can be rented for the county jail and the criminal courts.

Since there is sufficient land, a building with wings for cell blocks could be constructed to the greatest advantage. If the commission wishes to have interior cell construction of the modernized Auburn type for so-called desperate criminals awaiting trial, a small section of one wing could be utilized for this purpose, leaving the remainder of the building with the outside cell construction, thus providing complete classification, which is not possible under the Auburn plan. The great advantage of the outside cell for most cases awaiting trial is too obvious to require comment here. The Westchester County (N. Y.) institution has demonstrated that such a building can be made as secure as the inside cell construction of the Auburn type.

If the plan of the building is changed in the manner suggested, the three wings containing three cell blocks of outside cell construction should be separated from police headquarters, Municipal Court, and Common Pleas Court by corridors with exits and entrances on appropriate floors, in accordance with the typical floor plan of the cell blocks of the Westchester County penitentiary and workhouse at White Plains, New York, the plan of which is shown in Fig. 1. The space between the three cell blocks can be used as two outdoor exercise courts for the prisoners of different classes to exercise at different times. If this plan is used, space should be left between the ends of the cells and the cell block side of the corridors so that prisoners on each tier may be served food at tables, in order to avoid feeding prisoners in their cells or in a common dining-hall. This cell block construction not only provides a maximum of light and air, as is indicated by Fig. 1, but secures the best type of cell. (See typical cell, Fig 4.) In order to prevent prisoners from letting down strings from outside windows to the sidewalk on the sides of such a building, it will be necessary to erect a wall as high as the top of the second tier of cells. With such a system as the one outlined, Cleveland would avoid creating criminals while waiting to determine innocence or guilt. It is not tenable to argue

[59]

that this jail system cannot be made architecturally desirable, for the general view of the Westchester County penitentiary and workhouse shown in Fig. 3, proves the contrary. Moreover, the low cost of the Westchester County structure shows clearly that it cannot be ruled out on the grounds of expense.

RECOMMENDATIONS

The summary of recommendations is as follows:

1. Police headquarters, criminal courts, prosecutors' office, and county and city jails should be housed in a single building of the office building type.

2. The jail section should be included in three wings containing three cell blocks, with a complete separation of each tier of each block by utilizing outside cell construction, reserving the space between these blocks for exercise courts.

3. Wherever the sides or ends of the cell blocks are on the sidewalk line or may be approached from the ground level, they should be surrounded by a wall extending from the top of the second tier of the cell block.

4. All food should be prepared in a single kitchen for both the city and county jail sections, and it should be served at tables set up in spaces at the corridor ends of the cell blocks.

5. The two jails should be served by one laundry and one emergency hospital.

6. A single system of identification and other primary records should be maintained. These should be open to constant use, under proper regulations, by all the courts, the police, the prosecutors, and the probation officers.

7. The Juvenile Court should be eliminated from the plans for this building and provided for as previously recommended, either in a new building to be erected adjacent to the Detention Home or in a public school building.

8. If the Group Plan Commission cannot be prevailed upon to allow an office building type of construction on the Mall, this structure, as recommended, should be placed upon the site of the present county jail and criminal court building.

9. The county building commission should avail itself of the services of consulting architects, so that the most economical and modern type of structure may be provided. In carrying out this plan the studies of the present architect should be utilized as far as possible, and the building commission should not feel bound by any previous mistakes.

The consideration of expenditures made up to the present should not outweigh that of present savings of cost, improvements in service, and permanent economy of operation and maintenance.

10. Legislation should be passed to keep the court from sentencing any one to a term of imprisonment in the existing county jail or any new county or city jail which may be erected.

APPENDIX

SENATE Bill No. 8, of the Eighty-fourth General Assembly Regular Session, 1921, of Ohio Legislature, introduced by Senator Norwood, and which became a law without the Governor's approval:

A BILL

To amend section 2166 of the General Code, relative to indeterminate sentence to the Ohio Penitentiary.

BE IT ENACTED BY THE GENERAL ASSEMBLY OF THE STATE OF OHIO:

Section 1. That section 2166 of the General Code be amended to read as follows:

Sec. 2166. Courts imposing sentences to the Ohio penitentiary for felonies, except treason, and murder in the first degree, shall make them general, . . . *but they shall fix within the limits prescribed by law, a minimum period of duration of such sentences.* All terms of imprisonment of persons in the Ohio penitentiary may be terminated by the Ohio board of clemency, as authorized by this chapter, but no such terms shall exceed the maximum . . . *term provided by law for the felony of which the prisoner was convicted, nor be less than the minimum term fixed by the court for such felony.* If a prisoner is sentenced for two or more separate felonies, his term of imprisonment may equal, but shall not exceed, the aggregate of the maximum terms of all the felonies for which he was sentenced and, for the purposes of this chapter he shall be held to be serving one continuous term of imprisonment. If through oversight or otherwise, a sentence to the Ohio penitentiary should be for a definite term, it shall not thereby become void, but the person so sentenced shall be subject to the liabilities of this chapter and receive the benefits thereof, as if he had not been sentenced in the manner required by this section.

Section 2. That said original section 2166 of the General Code and all laws or parts of laws inconsistent with this act be, and the same are hereby repealed.

MEDICAL SCIENCE AND CRIMINAL JUSTICE

MEDICAL SCIENCE AND CRIMINAL JUSTICE

BY

HERMAN M. ADLER, M.D.

STATE CRIMINOLOGIST OF ILLINOIS

PART V

OF THE CLEVELAND FOUNDATION SURVEY OF

CRIMINAL JUSTICE IN CLEVELAND

FOREWORD

THIS is one of eight sections of the report of the Cleveland Foundation Survey of Criminal Justice in Cleveland. The survey was directed and the reports edited by Roscoe Pound and Felix Frankfurter. Sections which have been published are:

The Criminal Courts, by Reginald Heber Smith and Herbert B. Ehrmann

Prosecution, by Alfred Bettman

Other sections to be published are:

Police, by Raymond Fosdick

Penal Treatment and Correctional Institutions, by Burdette G. Lewis

Newspapers and Criminal Justice, by M. K. Wisehart

Legal Education in Cleveland, by Albert M. Kales

Criminal Justice in the American City, a Summary, by Roscoe Pound

The sections are being published first in separate form, each bound in paper. About November 1 the report will be available in a single volume, cloth bound. Orders for separate sections or the bound volume may be left with book-stores or with the Cleveland Foundation, 1202 Swetland Building.

PREFATORY NOTE

THIS section of the Cleveland Foundation Survey of Criminal Justice which deals with Medical Science and Criminal Justice was designed by Dean Pound primarily to answer the question, "How far are modern methods of psychological and psychopathic investigation and treatment made use of or available in Cleveland?"

While the original conception of Dean Pound has been kept practically intact, the scope of the inquiry has been slightly enlarged so as to include not only the mental phases of medical relations, but all questions of health which had any direct relation to the administration of justice. This was necessitated partly by the fact that one very important chapter in the inquiry, namely, the office of coroner, had little, if any, primary connection with psychology or psychiatry, but, above all, by the fact that, once the survey was under way, it appeared that medical relations must be interpreted in the broadest possible way in order to comply with the program outlined by Dean Pound.

In the collection of data and in making special investigations thanks are due to Maurice R. Davie, of the Department of Sociology of Yale University, for his valuable contribution; to Miss Helen Chew, of the staff of the Cleveland Foundation, for assistance both in the collection of information and in the planning and execution of the report; to E. K. Wickman, Psychologist in the Division of the Criminologist of Illinois, for his work in connection with the intelligence survey of the Cleveland police force and the Cleveland House of Correction; to C. E. Gehlke, Leonard V. Harrison, and all the members of the Survey staff for much help for which specific acknowledgment is impossible.

The work of this section complements in some measure that of the section on Penal Treatment and Correctional Institutions, and the author has had the coöperation of its director, Commissioner Burdette G. Lewis, of New Jersey, to whom he is deeply indebted for assistance and advice.

To the Medical Sub-committee of the Advisory Committee, the author wishes to express appreciation for kindly support and helpful suggestions. To Chairman H. L. Sanford and Dr. Howard Karsner the author is especially indebted for information and assistance in dealing with the subject of the coroner's office.

The author is glad to acknowledge here his indebtedness to two previous surveys conducted in Cleveland, and especially his personal debt to Colonel Leonard P. Ayres, who directed the Cleveland Foundation Educational Survey, and Dr. T. W. Salmon, of the National Committee for Mental Hygiene, who directed the Mental Hygiene Section of the Cleveland Hospital and Health Survey, for assistance and information without which this section of the present survey could not have been written.

HERMAN M. ADLER, M.D.

TABLE OF CONTENTS

LIST OF TABLES

LIST OF DIAGRAMS

MEDICAL SCIENCE AND CRIMINAL JUSTICE

CHAPTER I

PSYCHIATRY AND CRIME

C LEVELAND, like many other communities, is beginning to recognize the medical and more especially the psychiatric aspects of delinquency and crime, though as yet this recognition is confined to a relatively small part of the community, even of the official community. Some provision has already been made for psychiatric service, but only in more or less isolated centers which are not as yet correlated, and which, therefore, fail to give comprehensive attention to the entire field. The immediate problem, therefore, is to determine upon a policy which will utilize all the existing elements and yet insure expansion and development.

Specialists in the different fields of delinquency, dependency, and criminality are fully awake to the problem; there is even some general public interest in the subject as a result of the publicity given to it during the war. In Cleveland this is especially true, because the education and health surveys have dealt with the question, each from its particular angle.

Nevertheless, from the special point of view of the administration of criminal justice much more must be done to remove the general belief that delinquency and crime are entirely under the volitional control of the individual. The result of this attitude has been to make the treatment applied in each case dependent in a large measure on the degree of anger or annoyance to which the community has been aroused. Vindictive and punitive treatment, even though exercised by a group, loses little of the personal element. The community says to the delinquent: "You could behave yourself if you wanted to. If you break the laws, it is because you intended to, and therefore we are going to get even with you." The delinquent says to the community: "You do not need to be so rough with me, because it is in your power to be more lenient. If you

2 [1]

are rough, it is because you want to be unfair to me, and therefore I have a perfect right to hit back if I can."

There was a time when medicine was practised on much the same basis, and even when chemistry was regarded from this point of view. All the ailments of the human body were believed to be the machinations of evil spirits. The reactions of chemical substances in the retort were thought to be presided over by good and evil spirits. The scientific attitude which has removed these personal elements in the fields of pure science and of medicine is capable of doing the same in criminology. The introduction of exact methods in medicine has never interfered with the highest effectiveness of personality and character in the application of the science to the individual sufferer. In the same way the introduction of knowledge into the field of delinquency does not diminish the value of personal skill and of the so-called "human element" in its application to the administration of justice.

When the public becomes convinced that there are in the community specially trained persons who understand delinquency and are able to evaluate the various factors in a case of behavior difficulty, the result will be like that already witnessed in the field of public health. Few persons today have to be coerced to be protected against disease or to be treated when they are ill. Our dispensaries and hospitals clearly testify to that fact. When the public has learned to regard behavior difficulties, delinquency, and crime as manifestations of mental difficulties requiring treatment, just as physical ailments do, and provides institutions and officers to deal with these troubles as mental disease, rather than from the point of view of punitive justice, we shall be able to record advances as notable as those of the public health movement. And just as public health machinery has made large cities and small country villages *healthy* places in which to live, so this new public mental health movement will make our communities *safe* and *sane* places in which to live.

CHAPTER II

JUVENILE BEHAVIOR PROBLEMS

The Need for Mental Health Stations

THERE is probably no one who has not passed through difficulties during childhood. Indeed, the great majority believe they have been saved from becoming delinquent by some fortuitous circumstance, by the strict discipline of their parents, by the friendly offices of others, or perhaps that they were not saved but have in some way merely outgrown delinquency or "gotten by" in other ways. To those who look back from a secure position in society upon an adventurous and unlucky childhood or youth, it must appear that every individual has been, at one time or another, more or less delinquent. "There, but for the grace of God, goes John Bunyan," expresses their unconscious feeling when they consider criminality. Whatever truth there may be in this, it does not adequately explain the phenomenon of delinquency in its serious forms to one who differentiates between the significance of a single act and a series of reactions as disclosed by a study of the career of a delinquent individual. Regarded with the objectivity of the behaviorist, acts which may appear to be identical are found to have an entirely different significance. This is a point of view which the law—the emphasis of which is on the crime rather than on the criminal—does not, as yet, sufficiently recognize, though the law, to be sure, does recognize two groups of offenders needing special treatment—the irresponsible and the juvenile.

In dealing with adult criminals, a finding of feeble-mindedness or of insanity seems to some like condoning the crime, while to others that decision is merely the pronouncement of what they believe to be a well-established truth, namely, that all criminals are *ipso facto* insane or feeble-minded. However, all the partisanship and bitter feeling often aroused in cases of serious adult criminality are either absent or in abeyance in the case of juvenile delinquents. The entire development of the Juvenile Courts rests on the willingness of the community to believe that the child is not accountable for his misconduct in the same sense as the adult.

From the point of view of the behaviorist, one cannot hazard any

[3]

generalizations as to the causation of delinquency, but must make each case the subject of independent study. These considerations, pushed a little further, make us realize that similarity of behavior between youthful individuals does not imply identical causes, and therefore does not demand identical treatment. Perhaps nothing will help this point of view to gain general recognition so much as the introduction of facilities for consultation with mental and behavior experts, of which the general public may avail itself.

Parents, teachers, even children themselves, may be taught to consult the mental health station about their private affairs without fear of hostile criticism or condemnation, confident that though the experts may not be able to solve their problems, they will at least give non-partisan counsel. There will be no question whether the expert is for or against them any more than in the case of the hospital physician. The question will be merely what is the matter and what can be done.

In this work all the agencies of the community should assist. The public health system, especially with its public health nurses reaching into the homes, should direct cases suited to the mental health station. All the welfare agencies, through their social service, should daily discover cases requiring the assistance of a mental health officer. The police could easily be instructed in the nature of the cases that should be directed to the public health stations.

All of this field work, however, depends upon the existence of properly equipped mental health stations as bases. These stations, as a rule, so far as they exist in Cleveland and other communities, resemble dispensaries more than hospitals. This out-patient service, if properly conducted and enlarged, will take care of a large percentage of the cases. There are certain cases, however, which either for diagnosis or for temporary or preliminary treatment, require something more than out-patient treatment. For these, observation or temporary care stations should be provided.

The present plans in Cleveland include a psychopathic hospital as part of the city hospital, and ultimately a psychiatric institute in connection with Lakeside or Fairview Hospitals. The psychopathic hospital will take care of certain cases of juvenile delinquency in which the psychotic and psychopathic factors predominate. It is not likely, however, that such institutions will be able to care for a large number of behavior cases which require observation, but in which, nevertheless, the psychotic factor is either of minor importance or absent altogether.

In order to meet the requirements of the situation the Boys' School and the Detention Home would either have to be converted into behavior observation clinics with assistants and staff suitably trained in psychiatry; or, if they are to be retained as custodial or educational institutions, a new type of institution would have to be provided. The Bureau for Juvenile Research at Columbus, which is a link in the institutional chain, might serve in certain respects as a model for a local institute. The chief defect of the bureau, as was emphasized by Dr. Thomas W. Salmon in the health survey, is that it deals with cases only after they have been committed.

What is needed, then, in addition to the psychopathic hospital at Cleveland and the Bureau for Juvenile Research at Columbus, is a Children's Institute at Cleveland, either as a branch of the Columbus bureau or of the psychopathic hospital, or an independent unit affiliated and coördinated with the Juvenile Court, the Department of Education, the psychopathic hospital, and the University. It is preferable to keep such an institute distinct from the psychopathic hospital because the emphasis on mental disease has a deterrent effect upon the public, and also because the work of such an institute is sufficiently important to merit exclusive attention.

With some such provision the city of Cleveland would be able to deal effectively with the general problem of "criminal behavior" by attacking the problem at its source—in childhood. The saving in human careers, quite aside from the effect upon the safety of life and property, would more than repay the community for the relatively small expenditure involved.

THE JUVENILE BEHAVIOR PROBLEM IN THE SCHOOLS

Speaking solely from the point of view of the relation of mental studies to delinquency, the Cleveland schools are now very inadequately equipped to deal with behavior difficulties and the educational treatment of such cases. The facts which compel this conclusion have already been indicated by Dr. Salmon in Part VI of the health survey.

The Department of Education, as in all our larger cities, has provided special classes for children with retarded or low intelligence. The Boys' School might be considered a special class for behavior difficulties in boys. Educational and vocational questions are considered in practically all cases of juvenile delinquency, especially at the Boys' School, and the physical condition also is carefully considered by the school physicians. But all this is done in a more or less uncorrelated way. The physician works from too narrow a point of view. To him a boy who is a ward of the court on account of delinquency, if he has any physical defect or ailment, is exactly the same as any other case suffering from the same

[5]

physical troubles. The intelligence rating, as well as the educational and vocational tests, are made in the same way. What is entirely lacking is the *interpretation of the behavior difficulties*, and for this the social factors, which are fully as important as the physical or intellectual factors, must be studied. A careful analysis, not only of the environmental conditions under which the child is living, but also of his antecedents, his inheritance, and his social past, must be made. So far as this is done at all in Cleveland it is done by the overworked and understaffed Probation Department of the Juvenile Court and by the Boys' School.

From this point of view it is obvious that the community must assume an entirely different attitude toward its correctional and reformatory institutions. When it comes to treating juvenile behavior problems, we have an even blinder faith in the curative effects of punishment than have the criminal courts themselves. We erect buildings in which we gather the children who have had trouble at home or in school, or in the streets and parks of our cities, and by the application of what is commonly referred to as "strict discipline," we propose to relieve them and ourselves of their difficulties.

The officials who preside over these institutions are usually as ill equipped for constructive and scientific work as the domestics and window-washers of a hospital to carry out medical and surgical measures of relief. It would never occur to any one, in these days of modern medicine, to entrust a ward full of sick persons to the professional care of a cook, and yet that is what we do over and over again in our correctional and reformatory institutions. When we examine their provisions for grappling with this sort of work, is there a single institution in this country which has provided for its wards the same grade of personnel, the same training and expertness, that we find in a good general hospital?

Recommendations

1. A Division of Mental Health should be created in the Department of Education.

2. This division should be either coördinated with the division dealing with physical health, or be kept distinct from it so that mental health shall be given independent importance and authority.

3. The Mental Health Division should include the present psychologic clinics.

4. The mental health work should be closely coördinated with the Division of Special Education, or even merged with it, provided the mental health work does not thereby suffer partial or total eclipse.

5. The mental health staff should be under the direction of a competent psychiatrist.

6. The director and staff of the Mental Health Division should devote full time to the work.

7. A sufficiently large and comprehensive staff should be provided to assure that the work is performed in a satisfactory manner.

8. The Division of Mental Health should coöperate with the Juvenile Court, the Detention Home, the Welfare Federation, and the Department of Public Welfare, and all such public or private agencies as deal with problems of child welfare.

THE JUVENILE BEHAVIOR PROBLEM IN THE COURTS

The Juvenile Court is practically dependent upon the city health department and coöperating private organizations for the physical welfare of the children passing through the court, and largely on the Department of Education for mental tests. There are no regularly appointed medical or mental examiners attached to the court.

In regard to physical health, only children committed to the Detention Home or the Boys' School are examined. A physician and a nurse serve on part time in connection with these two institutions. There is a full-time dentist. In addition, the court often sends cases to hospitals, namely, the city hospital, Fairview Hospital, and Lakeside Hospital. The Humane Society furnishes the services of a physician for occasional cases. Judge George S. Addams, the Juvenile Court judge, hopes to have a nurse on duty at the court who will give a preliminary examination to all children, whether committed or not, as they pass through, and also a physician to examine all cases in the court every day. At present there is no money to permit such an arrangement.

The mental examinations connected with the Juvenile Court consist almost entirely of mental tests. These are applied under the direction of Dr. Bertha L. Luckey, the chief psychologist of the Board of Education. Dr. Luckey and her assistants examine especially children who have turned out to be problem cases in the special schools. Boys sent to the Boys' School by the court are examined by Miss Claire E. Walters. Miss Walters has her office in a temporary building at the Boys' School. She also examines the girls and dependent boys at the Detention Home nearby. If, in the opinion of the psychologist, a case requires further study, it is referred to the Bureau of Juvenile Research at Columbus, or a psychiatrist may be called in to make a special examination. There is no psychiatrist on the staff of the court, the school board, or the Department of Health, so that, naturally, these special examinations are made

[7]

but rarely. As a result, the reports of examinations which come back to the judge are confined merely to a statement of the findings and only in the more serious cases of feeble-mindedness is a recommendation for commitment to the State institution risked by the examiner.

The Juvenile Court is officially without equipment for making medical and special mental examinations. Whatever is done is at the personal request of the judge. The results of the various examinations are reported to him, and frequently Miss Walters appears as a witness. Neither Miss Walters, Dr. Luckey, nor their assistants receive any extra compensation for this work. Other psychiatrists and medical examiners, if they appear as witnesses, receive ordinary witness fees.

In spite of all these handicaps the work is extremely well done, although necessarily limited by inadequacy of equipment. Judge Addams recognizes the value of the work, however, and is not only inclined to follow recommendations made, but strongly recommends an extension of this work. The relation between the judge and the special examiners is one of close coöperation on both sides. The relation of these examiners to the probation officers is less close, although through the influence of the judge and the chief probation officer the facts disclosed by examination are utilized by the latter in selected cases. Much, however, could be done to improve this part of the work. The same may be said of the relation between the special examiners and the officers of the Detention Home.

Recommendations

1. A mental and physical examination should be made of every child brought to the attention of the Juvenile Court, and careful records should be kept of the results of each examination.

2. The examinations should be made whenever it appears advisable to the examiners.

3. The present excellent coöperation between the Juvenile Court and the Department of Education should be extended so as to make available for both such facilities as each may be able to provide. This applies especially to the suggested creation of a Division of Mental Health in the Department of Education. Such a division might profitably, and with little increase of staff, contribute to the Juvenile Court much needed information in regard to the intelligence, mental qualities, and personality of each child under consideration by the court.

CHAPTER III

THE ADULT CRIMINAL

PROGRESS OF MENTAL EXAMINATION

A DISCUSSION of the medical relations bearing upon the adult criminal is a matter of few words, so far as the present practice in Cleveland is concerned. Except for the occasional perfectly obvious case, practically no use is made of medical and more especially mental treatment in dealing with adult offenders. The majority of citizens and officials no doubt believe, as a high prison official in another State said—"Of course, the out-and-out feeble-minded or insane prisoners need special attention, but surely the doctors have no interest in the *normal* prisoner." Does it not depend upon the attitude with which one approaches the question of treatment whether mental experts are to concern themselves solely with the end stages of mental disease or deficiency, or with the interpretation and treatment of *all* cases of behavior difficulties, assuming them to be in the main problems of mentality? The use of the word *normal* should be prohibited as misleading in the field of behavior difficulties.

Experience in some of our reformatories and penitentiaries has conclusively shown that the study of mentality yields information which no modern institution can neglect. One need merely refer to the well-known work at Sing Sing, Concord, Elmira, and Bedford Hills, not to mention the institutions of New Jersey, Michigan, and Illinois, and especially the United States Disciplinary Barracks at Fort Leavenworth, Kansas. The elaborate plans for a psychiatric clinic in the new prison at Sing Sing clearly indicate what the New York State officials think of this work as an adjunct of the penal system. And what has come more and more to be considered indispensable in an institution has proved itself of similar value to the courts. Mental examinations and personality studies are now insisted upon as a *sine qua non* in the work of practically all the Juvenile Courts of the country.

There is every indication that this work has so far established itself that criminal and police courts are also availing themselves of the advantages. Thus, the Municipal Courts of Chicago, Boston, Detroit, and

Baltimore have psychopathic clinics or laboratories to which are referred all doubtful cases. No city has as yet worked out a system by which all cases coming before the court are considered from the mental angle. When, as often in court work, selection is made by untrained persons, important cases are frequently overlooked. Routine sorting examination of all cases, with more intensive study of those shown by first examination to require further investigation, is the only safe way.

As long as the public regards this work as a mere frill or an expression of maudlin sympathy for the criminal, of course, it will not be encouraged. What the uninitiated do not realize is that work of this kind is a very matter-of-fact and practical step toward the better administration of the law, as well as real economy.

THE NATURE OF MENTAL EXAMINATIONS

Although in general the public has become familiar with the fact that mental examinations are made in many cases where there is no reason to suppose that insanity exists, there is a great deal of doubt in the minds of many as to the nature of the methods and the information they may be expected to yield. It may not, therefore, be amiss to give briefly the outlines of this work.

Mental examinations, as they are now made, may be divided into two main groups: The first, or psychometric method, sometimes called the psychological tests, consists in the application of certain standardized sets of tests with the object of determining the native mental ability, or, as it is called, the "intelligence" of the subject. Various forms of tests are now used, but practically all of them are based upon the work of the French scientist, Alfred Binet, who, together with his collaborator, Theodore Simon, published in the years 1905 to 1908 the first scale for the measurement of intelligence in children.

This scale is arranged in accordance with the idea that as a child grows older and his mentality develops he is able to perform more and more complicated acts and to carry out more and more complex intellectual processes; so that, if we arrange a series of tests, questions, and problems in the order of their difficulty and present them to a child, we may be able to infer his degree of development by the point in such a series beyond which he is unable to answer questions satisfactorily. The scale thus arranged by Binet has since been tried out on a large number of school children, and as a result of this experiment it has been possible to arrange the tests in groups of six for each year. Since publication, these tests have been used to such an extent as to indicate thoroughly the existing need of such measurement.

It soon developed that there were in the schools and elsewhere individuals who, on being subjected to these tests, failed more or less widely to come up to the grade corresponding to their actual age, and since the tests had originally been arranged for age groups, it was said that their chronological age or actual age was, let us say, twelve years, and the mental age as determined by the scale was, let us say, nine years.

As the tests have become more definitely standardized, and as new tests have been devised and come into use, the exact definiteness with which the mental ages were stated ten years ago has gradually become subject to modification. Thus, while in the case of school children of twelve or less it is reasonably satisfactory to express their deviation or subnormality in terms of years, it is not so clear when the method is applied to older persons. When applied to adolescents, and especially to adults, these methods have frequently given rise to incredulity on the part of many; an instance of such a case is when an individual of twenty-five years who is guilty of a felony, and perhaps has a wife and children, and in other respects appears to be mature, is said to have the mind of a child of nine years as determined by the mental tests.

The reason for this apparent discrepancy is the fact that the original Binet scale and its modifications and amplifications hold with considerable accuracy for children of twelve and less, because the innate intelligence reaches its full development at about the age of puberty. This statement is not true in an absolute sense, but for present purposes is sufficiently accurate. The development which goes on after the age of puberty, during the age of adolescence, and until full adolescent maturity is reached, is a growth in strength, power, and the *use* of the innate ability through acquired habits and experience.

As this is the period during which the greatest apparent progress is made, when the change from childhood to adult maturity is visibly going on, it is difficult at first glance to reconcile this fact with the previous statement in regard to the maturing of intelligence. A child of twelve or fourteen may have as much intelligence as an individual of twenty-five or thirty years, and yet the adult will far exceed the child in intellectual performance and ability. This is because the older person is able to use his intelligence much more effectively because his emotional control, equilibrium, and judgment are much greater than those of a child. Less difficulty would undoubtedly be experienced in this regard had we a measure of the development which takes place during the adolescent period corresponding to the one we now have for the mental development during childhood.

The psychometric tests, therefore, give us a fairly accurate statement of the degree of intelligence of any individual. All inferences regarding the maturity of the individual in other respects, namely, emotional control, forbearance, responsibility, honesty, self-denial, respect for others, and the other attributes of personality which determine an individual's place in the social scale, can be determined only roughly. We can compare one individual with another in regard to his intelligence rating and can say with considerable precision by how much one excels another. For the period of adolescent development, no such exact measurement is possible, and we have to be content with a "more or less," "better or worse," standardization.

So striking have been the results achieved by means of the Binet-Simon tests that in the ten years since the first publication this type of measurement has become firmly established in schools, courts, and institutions, in fact, wherever child welfare is concerned.

Other scales have been devised which furnish the information in a somewhat different way, perhaps with greater precision than the original Binet scale. Aside from the first important modification of the scale, the so-called Stanford Revision, by Professor Terman, of the Leland Stanford University, there has been developed a point scale by Professor Yerkes, and a number of special tests, such as those of Dr. William Healy, Dr. Guy Fernald, Professor Whipple, and many others.

The problem of giving an intelligence rating to the soldiers of the draft army during the late war gave an impetus to another form of test which has been claiming attention in the schools, namely, that of the so-called "group tests." This method, based in general upon the same logic as the Binet tests, was so arranged that any one who can read and write may perform the test. The method consists in an instructor reading certain instructions to the group, who are equipped with pencils and test blanks, and who then carry out the instructions, answering questions and solving problems in accordance with printed statements, while the instructor keeps time. In this way as many as 1,000 men can be examined simultaneously.

The scores made on these tests, which are now usually referred to as the army tests, are expressed in figures: the highest possible score, for instance, was 212. The performance varied throughout the entire range from 0 to 212. In order to express the result in a usable form the score is divided into five groups, designated by the letters A to E as follows: A, very superior; B, superior; C, average; D, inferior; E, very inferior. It was found that so many men fell into the C or average group that it became necessary to divide this into two more groups, C plus and C minus, high average and low average respectively. The score necessary for a commission was judged, as a rule, to be either A or B. The men of E intelligence included the feeble-minded, the defective, and, in the main, men not fitted for the army because of low mentality.

In evaluating the mental status of an individual who, for one reason or another, is a subject for examination, more than intelligence rating is required. This further information is obtained by means of certain mental examinations which have as their object the determination not so much of the qualitative mental ability as of the existence of diseased or abnormal functionings or reactions. We might visualize this by saying that in the intelligence field we are taking a measure, just as we might measure the height of an individual, and that the differences are differences in mental stature. In the second form of examination, namely, the psychiatric examination, we are looking not for differences in height, but for pathological processes comparable to disease processes in the field of physical health. This type of examination seeks to determine the existence or absence of certain symptoms of disease, and when found, to evaluate their significance and the severity of the condition. It yields information upon which may be based such diagnosis as mental disease or the less severe pathological conditions, sometimes called psychopathic personality.

The study of the mentality of an individual from the point of view of psychiatry requires something further, however, than merely testing the mind or the nervous system. One cannot dissect the living human being and deal with one portion only. One of the characteristics of a living organism is that every part is in relation with every other. Nowhere is this more important than in the pathology of the mind. Of late a great deal of attention has been paid to the influence on mentality of certain factors which lie outside the nervous system. The existence of physical disease elsewhere in the body, as, for instance, in the delirium of fever, various intoxications and auto-intoxications, the effect of digestive disturbances, and, above all, the more newly disclosed effects of various glands and organs, such as the thyroid and the sex glands, are examples of these factors. It will be clear, therefore, that the examination of mentality from this point of view cannot be conducted with the same apparent exactness as is often possible in the investigation of the mental age. It must also be clear that this type of investigation requires the application of all the medical knowledge available and must, therefore, be made by a medical man with special experience in this field.

There is another point which must be understood in order to appreciate why medical, especially psychiatric, knowledge must be applied in addition to the intelligence rating. As we have seen before, the intelligence test is a matter of measuring mental stature. While these methods must be applied with the greatest care in order to be of any value and, therefore, require the services of a highly trained specialist, they nevertheless do not require any medical or pathological knowledge. In the elucidation of behavior difficulties we are confronted with a problem which is comparable less to an educational problem than to a problem of health. Even though our object is not to pin a label on the individual and find him either insane or feeble-minded, nevertheless we must arrive at a diagnosis of health by exclusion, for in no other way can a diagnosis be made. We cannot make a diagnosis of health or of sanity. We can only make a diagnosis of "no evidence of disease found." We can positively identify only the signs and symptoms of disease. In the absence of such we are justified in *assuming* that a person is healthy. It must be clear, therefore, that in making this sort of judgment upon the mentality of individuals and in elucidating the mental factors in behavior reactions a true knowledge of mental pathology is necessary in order to allow this judgment by exclusion.

The fact that psychiatrists are interesting themselves more and more in the behavior problems of the non-insane should not be interpreted as an indication that the psychiatrist is endeavoring to adjudge everybody insane. But, on the other hand, the commonly held fallacy that the psychiatrist has no interest in the problems of the non-insane or mentally healthy individual should be also dispelled.

CRIMINAL DETECTION BY THE POLICE

1. Departmental Health Work

The only medical officer officially connected with the Division of Police is the police surgeon. Only one police surgeon is employed. The present surgeon, Dr. G. P. O'Malley, has held this office since December, 1920. The duties of the police surgeon are, first, physical examination of all applicants for appointment to the police force, and, second, care of sick and disabled members of the force. It will be seen from this that he is concerned only with the health of members of the force itself and not at all with medical or health problems connected with the work of the police.

Even in this restricted application the work of the police surgeon is not adequately provided for. There are too many men to be examined and the equipment provided is in many respects inadequate. During March, 1921, there were 800 men to be examined. Blood tests are not being made, although the police surgeon believes that such tests should be made in every case. Neither the physical examinations of applicants

[14]

to the force nor the examination of men representing themselves as sick can now be made in any but a superficial way.

The police surgeon has no office—merely a desk in the office at the central station. There is no room where men can undress, and as a result the examinations cannot satisfactorily be made. A change is contemplated in this respect, and new quarters are to be provided at the Eighth Precinct.

The present officer, Dr. O'Malley, offers the following criticisms and recommendations:

1. Better working facilities with complete equipment for making thorough examination and also for emergency treatment.

2. Medical and clerical assistance. The city should be redistricted and a police surgeon hired for each district. There should be two assistants hired immediately to enable the city to be divided into three districts.

3. A card index and records of all cases entered should be kept, and for this office space and help are required. There should be a system of records to show exactly the number of times each man reported sick and how much time he loses.

4. To obviate the possibility of malingering there should be a constant checking up of the records. These should also show whether or not a man is in such poor health that he is unable to perform active duty.

5. If an officer is sick too often, he should be called before a medical board and given a thorough examination, at which time his family physician should be present, if desired.

6. All cases of pension should be handled by such a board.

7. The police surgeon as well as the police officers should be entitled to pension. This is not the case at present.

Malingering in the police department seems to be somewhat of a problem from the point of view of health work. The men live scattered throughout the town and at times it is impossible for the surgeon to call upon all of them on the same day they report sick. Sometimes it is two days or more before the surgeon can see a case. The men are aware of this, and the surgeon believes they take advantage of the fact to take a day off. Dr. O'Malley believes that as much as 12 per cent. of the sickness might be designated as malingering, although he has no means of saying definitely, because no records other than the daily sick report have been kept.

2. Public Health Problems

For all health work outside the department itself, including general cases coming to the attention of the police and the examination of suspects and prisoners, the police depend upon the Division of Health.

The city is districted, and the Division of Health maintains district physicians. The police may call upon these in cases requiring medical attention. The district physicians are supposed to confine themselves to the care of the indigent sick in their homes and to protect the community from contagious disease. In actual practice the police call upon the district health offices in many cases other than those specifically mentioned.

The police, furthermore, are instructed to remove any arrested person who requires medical treatment to the nearest hospital, preferably the city hospital, and a police guard is furnished in case such a person is kept at the hospital. There is a special ward at the city hospital for such persons, in which windows are barred, doors locked, and a guard constantly in attendance.

The police, however, render assistance to the general public in health matters. Owing to the fact that the police are always available for call, people refer cases to them, especially emergency cases, which should properly be taken care of by private physicians. The police keep on file the names and addresses not only of the district physicians, but also of certain private physicians who have certified their willingness to take emergency cases. Vice cases are referred to the Public Venereal Disease Clinics and to the Woman's Protective Association. The Division of Health maintains a diagnostic clinic for venereal diseases at No. 64 Public Square and the Fairview Clinic for Social Diseases at 3305 Franklin Avenue, mainly for treatment. The diagnostic clinic, under the federal government during the war, was taken over by the city in September, 1919. The Fairview Clinic was started August 16, 1920. These clinics handle private as well as court cases. Under the general code all vice cases are to be referred for diagnosis at the discretion of the judge. There seems to be considerable laxity, however, in referring cases. Rape cases are occasionally handled at these clinics, although, as a rule, such cases are referred to the city hospital.

It appears, therefore, that the problems of health, either of the police force or of the general public, in so far as the latter comes in contact with the police and the courts, are provided for adequately—if not in practice, at least in theory. The further improvement of this service and the raising of the general level of its efficiency is a question of applying present knowledge and furthering development along well-established lines.

3. Examination of Suspects and Prisoners

There are certain other problems of medical relations, however, of growing importance in connection with crime detection which concern the police and the crime-detecting agencies more than is commonly supposed.

The police have contacts with criminal and semi-criminal elements, which in many cases, if properly utilized, might result not only in better understanding of the general subject of crime, but actually in a more effective dealing with it. A patrolman on the beat can no longer adequately perform his full duty in a city such as Cleveland by merely representing in theory, and not in practice, the majesty of the law. To be the eyes of the law and of the community his powers of observation must be trained, so that he may be able to distinguish the significant from the adventitious.

This is not the place to discuss the details of police administration and police personnel. But it is relevant to consider here the equipment and skill necessary for individual police officers to secure the information needed to determine many important problems of the mentality and reliability of witnesses, and the relative honesty or dishonesty of witnesses, suspects, and prisoners. One cannot depend upon chance in this matter nor the haphazard school of experience. A very precise preparation must be made by the authorities to provide the necessary training. There seems to be no escape from the conclusion that the Division of Police should in some way be provided with the services of a specialist in mental science, particularly in its application to the problems of criminal behavior.

The work of the police surgeon in his professional supervision of the health of the police force; of the district health officers, in their relation to the physical health of the community in general, and of prisoners, suspects, and accidental cases in particular, should be strengthened by the introduction of three health officers—two to act as assistants to the present police surgeon in his routine work, and the third a specialist who should devote his time and energies to the mental aspects of the police department both within and without the force. Such a specialist would serve not only as an advisor in the department, but also as a teacher. Mental health work should really be a subdivision of the health department, and it is not unlikely that before long the health department of every large city will develop a special division for mental health.

The problems which present themselves for solution by mental science in connection with police work are:

First, the general problem of the existence of mental disease or mental defectiveness in persons under observation.

Second, the very important and broad problem of pathological personalities. In a great number of cases this seems to be one of the impor-

3   [17]

tant underlying factors in the interpretation of behavior disorders. A greater interest in these problems and a more intelligent application of the knowledge obtained in their scientific solution are essential if we are ever to reduce the seriousness of a large group of problem cases. In order to make clear the meaning of this one needs merely to refer to the relationship between the psychopathic personality and vagrancy, non-support, desertion, inebriety, drug addiction, and the types of delinquency in which sex difficulties are a decisive factor.

There are certain special relations in addition to these general ones in which mental science may be of assistance to the police. Two especially demand attention:

First, the general question of malingering, which is to some extent a factor within the police force and is of the utmost importance in relation to the analysis of individual delinquents and criminals. The value of a testimony, the reliability of a witness, the question whether an individual is shamming insanity, injury, or disability, may often be solved or at least determined by applying the rules of mental examination to the individuals under observation.

The second has to do with forced confessions or the so-called "third degree." A suspect is apprehended and many points of circumstantial evidence point to his being the criminal or at least implicated in a criminal affair. But the chain of evidence is by no means complete, and the suspect denies more or less successfully his guilt or complicity. Under such circumstances a confession, if gained, may be corroborated by evidence now easy to secure. Such a confession almost invariably simplifies the work of the police to such a degree that in many cases they are bent on securing a confession rather than objectively securing the available evidence.

It is not our wish here to discuss this method from the legal nor the police aspect. From the point of view of the scientist it is a clearly ineffectual and dangerous method. Not only is it apt to be misleading, but its chief fault is that it tends to accustom police officers to seek the easiest way out of a difficult situation, rather than to apply the best methods of scientific investigation.

However, confessions probably will continue to be sought, and in connection with this work a specialist in mental examination would prove of assistance. A careful mental examination will disclose whether a person is able to give reliable information, whether he is suggestible and to what degree, and therefore whether he will accept readily the suggestions of the "third degree." Furthermore, laboratory methods are of considerable aid in determining whether a person is withholding information, whether he shows well-marked emotional reactions, and many other points now too often ignored in the prosecution of unscientific investigations.

Recommendations

1. Three additional police surgeons should be appointed to serve as assistants to the police surgeon.

2. These surgeons should be employed on full time.

3. They should include in their duties medical and surgical attention to the suspects and prisoners lodged in the police jail.

4. One of the assistant police surgeons should be an expert in psychiatry, and should be known as the mental health officer.

5. The mental health officer of the police department should serve full time.

6. The mental health officer should devote his time to the mental problems in connection with the *police force* and the *police work*.

7. The mental health officer should make a mental and personality examination of every candidate for appointment to the police force and should record his findings.

8. Reëxaminations of every member of the police force should be made by the surgeon and mental health officer once every year.

9. The mental health officer should be present whenever possible at all special examinations of prisoners and suspects, especially in the case of examinations conducted with the purpose of obtaining so-called "confessions."

CRIME DETECTION BY THE CORONER'S OFFICE

"The office of coroner has long been a subject of comment and unfavorable criticism in this country. Physicians and medical societies have made frequent efforts to secure a more efficient administration of the duties devolving upon this office. Laws have been enacted establishing other offices as well as State boards and commissions which have gradually taken away many of the duties formerly belonging to the coroner. The importance of the office has so decreased that little attention is given by the political parties or by the voters to the candidates who seek election to the position. And even less attention is given by the public to the actual administration of the office by the men elected."

Thus begins the report of the investigation made by the Coroner's Committee of the Municipal Association of Cleveland in 1912, and in the nine years which have passed since the publication of this report practically nothing has been done to correct conditions or to apply any of the recommendations made at that time. With minor changes the report is valid today.

The office of coroner in Ohio is governed entirely by statute. The Ohio constitution of 1802 provided that one coroner should be elected in each county; but no provision for this office is contained in the present constitution. Under statute one coroner is elected in each county in the even-numbered years, who holds office for two years from the first Monday of the January following his election. The statutes make no provision for deputy coroners or other assistants, although reference is made to "the official assistant of the coroner," for whom, however, no appropriation is made. Because of the advantage of medical knowledge in this work it has been the custom to nominate physicians for the office of coroner.

The coroner's chief duty is to determine in cases of sudden or unexplained death the causes of death and whether it resulted from unlawful means, and, in the latter case, to fix responsibility for the crime and name the perpetrator. It is obvious, therefore, that a consideration of the office of coroner is well within the scope of a survey of the administration of justice.

Upon the proper execution of the coroner's duties depends, in no small measure, the strict enforcement of the law in homicide cases. A lax performance of these duties, whether due to carelessness, intentional neglect, or merely to ignorance, gravely affects the community. Public safety, especially in large and congested centers of population, requires now, as perhaps never before, that the inquiry into the cause of death shall be conducted according to the best modern theories and with the most expert knowledge and skill. It is easy to simulate an accident or suicide and therefore the definite determination that violence has been used may be well-nigh impossible unless the utmost skill and scrupulous scientific accuracy are brought to bear. It is clearly unsafe to trust such work to any but a highly competent pathologist and medico-legal expert.

The coroner's duties are given in the following excerpt from *The Coroner's Office, Efficiency Series, Report No. 2*, issued by the Municipal Association of Cleveland in December, 1912:

Inquests

The main duty of the coroner is holding inquests. Sections 2856 and 2857 of the General Code provide for the holding of inquests and set forth the method of procedure as follows:

"Section 2856. When informed that the body of a person whose death is supposed to have been caused by violence has been found within the county, the coroner shall appear forthwith at the place where the body is, issue subpoenas for such witnesses as he deems necessary, administer to them the usual oath, and proceed to inquire how the deceased came to his death—whether by violence

[20]

from any other person or persons, by whom, whether as principals or accessories before or after the fact, and all circumstances relating thereto. The testimony of such witnesses shall be reduced to writing, by them respectively subscribed, except when stenographically reported by the official stenographer of the coroner, and with the finding and recognizances hereinafter mentioned, if any, returned by the coroner to the clerk of the Court of Common Pleas of the county. If he deems it necessary, he shall cause such witnesses to enter into recognizances, in such sum as may be proper, for their appearance at the succeeding term of the Court of Common Pleas of the county to give testimony concerning the matter. The coroner may require any and all such witnesses to give security for their attendance, and if they or any of them neglect to comply with his requirements, he shall commit such person to the prison of the county, until discharged by due course of law.

"Section 2857. The coroner shall draw up and subscribe his finding of facts in writing. If he finds that the deceased came to his or her death by force or violence, and by any other person or persons, so charged, and there present, he shall arrest such person or persons, and convey him or them immediately before a proper officer for examination according to law. If such persons, or any of them, are not present, the coroner forthwith shall inform one or more justices of the peace, and the prosecuting attorney, if within the county, of the facts so found, in order that the persons may be immediately dealt with according to law."

The terms used in Section 2856 have been construed by the Ohio Supreme Court (62 O.S. 307) as follows:

"A death 'caused by violence' is a death caused by unlawful means, such as usually call for the punishment of those who employ them. A body 'is found' within the county when it is ascertained by any means that it is within the county."

"'Death is supposed to have been caused by violence,' whenever from such observation as he may be able to make, and from such information as may come to him, the coroner is, for reasons of substance, led to surmise or think that death has been so caused."

As thus interpreted by the Supreme Court, the statute, in referring to "death by violence," means intentional killing as distinguished from mere negligence. No criminal negligence act has thus far been passed in Ohio, and the terms of the present statute are certainly not intended to confer general jurisdiction upon the coroner in cases of accidental deaths by railroads, street cars, in manufacturing plants and the like, except in cases where death is supposed to have been caused by "unlawful violence" and not mere negligence.

However, there is one exception to the general rule, namely, that Secs. 926–7 seem to require the coroner to hold inquests in all reported cases of fatalities occurring by explosion or accident connected with a mine, regardless of the question of criminality. Moreover, the statutes now provide (Secs. 212–3) that in cases of death occurring without medical attendance it shall be the duty of the undertaker to notify the registrar of vital statistics of such death and, if such death appears to the registrar to have been caused by unlawful or suspicious means, he shall refer the case to the coroner for inquest.

The statutes further provide (Secs. 6268–9), in cases where the death of an inmate of a licensed maternity boarding-house or lying-in hospital is reported to the board of health, that such board of health shall forthwith call upon the coroner to hold an inquest unless the certificate of a legally qualified physician is exhibited specifying the cause of death.

The practical effect of Sec. 2856, giving the coroner jurisdiction to act in cases where "death is supposed to have been caused by violence" is to make it discretionary with the coroner in what cases he shall act; and renders it practically outside the power of the courts to regulate the actions of the coroner in this regard. The language of this section is so broad that the extent of the coroner's authority is left almost wholly to his discretion and good faith; and any criticism of his having assumed jurisdiction unnecessarily could be met with the general rule that a public officer's acts are presumed to be according to law and in good faith. In brief, the coroner is his own guide as to the number of inquests he will hold.

Autopsies

The statutes provide (Sec. 2495) that "The county commissioners may allow a physician or surgeon, making a postmortem examination at the instance of the coroner or other officer, such compensation as they deem proper." Although the coroner may determine in what cases autopsies shall be performed, and who shall perform them, the commissioners thus have entire discretion as to compensation, and in practice their wishes largely control as to the kinds of cases in which autopsies shall be made. Autopsy fees and the relative number of autopsies performed vary greatly, therefore, in different counties.

Formerly in Cuyahoga County the coroner distributed the autopsies among favored physicians or hospital internes. Under the present administration the coroner has assigned this work to his "deputy," Dr. Droege, and under an agreement between the county commissioners and Dr. Droege he performs all autopsies at a uniform charge of $15 and confines his examinations to cases of supposed homicidal death.

Further Duties

Where the coroner attends upon the body of a deceased person it is his duty (Sec. 2860) to notify friends or relatives of the deceased if known, or if not known, to advertise the fact of death in a newspaper.

He is required (Secs. 2859 and 2861) to make an inventory of all articles of property found on or about the body, and to return the inventory (Secs. 2861–3) and the articles described therein to the Probate Court, where such property other than money becomes subject to the order of the Probate Court, for its preservation or other disposition, the rights of administrators and executors (Sec. 2684) being fully recognized. The statute directs that such property (Sec. 2863) as is unidentified or unclaimed shall be advertised and sold at public sale annually by the Probate Court and the proceeds paid into the county treasury. However, money found shall be applied first (Sec. 2862) to paying the expenses of saving the body, and of the inquest and burial, and the remainder shall be paid into the county treasury, where, on proper proof being offered, such money as well as the proceeds of property sold shall be paid over to the claimant entitled to it.

Anomalous Duties of Ohio Coroners

In addition to the duties which it would seem properly belong to the office of coroner, he is by statute in Ohio made a process server, both for the Common Pleas Court (Sec. 2835), where the sheriff is an interested party, and for the Probate Court (Secs. 1596 and 1599), generally, and in certain cases (Sec. 11435) he may further be called on for summoning a jury. Moreover, he is given the additional duties (Sec. 13606) of endeavoring to arrest convicts escaping from the penitentiary, and (Sec. 9914) of apprehending persons selling liquor contrary to law within two miles of the place where an agricultural fair is being held.

In all these latter cases he is assigned duties—although his services in such instances are extremely rare—which are already enjoined upon other officers by law, or for the performance of which the courts are given the power to make special appointments in case of need. These special duties are clearly a survival of the days when deputy sheriffs were a rarity and when the office of coroner was not regularly filled by a practising physician.

Compensation

The coroner's office is the only office still maintained on a fee basis. His remuneration for his services is dependent entirely upon fees earned, the amounts of which are scheduled (Sec. 2866) as follows:

(a) For viewing a dead body, three dollars.

(b) For all necessary writings and the return thereof, 10 cents per 100 words.

(c) For traveling to the place of view, 10 cents per mile.

No special fee is provided for the hearing of testimony in connection with inquests, and the coroner's compensation in such cases, other than the fee for viewing the body, is dependent on the allowances for necessary writings connected with making up the records from the testimony and the other incidents of the case. The statutes do not contemplate the making of autopsies by the coroner in person and no fee is specified for this work.

The staff of the coroner is appointed by the county commissioners, the tenure of office being subject to their pleasure. The staff is under the jurisdiction of the coroner, although he has no authority to discharge individuals. There is little interest in the election of the coroner, the name of the nominee appearing usually at the end of the ballot.

The coroner receives no specified salary, his compensation being dependent on the collection of fees, the only county office still thus maintained. For viewing a dead body he receives a fee of $3.00, no matter where the body may be located nor the length of time consumed in reaching it. For traveling expenses 10 cents per mile is allowed. The statutes do not provide special fees for the performance of autopsies by the coroner. As a matter of practice, the county commissioners allow a fee of $25. There is no specified fee provided for the taking of testimony at inquests, compensation for this depending upon the allowance for the necessary clerical work. There is no provision for extra fees and no allowance to meet the expenses in especially complicated cases. Salaries and wages for the staff are as follows: morgue keepers, $137.50 per month; janitors, $110.

The present coroner of Cuyahoga County, A. P. Hammond, M.D., has been in office since January, 1921. Dr. Hammond has been a practising physician and still devotes some time to general practice. He keeps daily office hours at the Morgue, from 8.30 to 12 and from 1 to 3 o'clock. All who have come in contact with Dr. Hammond are unanimous in their commendation of his serious attitude toward his work and his desire to coöperate in every way. The community is fortunate in having such an officer in this very important position, especially in view of the antiquated conditions under which this work is being performed in Cuyahoga County.

The statutes lay down no requirements for the office of coroner except that he must not practise as an attorney or counselor-at-law.

The present practice in the coroner's office in regard to stenographic service is to secure a stenographer from a typewriter company on the authority of the county prosecutor. A fee of 10 cents per 100 words is all the compensation available, although this sum appears to be less than the salary of a regular full-time stenographer. It has been the practice in the past for the coroner to employ a stenographer at his own expense.

Autopsies are performed by physicians selected by the coroner for this duty. As a rule, a qualified pathologist has been employed for this work. For this reason practically all the autopsy work has been of a high order, a circumstance which is all the more fortunate since it is due to the good judgment of the coroner, rather than to the provisions of the law.

There are four morgue keepers and two janitors. One of the morgue keepers serves as a clerk, keeping and filing the records. He assists at autopsies and acts as coroner when the latter is absent. The present incumbent was formerly an undertaker and expert embalmer. He has held his present position for eight years. The other three morgue keepers do general utility work, such as answering the telephone, taking messages, receipting for property and money found on bodies brought in by the police, making entries in property books, etc. They work eight hours a day, seven days a week, as the morgue is never closed. No bond is required and no special qualifications are named for these positions. However, the feeling among the morgue keepers is that they should be licensed and bonded and that a qualification for this position should be experience as a licensed embalmer, especially on account of the possible danger to the community of careless handling of the bodies of persons who have died of contagious disease.

The two janitors are responsible for caring for the two floors of the morgue. One of the janitors serves as relief man to give the morgue keepers one day off a week. The morgue keepers and janitors are appointed and paid by the county commissioners. The discipline is not good, and the staff, as might be expected under the conditions, lacks *esprit de corps*. On account of the valuables and other property which is continuously passing through the morgue, the staff must often find themselves in positions where their honesty may be questioned, a circumstance which further tends toward bad morale and consequently lessened efficiency in the service.

In addition to the above, there is a special constable attached to the coroner's office who serves the necessary legal papers in subpœnaing witnesses. This officer is allowed considerable discretion in deciding which witnesses to subpœna. Usually the selection depends entirely upon his judgment. The fee for this work is paid by the county treasurer through the auditor, and the total sum varies considerably in amount in a year. It is said that formerly considerable sums were paid over annually for such service.

1. Relation to Police

The Division of Police sends the coroner a copy of its reports on criminal cases. The coroner also makes a report to the police of all cases coming to his notice. If a dead body is discovered in surroundings indicating violence, the police assume responsibility for all weapons and other objects which might serve as evidence and exhibits. The coroner takes possession of the body and personal belongings. The police later turn over to the prosecutor all property in their possession.

The police emergency or ambulance conveys bodies to the morgue in practically all cases. This has become the custom only of late, since the police emergency has superseded the old ambulance service which used to be in the hands of undertakers. Occasionally bodies are brought to the morgue in undertakers' wagons. A policeman accompanies the body and makes a list of the clothing and property found. The morgue keeper makes an examination of the clothing of the corpse in the presence of the police officer, making an inventory of all property found, and an entry in the property book which the policeman signs as a witness. There is thus a double check on all property.

In murder or suspected murder cases the clothing is put in a bag and kept in the morgue, available for use in evidence. In criminal cases clothing and property are released to relatives only on order of the prosecutor. Bullets taken from bodies are carefully·preserved and importance is attached to the necessity of proving that the bullet submitted as evidence was actually the one taken from the body. Some years ago a case occurred in which a person indicted for murder was not convicted because of careless handling of the evidence, which in this instance was a bullet. In the case of bodies which are in an unidentifiable condition, due to exposure or long immersion in water, or to trauma, the skill of the expert embalmer has proved of value to the morgue by so restoring the bodies that identification was possible.

In manslaughter and murder cases police officers or detectives are present at the autopsies. There is naturally a great deal of coöperation between the coroner's office and the police in detecting crimes, evidence often being obtained in the morgue in regard to the exact cause of death, the nature of the weapon used, and many other details which prove of value to the criminal detective agencies. The police sometimes bring suspects to the morgue for "third degree" purposes, suddenly confronting the suspect with the body of the victim.

2. Relation to Courts

The coroner and his assistants have relations with the Municipal Court, the grand jury, the Common Pleas Court, and the Probate and Juvenile Court.

The coroner or his assistants are subject to call as witnesses in the Municipal Court before the cases are bound over to the grand jury. The coroner testifies before the grand jury, submitting for its use copies of the report of the autopsy and the inquest. In all Common Pleas Courts the coroner or his assistants testify in murder cases. The present coroner is of the opinion that this testimony would be of more value if the coroner himself performed the autopsy. The coroner, as well as all the assistants and employees, are, of course, subject to subpœna in court to prove *corpus delicti*.

The Probate Court law of 1920 makes the coroner custodian of all property in coroners' cases. All unclaimed money is held for a year and then turned over to the Probate Court. A property list is made and must be filed by the morgue keeper and the coroner. Property of any amount or value may be released to relatives or other claimants upon order by the Probate Court. If, however, the property is of considerable value, it is turned over to an especially appointed administrator. The order from the Probate Court releasing property is carefully filed at the morgue in the property book.

The relations of the coroner to the Juvenile Court are of little importance, as the coroner and his assistants are rarely called upon to appear in this court.

3. Relation to Prosecutors

The nature of the coroner's duties and functions necessitates much contact with the prosecutor's office. The effectiveness of the service is somewhat influenced, therefore, by the personal relations existing between these officers. The present coroner and the city prosecutors are on friendly terms, and as a result, coöperate satisfactorily. The county prosecutor decides in which cases to hold autopsies. A representative of the county prosecutor's office is usually present to assist in coroner's inquests. The coroner and his assistants are often called to the police station to give information regarding the bodies and to aid the police in preparing cases. During the trial they are often called upon to testify in court. The coroner and his assistants are called in by the prosecutor to establish the *corpus delicti* and to bind the prisoners over to the grand jury.

4. Relation to the Bar

Lawyers acting as counsel in both civil and criminal actions may come to the morgue for information or evidence. A lawyer may attend the coroner's inquests and may question witnesses, but cannot enter objections.

5. Relation to the Medical Profession

Physicians report to the coroner cases of sudden death, usually by telephone. The coroner then decides whether or not to claim the case. When the coroner decides not to assume jurisdiction, the physician may perform the autopsy himself, either at the morgue or at his own office.

6. Administrative Relations

The coroner issues certificates to undertakers through the Board of Health. Sometimes the district physicians feel they cannot issue death certificates because of suspicious circumstances, and so report to the Board of Health, which in turn reports to the coroner. The city chemist analyzes stomach contents, secretions, and excretions obtained from the body in suspicious cases. In all cases of death occurring without medical attendance within the city limits the district physician may view the body and report "Cause of death unknown." In cases of sudden death without medical attendance occurring in the county outside of the city of Cleveland, the sheriff performs the functions which, within the city limits, are performed by the police. He notifies the coroner when such cases are found, and accompanies the coroner to the body. The sheriff takes the weapons and all suspicious objects; the coroner claims the body and the property on it. In the case of probable suicide the coroner also takes possession of the gun or other weapon.

The county commissioners "O. K." all bills of expense of the coroner's office. There is no supervision of the county work. At present both the municipal and county administration are Republican. One of the morgue keepers who is a Democrat stated to the investigator that there are no political troubles.

The present coroner is on friendly terms with the county prosecutor. They coöperate in inquests and in other activities connected with their duties. This has not always.been the situation, and difficulties have occurred because of strained relations between coroner and prosecutors.

7. Equipment

The public morgue was created by special statute passed in 1896 (92 Ohio Laws, 678). It was placed in care of the coroner, who is directed to see that all dead bodies received are properly preserved until identified or claimed for burial; to collect from friends or relatives of such deceased persons not residing in the county a sum not to exceed $10; and to have photographed all bodies not properly identified.

The morgue occupies a two-story building. On the first floor are the office of the morgue keeper and a safe for property, a well-equipped autopsy room, and a viewing hall. The morgue has capacity for 100 bodies at a time. This space is arranged in four sections, the first of which only is cooled by refrigeration, because of the fact that it is easier to embalm bodies which have not been frozen. Hence most of the bodies are kept in the non-refrigerated sections. On the second floor are the coroner's office, a safe for property, and the office of the assistant clerk, a well-appointed inquest room, and files and records which go back to 1828. These files and records are kept in the inquest room. The filing cabinets contain the following data in each case: viewing slip, inquest slip, a carbon copy of the police report of criminal cases, testimony of witnesses, and the autopsy records, all filed together in a folder.

8. Death Records

Only the knowledge that we are dealing with a very serious subject prevents us from treating in a lighter vein some of the results of the coroner's work as performed under present conditions. Indeed, we cannot entirely suppress a sense of the ridiculous when we read over the list of causes of death as officially recorded by the coroner of Cuyahoga County for the year 1919.

The first entry for the year is:

No. 22942: "Could be suicide or murder," a reassuring statement and one calculated to promote confidence in the guardians of public safety.

Again a few lines further along we read: No. 22957—"Auto accident or assault." Certainly this expresses a doubt which the public would be interested to have resolved further.

No. 23178: "Aunt said she complained of pneumonia, looked like narcotism." Is it necessary to dwell on the extraordinary convenience of having the subject thus obligingly perform the work of the coroner by confiding the diagnosis and thus settling at the same time the cause of subsequent demise?

No. 23203: "Believe strychnia used—viewed as suicide." Is it not possible to *know* whether strychnia was or was not used?

No. 23241: "Looks suspicious of strychnine poisoning," and this suspicion must forevermore poison the mind of anyone who turns the pages of the coroner's record because the county of Cuyahoga did not believe it important to *know* whether this was a case of homicide, suicide, or an accident.

Consider from the point of view of law enforcement and the public safety such records as these:

No. 22964: "Found dead."
No. 22987: "Found dead in shanty."
No. 22990: "Head severed from body."
No. 23035: "Could be assault or diabetes."
No. 23050: "Premature or abortion."
No. 23135: "Found dead in alley—lobar pneumonia." .
No. 23187: "Diabetes, tuberculosis, or nervous indigestion." ·
No. 23253: "Consider it tuberculosis."
No. 23300: "Found dead."
No. 23484: "Found crushed."
No. 23512: "Could be diabetes or poison."
No. 23551: "Died suddenly after taking medicine."
No. 23568: "Medicinal poisoning." .
No. 23574: "Body entirely burned."

No. 23577: "Found dead in bath-room."
No. 23605: "Died suddenly."
No. 23670: "Loss of blood."
No. 23686: "Shock."
No. 23687: "Body covered with sores."
No. 23731: "Acute arsenical poisoning-accident."

In none of these cases was an autopsy performed, although one would suppose that in some, if not in all, more precise information is needed not only to determine the exact cause of death, but definitely to exclude foul play.

9. Cost of Administration

The apparent cost of administration of the coroner's office appears to be about one-half what it was in 1912. The scattering of items throughout the county work makes it impossible to be exact, but it is safe to assume that the entire cost of administration, including the morgue and numerous miscellaneous items, is between $10,000 and $15,000 annually.[1]

REPORT OF AUDITOR'S OFFICE OF CUYAHOGA COUNTY ON THE EXPENSE OF THE CORONER'S OFFICE

	September, 1912	September, 1919	September, 1920
Coroner's fees	$6,101.75	$4,629.10	$1,876.82
Constable's fees	1,585.30	..	5.50
Witness' fees	1,801.90	14.40	12.60
Autopsy fees	1,155.00	1,290.00	2,760.00
Miscellaneous	127.61	..	44.55
Totals	$10,771.56	$5,933.50	$4,699.47

Even a cursory glance at the foregoing suffices to show that the work of coroner as now performed is far from adequate. It is indeed high time that the facts are faced and an effective arrangement commensurate with modern scientific efficiency be instituted.

This means abolishing the office of coroner.

10. The Remedy

During the recent (1921) session of the Ohio Legislature a bill was introduced through the efforts of the present coroner of Cuyahoga County, Dr. A. P. Hammond, which was designed to meet some of the objections

---

[1] The budget for the office of chief medical examiner of New York for the year 1921 is $127,303, of which $120,653 is for salaries and wages.

without abolishing the office of coroner. This bill allows the coroner, in counties having a population of 100,000 or more, to appoint an official stenographer, and "in counties where there is maintained a county morgue, the coroner may also appoint necessary assistant custodians of the morgue, in no case to exceed three in number." Above all, in counties having a population of 100,000 or more, "no person shall be eligible to the office of coroner except a licensed physician of good standing in his profession."

The principal objections to this bill are:

1. That the coroner is elected and not appointed. Keeping the office in politics makes it impossible to secure the quality of service required. No competent expert can be induced to subject his work or his professional career to the uncertainties of partisan politics. Continuity of service and freedom from extraneous interference are the *sine qua non* of scientific efficiency.

2. That the decision whether or not to perform an autopsy rests not with the coroner, but with the prosecuting attorney. This most pernicious custom makes the scientific determination of the cause of death subservient to the requirements of the prosecutor's office and dependent upon the state of his finances, instead of regarding such determination as a complete end in itself, the results to be used in whatever way may be considered proper by the prosecutors or anyone else.

3. That the coroner should be a physician, but not necessarily experienced in pathology. It is amply demonstrated by the history of the coroner's office in Cuyahoga County that securing a physician as coroner does not in itself constitute a sufficient safeguard against unsatisfactory results.

In 1877 the General Court of Massachusetts abolished the coroner and created in his place a medical examiner.[1] Dr. George Burgess Magrath, medical examiner of Suffolk County, Massachusetts, has kindly furnished the following statement in regard to the Massachusetts law and its functioning:

The Massachusetts Medical Examiner Law was enacted in 1877. It abolished the office of coroner, assigned to physicians appointed by the governor all of the responsibilities involved in the investigation of the cause and manner of deaths supposedly due to injury, and delegated to justices of courts of first instance the magisterial function of fixing the responsibility for a death due to an unlawful act. The only important modification of the original statute is one made a few years ago by an amendment which substituted for the word "violence" the words "act or negligence of another" in that portion of the law governing inquests.

---

[1] The Massachusetts law is appended.

The statute is not highly specific in its definition of the jurisdiction of a medical examiner, in that it merely provides for his functioning in the case of death of any person "supposed to have come to his death from violence." The interpretation of this statute by the medical examiners of the commonwealth is, however, such as to extend its provisions to include all deaths caused directly or indirectly by traumatism, including traumatic septicemia, deaths caused by the action of chemical substances, of thermal or electrical agencies; deaths' following abortions, irrespective of circumstances; deaths from disease resulting from injury or infection relating to occupation; deaths from neglect; sudden deaths of persons not disabled by recognized disease; and the deaths of persons found dead. This interpretation is, of course, necessary in order to make the law of any practical value, and brings within the scope of its operation deaths universally recognized as appropriate for medico-legal inquiry.

The principal advantages of the Massachusetts type of medico-legal inquiry over the coroner system are as follows:

(1) The separation of medical and judicial functions and the delegating of each to appropriate officials.

(2) The giving to the medical investigator the primary and full jurisdiction over the body of the decedent, thereby insuring to him ample opportunity to observe conditions or circumstances tending to show the manner as well as the cause of death. These often include facts susceptible of recognition and proper interpretation by a medical examiner only.

(3) The economy incidental to the use of existing courts which dispenses with the coroner's court and jury.

(4) The placing where it belongs, in the hands of a medical man, the duty of determining promptly the cause of death, whereby crimes against life may be immediately brought to light and the appropriate judicial and police authorities notified thereof; whereby also deaths from injury other than that incidental to the act or negligence of another, as well as deaths from so-called natural causes, may be recognized as such with equal promptness, without unnecessary publicity, and without the use and incidental expense of a court or coroner's jury.

(5) The opportunity existent is an appointive position of selecting therefor physicians qualified by special training and experience.

Dr. Charles Norris, Chief Medical Examiner of New York city, under the recently enacted law of New York[1] abolishing the coroner and establishing the office of chief medical examiner, has thus summed up his experiences and conclusions:[2]

General dissatisfaction with the work of the coroner of the city of New York

---

[1] Laws of New York, 1915, Chap. 285. "An act to amend the Greater New York Charter and repeal certain sections thereof." (See also: Laws of New York, 1882. Chap. 410.)

[2] "The Medical Examiner versus the Coroner," by Charles Norris, M.D., *National Municipal Review*, Vol. IX, No. 8, August, 1920.

resulted in many attempts in the legislature at Albany to abolish this office and to substitute an office to be known as medical examiner, after the fashion of that created many years before in Massachusetts. Finally on April 14, 1915, the office of the coroner was abolished and in its place the office of chief medical examiner was established.

THE CORONER'S OFFICE BREAKS DOWN

Unlike the coroner's office, the medical examiner's office was not given quasi-judicial powers, but was vested with sufficient authority to administer oaths and take affidavits, proofs, and examinations as to any matter within the jurisdiction of the office. The judicial functions formerly vested in the coroners were, under the medical examiner's act, transferred to the proper legal authorities, namely, the magistrates and the grand jury. Prisoners are now held by the magistrates, and the defendants are indicted by the grand jury upon presentation of the facts by the district attorney from the reports furnished by the medical examiner, the police and witnesses.

The judicial functions of the coroner's office are now more satisfactorily and quickly handled by the legally trained magistrates and by the grand jury under the guidance of the district attorney. In other words, the judicial functions of the coroner's office are redundant and have no proper place.

The correct determination of the cause of death is designated as medical jurisprudence, the science which correlates our medical knowledge to the purpose of the law. Thorough equipment in medicine and surgery must be supplemented by a knowledge of firearms, the effect of bullets on the human body, recognition of powder marks and burns, etc. Familiarity with the biological methods employed in testing suspected blood, semen, and other stains; practical knowledge of botany in the examination of dust and foreign material upon the clothes of suspects and in the examination of the intestinal contents for particles of food, that is, plant seeds and fibers of animal and vegetable origin; an acquaintance with the flora and fauna of waters, namely, diatoms, etc., may be of great assistance in the microscopic examination of the contents of the lungs and stomach of persons supposed to have been drowned; and again, the determination of the freezing-point and the differences in the salt content between the blood of right and left side of the heart may be of use to confirm or negate the diagnosis of drowning. Entomology also may be of considerable assistance in establishing the date of death through the cadaveric flora and fauna.

This incomplete summary of the duties of the pathological expert serves to emphasize the point I wish to make. That the officer whose duty it is to make such examinations which have as their one and single aim the determination of the cause of death and a correct and analytically interpretative analysis of the surrounding circumstances attending, must be a physician by education, technically and practically trained in these branches. No lay or professional man other than a well-trained pathologist as above defined possesses the requisite natural or legal qualifications to discharge properly the duties of such an office.

4

The records of the medical examiner's office are open to the public, and daily use of such records is made by representatives of insurance companies, the families or representatives of the deceased, the army and navy authorities (especially during the late war), and the State Industrial Commission. Whereas under the coroners, the chemical examinations, even in poison cases, were not made except here and there, when the services of the pathological chemist of Bellevue Hospital in Manhattan were called upon to aid in a scientific inquiry, the office at the present time is constantly required to furnish evidence of the presence or absence of alcohol and of poisons. We are furnishing constantly to the department of health, the census bureau at Washington, and the various insurance companies, information in order to give them accurate data for purposes of classification, etc. The educational value of our reports is illustrated by the curious fact that the office is now criticized in those instances where chemical examinations are not made.

Without the aid of a properly organized chemical laboratory many certificates of death would be signed improperly. A most noteworthy illustration of this point is the fact that before the attention of the country was called to the so-called epidemics of wood alcohol poisoning, this office had become aware of the iniquitous sale of methylated spirits in place of grain alcohol through the routine chemical examination of cases which had come to autopsy in which the pathological lesions were indefinite.

The difficulty in abolishing a long and well-established office, as was the coroner's, is abundantly illustrated by the discussions which took place before the senate committee on city affairs in 1915. The arguments presented by the representatives of the coroner's system were that the coroners' physicians had surveyed a very large number of cases, that they were competent in view of this fact, that the establishment of a medical examiner's office would entail an extraordinary expenditure of moneys—some claiming that a satisfactory substitute of the system could not be maintained under less than half a million dollars a year. As a mere matter of fact, the medical examiner's office was created with a budget of about $65,000 less than the coroner's budget for Greater New York. The favorite arguments of the coroners were that they were the protectors of the rights of the people, that the new system was instituted purely for the benefits of the medical colleges and that the introduction of a new system was merely a scheme to obtain sufficient autopsies for medical purposes. Glaringly false statements were made in the hearing.

THE MEDICAL EXAMINER FACES PERPLEXING PROBLEMS

One of the most serious tasks that the medical examiner performs is the determination of criminal negligence in accident cases. This consists in the investigation of the circumstances surrounding the deaths in various industrial accidents, the analysis of poisonous fumes in manholes, the deaths resulting from careless cyanide disinfection, either in rooms or in the holds of vessels, deaths resulting from salvarsan poisoning, deaths resulting from structural defects in wood from dry rot and in the careless construction of buildings and other structures in general. In fact, the policy of the office is to bring out all the facts, medical, pathologic, or chemical, and to present all such evidence in proper fashion, making direct and trustworthy inferences and at the same time to avoid the danger of looking at facts through the spectacles of theory.

The numerous cases of asphyxiation by illuminant gas which this office handles yearly present a subject of considerable importance to the commonwealth. The duty of the office is not merely to give a correct determination of the cause of death, namely, whether accidental, suicidal, or homicidal, but to report to the proper authorities any negligence or carelessness on the part of the landowner or tenant in connection with the attachments of the gas tubing to the heating and illuminating apparatus or structural defects causing leakage of coal gas from water heaters or furnaces. There have been a number of accidental deaths due to the habit of a few of the keepers of boarding-houses of turning off the gas at stated hours and again turning on the gas in the early morning hours when the tenants are still asleep, the burners being turned on. One of the difficulties we have experienced is that there is no single department which has responsibility to whom such cases can be referred with a certainty they will receive prompt attention and action. The inadvisability of the use of rubber tubing for gas connections was called to the attention of the board of aldermen a few years ago and it is expected that action will be taken to prohibit its use in connections of this kind.

I wish to call attention to the necessity of performing autopsies upon all suspected cases, namely, all those cases in which the diagnosis cannot be made beyond reasonable doubt. Curious illustrations have occurred in this office to indicate how important a matter this is to the community. For instance, we have had two cases within the past several months of supposed criminal abortions in women in their early forties, upon whom criminal abortions have been performed, and who at autopsy were found not pregnant. The department examines cases rejected by the department of health and death certificates signed by apparently reputable physicians have disclosed cases of acute gastroenteritis which turned out to be peritonitis following criminal abortion, and cases of suicide in women supposedly pregnant (one case up to the seventh month, in an elderly married woman), autopsy revealing that there was no pregnancy, pregnancy being feared due to the appearance of the menopause and poison being taken to deliver a supposed fœtus.

Recommendations

1. The office of coroner should be abolished.

2. A law similar to the New York or Massachusetts law creating a medical examiner should be enacted.

3. The medical examiner should be a physician, expert in pathology and in medico-legal investigations.

4. The Board of County Commissioners should appoint from a civil

service list a medical examiner, and in counties having more than 100,000 inhabitants should appoint a chief medical examiner.

5. The chief medical examiner should have the power to appoint and to remove such deputies, assistant medical examiners, scientific experts, officers, and employees as may be provided for by law.

6. The medical examiner or his deputy or assistant should take charge of the body of any person who has died from criminal violence, or by a casualty, or by suicide, or suddenly when in apparent health or when unattended by a physician, or in prison, or in any suspicious or unusual manner.

7. If, in the opinion of the medical examiner, an autopsy is necessary, it should be performed by the medical examiner or his deputy or assistants.

8. The medical examiner should be in charge of the morgue.

9. Suitable laboratories, autopsy rooms, record rooms, and vaults, properly equipped for the performance of whatever investigations may be required in the course of the medical examiner's work, should be provided at the morgue.

10. A budget should be drawn up for the office of medical examiner each year, based upon the total amount of work to be done and not upon any proportionate relation to other public expenditures.

Prosecution

There is no provision for special medical examination in connection with prosecutions. It is left to the discretion of the prosecutor to call in physicians or other specialists to serve as expert witnesses. This is in accordance with the course pursued almost everywhere, and probably is satisfactory, according to present standards. There are certain individual prosecutors who consult and who may even be advised by experts throughout a trial without placing them upon the witness-stand. While this is a little more progressive than the general practice, it has the disadvantage of being partisan.

Prosecutors, in common with others, would benefit if there were available a body of expert opinion which could be invoked, as a routine measure, in all criminal cases.

Adjudication

1. Municipal Court

In the Municipal Court no special provision is made for expert medical or mental examinations. Cases dealt with by this court are in the main minor ones. They do not attract attention, and are passed through the court in a more or less routine fashion, on the general assumption that a delinquent requires punishment.

That the Municipal Court should constitute a process of weeding out socially incompetent individuals or serious delinquent types not yet guilty of a major crime is not comprehended. In a community in which public opinion on this subject is more advanced the Municipal Court is regarded as the most important clearing-house and sorting station for keeping the stream of civic life pure.

2. Common Pleas Court

The Common Pleas Court, criminal branch, hears cases of insanity under certain conditions. There are three ways in which such cases come before this court:

1. According to Sec. 13577, General Code, the grand jury may, if it finds the accused person insane, report that finding to the Common Pleas Court instead of indicting the person. The court then, as provided by law, impanels a jury to try that fact, whether or not the person is insane. If found insane, he is committed to Lima State Hospital for the criminal insane. The Ihlenfeld case is the first and only case to be dealt with according to the provisions of this section. Judge Baer, who tried the case, says this method saves time and money.

2. After a person has been indicted, and before sentence, his attorney may present to the court a certificate from a reputable physician to the effect that the person accused is insane, whereupon a jury is impaneled to decide the matter. The burden of proof rests on the defense. If three-fourths of the jury find the accused insane, he is committed to Lima State Hospital. (Sec. 13608 ff.)

3. The defense of insanity may be made at a regular trial. If the person tried upon an indictment for an offense is acquitted on the sole ground that he was insane, he is committed to Lima State Hospital, Sec. 13679. In all cases, if restored to reason, he may be prosecuted for the offense.

These seem to be the only ways in which such cases come before the Common Pleas Court. The number of such cases is small. During 1919 there were but seven cases. No separate or special records are kept; the records of the number of such trials and disposition of cases are found in the general Common Pleas docket. The prosecution can oppose the plea of insanity and call in doctors or other specialists as witnesses. There is no special provision in law for calling in experts or for their compensation in such cases. Judge Levine and Judge Baer are of the opinion that the Common Pleas judge can order examination to be made as to an accused person's sanity. No specific powers of that nature are mentioned in statutes.

In Judge Baer's opinion there should be a laboratory to investigate the mental condition of persons indicted, especially in the case of recidivists. Such work he considers belongs to a specialist and not to the judge, who cannot detect such cases when they appear in court.

3. Probate Court

There are no medical experts specially attached to the Probate Court to act in lunacy and feeble-minded cases. The law requires that in every case of feeble-mindedness, epilepsy, or insanity two reputable physicians shall be called in as medical witnesses. Technically, these are selected by the probate judge in each case, and serve only for that case. As a matter of practice, of course, physicians appointed to this commission are almost always the same; but this is purely dependent on the judge's choice and judgment. The medical witnesses are paid $5.00 for each case in which they testify, or, in other words, $5.00 for each certificate. At present the two physicians appointed by the judge are experts in mental diseases, having had experience in State hospitals.

There is no equipment for this work; the court does not control any offices or laboratories, though when it is not possible to arrive at a decision without special observation, the court is able, as a rule, to send the patient for examination to the psychopathic ward of the city hospital, which is the so-called Detention Hospital.

No selection of cases is possible; the examinations are made in those cases which are brought into the Probate Court on a complaint of insanity, epilepsy, or feeble-mindedness. Every complaint made is examined. The original papers in all cases are kept in the office of the court. Certified copies are sent to the hospital or other institution to which the patient is sent for examination and observation or to which he is committed. Reports of work are also made to the Secretary of State.

The examiners perform their work wherever necessary, according to the requirements of the case. They visit patients in their homes and in hospitals, at the State hospital, in jails, or wherever else they may be. The recommendations of the medical examiners are nearly always carried out. The judge acts upon the medical experts' advice also, and has confidence in the examiners whom he selects because they, in his opinion, are careful and conscientious in their work. Since the medical examiners are appointed by the judge, their mutual relations are very close. Apparently no other consideration than their fitness for the work enters into their appointments.

This system, which is obviously open to many theoretical objections, especially the opportunity it affords for political and other considerations to play an important part, is safeguarded by the fact that the present probate judge is above allowing such factors to influence his judgment. The medical examiners are free from the objection of being interested in the State hospitals, especially since the law requires that no physician officially connected with these may serve as examiner for the Probate Court.

In regard to the relation of medical examiners to commitment of insane persons, there is this to be said: The law which authorized the payment to the medical examiner of a fee for each case committed obviously places a premium on committing individuals; it would seem that the interest of the physician was to commit persons rather than to keep them out of institutions. Any possible tendency in this direction is counteracted, however, by the equally potent restraint of laws concerning malpractice and other legal actions.

Nevertheless, the recompensing of these special witnesses is a bad practice. Physicians are not only open to the influence above mentioned, but personal considerations enter in which have no place in this connection, such as the fact that these fees, which are paid through public funds, are in the nature of a largesse and should, therefore, be distributed among as large a number of physicians as possible. In the eyes of the more unscrupulous it will appear as a downright "graft," which may be connived at only if every one gets his full share. In Cleveland, as in other cities where this system is used, the work is done with little, if any, evidence of bad influences. Nevertheless, from the point of view of efficiency, and above all that of educating public opinion, it should be changed.

The tendency in all matters pertaining to insanity, at least since Charles Reade published *Hard Cash*, has been to remove all specific incentive in the matter of commitments. This fact, probably more than any other, has resulted in the respect shown for the State hospital and the prejudice in favor of this institution as compared with private institutions for mental cases.

The decision, whether a person should be segregated to a certain extent and deprived of his liberty, should be made on purely objective evidence, and while it is true that the court makes the final decision and examines the records, it is nevertheless upon the evidence submitted by the medical experts that such a decision is made by the court. If, then, medical examiners are swayed, either consciously or unconsciously, by other reasons than those based upon purely objective evidence, the court, even if ignorant of this, cannot act in an unbiased way. The result is that medical examiners should be paid either a salary or a fixed fee for every examination they make, regardless of whether commitment is recommended or not. At present they are paid for the certificate issued and not for the examination made.

The same statements which apply to the question of expert witnesses in general apply here. There may be, and probably should be, two kinds of experts available to the courts, the one serving as a public official on salary, for either full or part time, the other physicians who, in addition to the usual medical qualifications, have qualified and been appointed as experts. When a court or other public official or a private individual requires the services of an expert other than the officially salaried expert, he may select one from this qualified list. This system does not force any expert upon either courts or private individuals, nor does it require the poor man to suffer because he cannot afford the expensive specialist. Furthermore, it guarantees that the public official will be non-partisan and that the privately retained expert will at least measure up to the minimum standard requirements.

There is another phase of the relationship between the medical and particularly the mental expert and the Probate Court. In the Probate Court questions of property rights, guardianship, and conservatorship continually arise. While the question of mental disease or mental deficiency may not arise, there may, nevertheless, be important considerations in which the expert knowledge of the qualified psychiatrist would be of considerable value to the court. This refers particularly to that very large field of personality factors which we are just beginning to study scientifically. Every judge of the Probate Court will readily recognize what is referred to here, and probably every judge who has served in the Probate Court has made use of his experts in non-insane and nonfeeble-minded cases, for the purpose of evaluating the personality factors before making a decision.

This important work requires specialization and, furthermore, cannot be done satisfactorily unless experts making the examinations are employed on full time; that is, the experts cannot be expected to be efficient if they are called in only occasionally on such cases—they must be dealing with them as a matter of daily routine.

In the last year 560 cases have been examined by medical commissions for the Probate Court at $10 a case, or a total expenditure of $5,600 for medical fees alone. This does not include the sheriff fees, witness fees, and other incidentals.

Recommendations

1. A chief psychiatrist should be appointed by the judge of the Probate Court from a civil service list.

2. The chief psychiatrist should be empowered to appoint from a civil service list three assistant or deputy psychiatrists, one psychologist, and one assistant psychologist.

3. Suitable salaries should be provided to attract properly qualified experts.

4. The necessary clerical assistance and office quarters should be provided in the new court-house office building or county jail.

5. The chief psychiatrist should examine and pass upon all cases coming from the Probate Court, the Municipal Court, and the Court of Common Pleas, in which the question of sanity or insanity, epilepsy, or mental deficiency is raised.

6. The chief psychiatrist should cause to be examined, physically and mentally, in so far as possible, all persons coming before the Municipal Court.

7. The chief psychiatrist should present to the courts in writing a statement of the findings and opinion of the psychiatrist in each case examined.

8. In cases of dispute or doubt the court should be able to appoint a special psychiatrist to examine a case.

9. The person to be examined, his counsel, relatives, or friends, should be permitted to be represented by a psychiatrist who should have access to the findings of the chief psychiatrist, and who may be present at and participate in the examination by the chief psychiatrist, but who may not interfere with the conduct of such examinations.

10. The sheriff of Cuyahoga County and the Director of Public Welfare should be able to call upon the psychiatrist to examine any person in their custody and to enter a petition for commitment of any person thus examined who shall be found to be insane, epileptic, or feeble-minded.

11. Whenever, in the opinion of the psychiatrist, any person examined requires more extended study or observation than can be given at the county or city jail, application should be made to the court having jurisdiction, for temporary care at the city psychopathic hospital for a period of ten days, or not more than three months, or until such time as the director of the psychopathic hospital shall depose in writing that the examination or observation has been completed.

CHAPTER IV

PREVENTION

EARLY DETECTION OF SPECIAL CASES

IF WE may correctly assume that delinquency in most instances is not merely accidental, but is associated with characteristics and personal peculiarities inherent in the individual, it must follow that any attempt at prevention must include elimination at the source. By this we mean the examination of children of school age and even younger from the point of view of mental and personality characteristics, as manifested especially in behavior. It is by no means a certain or a simple matter to determine, even after careful examination, which children will present major behavior problems later in life. But it is certainly possible to determine which ones are in need of immediate special training and which show present behavior or mental deviations.

A careful study of this kind, followed by intensive training and observation of the physical, mental, and social factors involved, will, if applied to enough children, be comparable to the results obtained in the same circumstances by the methods of physical health training. If these methods now succeed in the Juvenile Courts, where they are applied after delinquency develops, there is every reason to expect even more satisfactory results when applied earlier, before the major problems of delinquency appear. When such a plan has been in operation for a generation, it is not unlikely that the problem of delinquency in the community will have changed so much as to make jails, as we now know them, quite unnecessary. We shall probably always require places of detention, but with a better understanding of the real causes of delinquency and crime and with more effective methods of prevention and treatment it is fair to assume that future detention institutions will differ from the present ones as modern hospitals differ from the ancient pest houses.

Meanwhile the police will continue to pick up and detain a large number of individuals who are a source of trouble and loss to the community and of little profit to themselves. Even in these cases an intelligent attitude requires that suitable studies shall be made of each individual case in order really to solve the problem, instead of depending entirely on forcible detention and segregation and the supposedly curative effects of

[42]

punitive imprisonment. The number of recidivists who pass through our jails is ample evidence against such misplaced confidence.

Even if a thorough examination of each prisoner is not possible, a sorting by simple examinations will identify extreme types of feeble-minded or psychopathic individuals. Individuals who are brought to light by these sorting examinations cannot be properly disposed of without treatment, and the treatment which may be given is one of three general types or combinations of these, namely, physical, mental, or social.

Physical treatment is directed against physical disease, on the one hand, and physical handicaps and defects, on the other. It is not necessary to enlarge upon this familiar topic. The main thing to emphasize here is the importance of correcting all physical disabilities, even those of apparently minor significance, in the interest of improving the mental and behavior reactions. Physicians often err in minimizing the effects of minor physical ailments.

For example, in the field of the psychoneuroses, as exemplified by the cases of so-called shell-shock during the war, the slighter the physical injury, the greater the psychic disturbance. In the field of behavior difficulties this is often markedly true. It is obvious, therefore, that physical examination must be performed with subtlety and niceness of observation. Clearly a physician, to be effective in the physical examination of behavior cases, must approach his work from a different angle from his general medical practice. The examination thus performed must then be correlated with the mental and social factors of each case in order that suitable physical treatment may be prescribed.

Mental treatment consists in the main of two kinds: first, education and training of various mental faculties or talents, which are carried out in accordance with established principles of educational training and certain sorts of habit formation; second, treatment by various means of what may be considered pathological mental traits. Psychotherapy, hydrotherapy, mechanotherapy, occupational therapy, and other modern forms of treatment may be applied by trained experts to good effect.

Social treatment is perhaps the most modern and least well defined of all the various forms of treatment. As applied to delinquency, it consists mainly of adjusting environmental conditions to the needs of the individual case. The important point is not merely to change the environment, but to adapt the environment to the needs, temporary or permanent, of an individual more or less incapable of adapting himself. This form of treatment is consequently varied, and includes the adjustment of the individual to living conditions in his particular community, as well as social relief, recreation, or employment.

[43]

One of the most potent influences in prevention is, of course, public education. As in public health, the only effective way to educate the public is by spreading broadcast the knowledge now available to which the public is entitled.

Unfortunately, in this era of advertising, everyone is becoming suspicious of propaganda conducted under the guise of public education. It is, therefore, necessary to force upon the public something more than off-hand opinions and prejudices. Ultimate progress depends upon the strict adherence to facts. For example, during recent years considerable propaganda has been adopted to prove that feeble-mindedness is one of the principal causes of criminality. It has been contended that if we detect and segregate the feeble-minded early in life, we can reduce crime by one-third to one-half, if not more. This belief was based upon the finding that in certain institutions from one-fourth to one-third of the institutional population was rated feeble-minded by intelligence tests.

This contention was given a most favorable reception, and for a time promised to induce a more scientific attitude on the part of officials toward the various phenomena of crime, and also to arouse a greater interest in and support of the institutional care of the feeble-minded. Certain officials—police, prosecutors, attorneys, prison authorities, in short, all who were brought in close contact with the criminal population—were reluctant to accept these statements, but their attitude was ascribed to natural conservatism.

More recent work has shown that while figures for the institutions were undoubtedly correct, the interpretation placed upon them was not correct, because it failed to take into account the nature of the population from which the prisoners came. From information now available in regard to the intelligence distribution throughout the United States it appears that the prison populations are probably fairly representative, so far as intelligence goes, of the communities from which they come. It may be true, therefore, that a quarter of the persons in a given institution are feeble-minded, but, in order to reduce crime by 25 per cent. not only would 25 per cent. of the prison population have to be committed to an institution for the feeble-minded, but 25 per cent. of the population from which they came would have to be segregated, which is clearly ridiculous.

This illustrates one of the dangers of the proposed methods, even when applied to a worthy purpose. Nothing could be more desirable than the scientific treatment of criminals and the application of psychological, psychiatric, and other mental methods to criminals and delinquents. But it is a mistake to make the success of such a venture depend upon arousing the public's interest by unwarranted statements. In the business world, where an effect is desired for a short time, such methods may be legitimate, but in the case of treatment of crime, where we are building for generations ahead, they are nothing short of dangerous. The psychology of salesmanship has no place in the sphere of science. The reaction in the public mind of arousing interest on the basis of statements which are only partly true causes a loss of confidence which retards progress more than initial conservatism.

RESEARCH

Where shall the facts and information be obtained upon which a campaign of public education may be based?

Obviously, in an experimental subject, such as criminology, and one in which science is just beginning to make itself felt, concrete information is extremely scanty. In order to keep pace with the progressive demands of modern community life and the growing public interest, provision must be made for investigation and research into the nature and treatment of delinquency and crime.

Such scientific research requires the same arrangements as any other sort of scientific investigation. In the first place, there must be properly trained and equipped experts. They must have a place in which to work which is officially designated the laboratory, and in which are provided all the necessary paraphernalia for scientific research. This is not the place to enter into detailed statements as to the exact size or arrangement of such laboratories or staff. These depend largely upon the resources which the community makes available for the purpose and the interest which it arouses.

Since scientific research is at best an uncertain matter, a liberal allowance or *margin of safety* is advisable in order to insure a minimum of return. There are no rules for this work, and there is, as yet, no standard. It would be better, however, for Cleveland not to venture into this field at all unless the start can be made on a scale commensurate not only with the size and importance of the city, but with the size and menace of the problem.

A research laboratory or institution, properly staffed and equipped, could conduct scientific investigations into behavior problems for the police, schools, public health bureaus, courts, jails, correctional and penal institutions, and the numerous public and private social agencies.

In another part of this section of the survey there is a brief account of a psychological analysis of the population of the Cleveland workhouse.

It will be seen from this analysis that the workhouse has a large number of low-grade feeble-minded men. Reference to the chart will show that the number is out of proportion to the rest of the community. Clearly, here is a problem for mental science—for the student of the pathology of human behavior. We are spending several hundred million dollars in the United States annually in dealing with the end results of criminality and behavior disorders. Probably not $500,000 is being spent in a scientific attack upon the *causes*.[1]

TRAINING OF WORKERS AND EXPERTS

The plan outlined thus far has discussed: (a) The workers for practical daily routine; (b) the research institution and staff, where new knowledge may be sought and gained; and (c) the dissemination of information to train and direct public opinion. There is left one more item to round out the scheme, and that is a provision for the training of workers and experts who are to take their places in the ranks.

Whenever a community has been aroused on the subject of mental problems, and particularly behavior problems, and has finally decided to establish scientific work, the perplexing question presents itself: "Where shall we find the workers?" It must be admitted that the workers available for immediate employment in this field are limited in number. This is, however, not to be wondered at, nor is it an indication that the subject does not appeal to scientific minds.

Rather it is a manifestation of one of the many vicious circles in our social organization. There must be a demand for this work and a realization on the part of the public of its importance great enough to insure a career for the workers. This, in turn, depends upon the attainment of results of a concrete and practical sort, to stimulate public interest. Many who might have been glad to devote their lives to this science have been compelled to seek other fields by a failure to obtain either opportunity or remuneration enough.

In order permanently to break up this vicious circle and to make the scheme outlined here quite clear, we must, therefore, add a provision for the training of workers and experts. This training should be given in the

---

[1] It is as well, perhaps, to state here that the term "scientific," as used repeatedly in this report, is not used as applied to the worker in the exact sciences. The scientist referred to here is not a man manipulating test-tubes and galvanometers alone. The investigation of behavior problems requires scientists equipped to deal not only with the methods of exact science, but also those who are capable of devoting themselves to problems of education and social organization.

main under the auspices of a research laboratory, as we suggested, and in connection with the schools and universities of the community. Such training should be offered, in the first place, to physicians, lawyers, psychologists, psychiatrists, social workers, administrators, and public officials. A flexible curriculum should permit these different classes of professional workers to obtain the training needed to make their particular contact with the problem of delinquency. In order to do this it might be desirable to utilize existing departments of the university, perhaps the medical school. The latter is preferable to the law school, but close correlation between the law school and such work in the medical school is essential.

In addition, special courses should be offered to social workers, parole and probation officers, police officers, teachers, and nurses. Here again the curriculum might be so arranged that police officers, for instance, should receive a brief and intensive training, whereas social workers and probation officers should receive a more extended training. A scheme such as this, furthermore, makes possible part time graduate work or special investigations, just as now a properly qualified student may enter a laboratory for post-graduate study on a special topic.

When an organization of this sort has functioned long enough to produce the first graduates, the community can equip itself in such a way as undoubtedly to reap the benefit in a continually lessened cost of administration of criminal justice; and not the least of the benefits to be expected from such an organization is that other communities, no less anxious to improve their crime statistics than Cleveland, and no better off for staff or special workers, will turn to Cleveland for their personnel.

Recommendations

1. If possible, a privately supported institute or clinic should be established either independently or, preferably, in connection with Western Reserve University.

2. The object of the institute should be:

(a) Investigation of the nature and treatment of human behavior difficulties.

(b) The training and education of special workers and experts in the field of behavior problems.

3. The institute should have a staff comprehensive enough to include the methods of physical and mental health and the social sciences.

4. The institute shall be equipped with the necessary laboratory space and apparatus and with bed capacity for a limited number of patients.

APPENDICES

APPENDIX I

REPORT OF INTELLIGENCE SURVEY OF THE CLEVELAND POLICE DEPARTMENT

BY E. K. WICKMAN
Psychologist, Division of the Criminologist, Illinois

A SURVEY of the intelligence of the personnel of the Division of Police of Cleveland was made in connection with the survey of the administration of justice conducted by the Cleveland Foundation. Mental ratings on 979 officers, detectives, and patrolmen were secured by the use of the army Alpha Intelligence Examination.

The survey was made with the coöperation of the Chief of Police, Frank W. Smith, who ordered the men of his department assembled for the examination and who lent his coöperation and influence to their effective administration and completion. The examinations were not compulsory for the men, with the exception of those in the training school. Orders by the Chief of Police were issued for all men who were on active duty during the three days of the survey to report for the examination, but the actual examination was taken voluntarily. There were, however, no men in the department who declined to submit to the tests.

The 979 men who were examined compose over 90 per cent. of the entire department, and the men who were not rated were not actually available for the examination during the three days of the survey. The general orders for the assembling of the men called for one-half of one of the four platoons for each group examination. The examinations were made on the salary time of the men, and the groups were assembled at 1, 2, and 3 o'clock in the afternoons, and at 7.30 and 10 o'clock in the evenings. The 979 men include officers (captains, lieutenants, and sergeants), detectives, men of the vice bureau, the traffic, mounted, emergency, and regular patrolmen, and the members of the training school.

The intelligence examination used was the army Alpha examination, the scale employed for literates in the examination of officers and recruits in the United States army. The army procedure in the administration of the examination was adhered to in all respects. The groups varied in size from 10 to 90 men. With the exception of the captains and detectives, the groups were assembled in the training school class-room of the Eighth Precinct Police Station. All five forms of the Alpha examination were employed, so as to avoid possible coaching.

The papers were later scored by special clerks, and intelligence ratings were assigned to all the men on the basis of the army letter rating scale, as follows:

Grade of intelligence	Explanation	Alpha score	Approximate mental age, years
A	Very superior intelligence	135–212	..
B	Superior intelligence	105–134	
C+	High average intelligence	75–104	..
C	Average intelligence	45– 74	
C—	Low average intelligence	25– 44	11–13
D	Inferior intelligence	15– 24	9–10.9
E	Very inferior intelligence	0– 14	Below 9

The distribution of intelligence ratings for the officers, detectives, and various divisions of the patrolmen is shown in Tables 1 and 2 and Diagram 1.

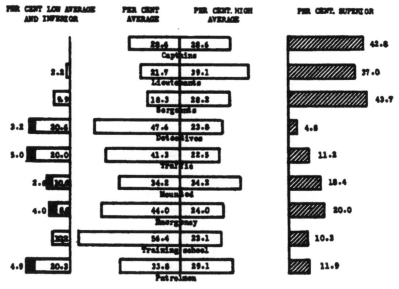

Diagram 1.—Intelligence ratings of divisions of Cleveland police department

About 40 per cent. of the officers of the department rate in the superior grades of intelligence. These ratings were secured by about 13.5 per cent. of the draft army. Another 32 per cent. of the officers are of high average intelligence; about 20 per cent. are average, while 6 per

5

TABLE 1.—DISTRIBUTION OF INTELLIGENCE RATINGS

	Captains		Lieutenants		Sergeants		Detectives		Vice Bureau		Training school		Traffic police		Mounted police		Emergency motorcycle		Patrolmen	
	No.	Per cent.	No.	Per cent.	No.	Per cent.	No.	Per cent.	No.	Per cent.	No.	Per cent.	No.	Per cent.	No.	Per cent.	No.	Per cent.	No.	Per cent.
A	1	7.1	4	8.7	7	9.9	.	.	4	15.4	1	2.6	1	1.2	1	2.6	1	4.0	17	2.9
B	5	35.7	13	28.3	24	33.8	3	4.8	9	34.6	3	7.7	8	10.0	6	15.8	4	16.0	52	9.0
C+	4	28.6	18	39.1	20	28.2	15	23.8	8	30.8	9	23.1	18	22.5	13	34.2	6	24.0	168	29.1
C	4	28.6	10	21.7	13	18.3	30	47.6	4	15.4	22	56.4	33	41.3	13	34.2	11	44.0	195	33.8
C−	.	.	1	2.2	7	9.9	13	20.6	1	3.8	4	10.2	16	20.0	4	10.6	2	8.0	117	20.3
D	.	.	.	.	.	.	2	3.2	.	.	.	.	3	3.8	1	2.6	1	4.0	22	3.8
E	.	.	.	.	.	.	.	.	.	.	.	.	1	1.2	.	.	.	.	6	1.1
	14	100.0	46	100.0	71	100.0	63	100.0	26	100.0	39	100.0	80	100.0	38	100.0	25	100.0	577	100.0

cent. are low average. There are no representatives among the officers in the inferior grades of intelligence.

TABLE 2.—SUMMARY OF DISTRIBUTION OF INTELLIGENCE RATINGS

	All officers		Vice Bureau		Detectives		All patrolmen		Total		Draft army
	No.	Per cent.	No.	Per cent.	No.	Per cent.	No.	Per cent.	No.	Per cent.	Per cent.
A	12	9.2	4	15.4	..	..	21	2.8	37	3.8	4.5
B	42	32.0	9	34.6	3	4.8	73	9.6	127	13.0	9.0
C+	42	32.0	8	30.8	15	23.8	214	28.2	279	28.5	16.5
C	27	20.6	4	15.4	30	47.6	274	36.1	335	34.2	25.0
C−	8	6.1	1	3.8	13	20.6	143	18.8	165	16.9	20.0
D	..	..	..	..	2	3.2	27	3.6	29	2.9	15.0
E	..	..	..	..	..	..	7	0.9	7	0.7	10.0
	131	100.0	26	100.0	63	100.0	759	100.0	979	100.0	100.0

Of the patrolmen, there are 12 per cent. in the superior grades, 28 per cent. are high average, while the greatest percentage (34) are average. There is a heavier percentage of patrolmen in the low average group than in the superior groups, and about 3 per cent. are definitely in the inferior grades of intelligence. Of the various divisions of the patrolmen, the emergency and mounted police have the higher intelligence distributions.

The detectives, a group of 63 men, rate lowest in the entire department. There are less than 5 per cent. in the superior grades, and about 23 per cent. are high average, while 70 per cent. are either average, low average, or inferior.

A further comparison of these divisions of police is shown in Table 3 and in Diagrams 2 and 3, by comparing their median scores and the range of scores of the high, middle, and low third of each division. The median scores of the officers varies between 95 and 98. These are high scores in the high average grade of intelligence. The patrolmen have a median of 67, which falls in the average grade of intelligence, while the detectives are the lowest of the divisions, with a median of 59.

At present the detectives are ranking, as far as salary is concerned, with the lieutenants, but a comparison of these two groups shows that the lieutenants have 37 per cent. of representatives in the superior grades of intelligence, as opposed to 4.8 per cent. of the detectives, and only 23.9 per cent. in the average and low average grades, as compared with 71.4 per cent. of the detectives. The lieutenants' median falls at 95, while the detectives' is 59. Furthermore, the low third of the lieutenants has a higher range of scores than the middle third of the detectives.

TABLE 3.—MEDIAN SCORES AND RANGE OF SCORES OF POLICE DIVISIONS

Rank or division	Median	Range of scores of each division		
		Low third	Middle third	High third
Captains	98 C+	50–75	76–104	105–154
Lieutenants	95 C+	36–81	82–108	109–165
Sergeants	99 C+	28–79	79–109	110–166
Vice squad	75 C−	23–61	64– 84	84–134
Detectives	59 C	23–50	51– 71	72–131
Training school	63 C	25–56	57– 74	77–138
Traffic	61 C	5–56	56– 74	75–137
Mounted	78 C+	22–59	60– 91	92–155
Emergency	67 C	19–64	65– 80	83–150
Patrolmen	67 C	6–52	53– 82	82–170

When compared with the results obtained from the recent draft army, there is, of course, a very small percentage (3.6 per cent.) of men in the police department who rate in the inferior grades of intelligence in which the lowest 25 per cent. of the men in the draft army were classified. The men of the police department group themselves closely about the average grade of intelligence, and the medians of the patrolmen are about identical with the medians of the draft army. With the exception of the officers, there is a smaller percentage of representatives in the police department in the superior grades of intelligence than were found in the draft army. The detectives have no representatives in the very superior grade of intelligence, a classification secured by 4.5 per cent. of the draft army, and only three individuals of the detectives have superior intelligence, as opposed to 9 per cent. of the draft. As a whole, however, the police department ranks somewhat higher than the majority of the men of the draft. This is evident in its somewhat larger percentage of representatives of high average intelligence.

Table 4 shows a distribution of intelligence ratings of patrolmen according to the date of entry into the police department. There is very little difference in the ratings of the first year groups, who entered between 1895–1919. There is a slight decrease with length of service, much of which may be attributed to the deterioration of increasing age. The table also shows that the men who entered during the present year, 1921, have a considerably higher percentage of men of superior intelligence. The war year, 1918, produced no men either of superior or of inferior intelligence. All of the entrants in that year rate in the average classes of intelligence.

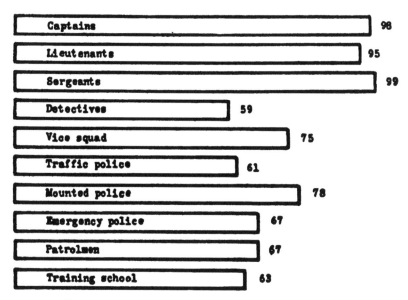

Diagram 2.—Median scores, Cleveland police department

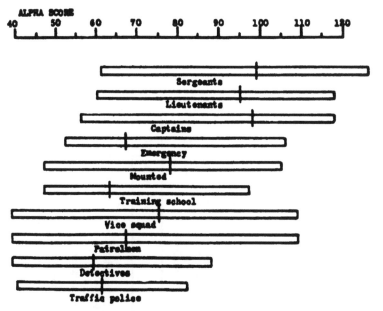

Diagram 3.—Range of scores between first and third quartiles of Cleveland police department. (The median scores are indicated by the cross lines.)

TABLE 4.—INTELLIGENCE DISTRIBUTION OF PATROLMEN BY DATE OF ENTRY INTO THE DEPARTMENT

Letter rating	Explanation	Entered 1921		Entered 1920		Entered 1918		Entered 1915–1919		Entered 1910–1914		Entered 1905–1909		Entered 1895–1904		Entire police dept.		Draft army
		No.	Per cent.	No.	Per cent.	No.	Per cent.	No.	Per cent.	No.	Per cent.	No.	Per cent.	No.	Per cent.	No.	Per cent.	Per cent.
A	Very superior	6	7.4	3	3.3	..	..	8	3.1	2	1.9	1	1.4	..	..	37	3.8	4.5
B	Superior	16	14.8	11	12.2	..	..	22	8.4	8	7.7	4	5.9	3	5.3	127	13.0	9.0
C+	High average	21	25.9	27	30.0	9	27.3	90	34.5	30	28.9	17	25.0	11	19.3	279	28.5	16.5
C	Average	25	30.9	33	36.7	20	60.6	92	35.3	36	34.6	23	33.8	24	42.1	335	34.2	25.0
C–	Low average	12	14.8	13	14.5	4	12.1	39	15.0	23	22.1	19	28.0	15	26.3	165	16.9	20.0
D	Inferior	1	1.2	3	3.3	..	..	9	3.4	4	3.9	4	5.9	3	5.3	29	2.9	15.0
E	Very inferior	..	..	..	..	..	..	1	0.3	1	0.9	..	..	1	1.7	7	0.7	10.0
		81	100.0	90	100.0	33	100.0	261	100.0	104	100.0	68	100.0	57	100.0	979	100.0	100.0
A B	Superior	Per cent. 27.2		Per cent. 15.5		Per cent. ..		Per cent. 11.5		Per cent. 9.6		Per cent. 7.3		Per cent. 5.3		Per cent. 16.8		Per cent. 13.5
C+ C C–	Average	71.6		81.2		100.0		84.8		85.6		86.8		87.7		79.6		61.5
D E	Inferior	1.2		3.3		..		3.7		4.8		5.9		7.0		3.6		25.0

[54]

APPENDIX II

INTELLIGENCE SURVEY OF THE CLEVELAND WORKHOUSE

By E. K. WICKMAN

Psychologist, Division of the Criminologist, Illinois

A N INTELLIGENCE survey of the workhouse of Cleveland, Ohio, was made in connection with the survey of the Administration of Justice, to illustrate some of the results which may be obtained by mental studies. The population of this institution was about 450 men, of whom about one-fifth were examined by the use of the Army Alpha Intelligence Examination. This one-fifth was chosen by assembling the men in single file and selecting every fifth man in line for examination. To this group were added all of the men who were at the workhouse on federal charges, and also the group of men called "long termers." One hundred and twenty-six men were thus assembled for the examination; of these, 32 were illiterate and were unable to take the examination, insofar as they claimed to be unable to read and write, and one other man was unable to take the examination because of poor vision.

Records were thus secured on 93 of the men, of whom 44 (47 per cent.) were native-born whites, 32 (34 per cent.) were negroes, and 13 (14 per cent.) were foreign born. Four men did not indicate birth or race.

The distribution of intelligence ratings as secured by the army Alpha examination is given in Table 5.

The literate native-born white group who took the examination fall mostly in the average grades of intelligence, but about 15 per cent. of them are inferior. The army statistics show about 14 per cent. inferior in this group of native-born whites. There are, however, only about 4 per cent. in the superior groups, as opposed to 15 per cent. in the army.

Of the negroes, 61 per cent. fall in the inferior groups of intelligence as opposed to 43 per cent. in the army.

The average rating for the white prisoners fall in the "C" or average group of intelligence, as it also did in the army, while the average for the negro prisoners falls in the "D" or inferior group, while the army average was "C—" or low average group.

[55]

TABLE 5.—DISTRIBUTION OF INTELLIGENCE RATINGS IN THE WORKHOUSE

	Native born white		Foreign born	All whites		Negroes		Race unknown	Total	
	No.	Per cent.	No.	No.	Per cent.	No.	Per cent.	No.	No.	Per cent.
A	..	..	..	..	..	..	..	..	..	..
B	2	4.5	1	3	5.3	..	..	..	3	3.2
C+	16	36.4	..	16	28.0	..	..	..	16	17.2
C	13	29.6	1	14	24.5	2	6.2	..	16	17.2
C−	6	13.6	3	9	15.8	7	21.9	..	16	17.2
D	2	4.5	4	6	10.5	9	28.1	..	15	16.2
E	5	11.4	4	9	15.8	14	43.8	4	27	29.0
Total	44	100.0	13	57	99.9	32	100.0	4	93	100.0

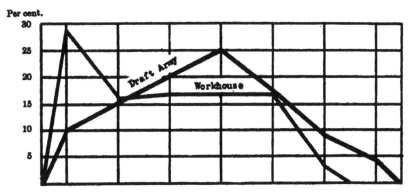

Diagram 4.—Comparison of intelligence distributions of Cleveland Workhouse and United States Draft Army

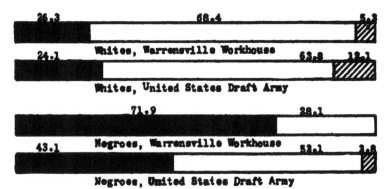

Diagram 5.—Comparison of intelligence ratings, Warrensville Workhouse with United States Draft Army

Diagram 4 shows the distribution of intelligence ratings of the Cleveland workhouse with the United States draft army. In Diagram 5 the same distribution is shown for whites and negroes separately.

These results would undoubtedly be lowered if ratings of the illiterate men were included, so that it may safely be said that the intelligence of these men at the Cleveland workhouse is somewhat below the draft army intelligence.

APPENDIX III

TEXT OF THE MASSACHUSETTS MEDICAL EXAMINER LAW

THE COMMONWEALTH OF MASSACHUSETTS
General Laws, Chapter 38

MEDICAL EXAMINERS

SECTION 1. The governor, with the advice and consent of the council, shall appoint for terms of seven years able and discreet men, learned in the science of medicine, as medical examiners in and for their respective counties, and as associate medical examiners in and for their respective districts in counties divided into districts, otherwise in and for their respective counties, in number as follows:

Two examiners and two associate examiners in Suffolk county, and one examiner and one associate examiner in Nantucket county and in each of the following districts:

Barnstable county, district one, comprising Harwich, Dennis, Yarmouth, Brewster, Chatham, Orleans and Eastham; district two, Barnstable, Bourne, Sandwich, Mashpee and Falmouth; and district three, Provincetown, Truro and Wellfleet.

Berkshire county, district one, comprising North Adams, Williamstown, Clarksburg, Adams, Florida, Savoy, New Ashford and Cheshire; district two, Pittsfield, Lanesborough, Windsor, Dalton, Hinsdale, Peru and Hancock; district three, Richmond, Lenox, Washington, Becket, Lee, Stockbridge, Tyringham and Otis; and district four, West Stockbridge, Alford, Great Barrington, Monterey, Sandisfield, New Marlborough, Sheffield, Egremont and Mount Washington.

Bristol county, district one, comprising Attleboro, North Attleborough, Seekonk, Norton, Mansfield and Rehoboth; district two, Taunton, Raynham, Easton, Berkley, and Dighton; district three, Fall River, Somerset, Swansea, Freetown and Westport; and district four, New Bedford, Dartmouth, Fairhaven and Acushnet.

Dukes county, district one, comprising Edgartown and Oak Bluffs; district two, Tisbury, West Tisbury and Gosnold; and district three, Chilmark and Gay Head.

Essex county, district one, comprising Gloucester and Rockport; district two, Ipswich, Rowley, Hamilton and Essex; district three, Newburyport, Newbury, West Newbury, Amesbury and Salisbury; district four, Haverhill and Merrimac; district five, Lawrence, Methuen, Andover and North Andover; district six, Georgetown, Boxford, Topsfield and Groveland; district seven, Beverly, Wenham and Manchester; district eight, Peabody, Danvers, Middleton and Lynnfield; district nine, Lynn, Saugus, Nahant and Swampscott; and district ten, Salem and Marblehead.

Franklin county, the northern district, comprising Orange, Warwick, New Salem and Wendell; the eastern district, Bernardston, Erving, Gill, Greenfield, Leverett, Montague, Northfield, Shutesbury and Sunderland; and the western district, Ashfield, Buckland, Charlemont, Colrain, Conway, Deerfield, Hawley, Heath, Leyden, Monroe, Rowe, Shelburne and Whately.

Hampden county, district one, comprising Brimfield, Holland, Palmer, Monson and Wales; district two, Springfield, Agawam, East Longmeadow, Longmeadow, West Springfield, Wilbraham and Hampden; district three, Holyoke; district four, Blandford, Chester, Granville, Montgomery, Russell, Southwick, Tolland and Westfield; and district five, Chicopee and Ludlow.

Hampshire county, district one, comprising Northampton, Chesterfield, Cummington, Goshen, Hatfield, Plainfield and Williamsburg; district two, Easthampton, Huntington, Middlefield, Southampton, Westhampton and Worthington; district three, Amherst, Granby, Hadley, Pelham and South Hadley; and district four, Belchertown, Enfield, Greenwich, Prescott and Ware.

Middlesex county, district one, comprising Cambridge, Belmont and Arlington; district two, Malden, Somerville, Everett and Medford; district three, Melrose, Stoneham, Wakefield, Wilmington, Reading and North Reading; district four, Woburn, Winchester, Lexington and Burlington; district five, Lowell, Dracut, Tewksbury, Billerica, Chelmsford and Tyngsborough; district six, Concord, Carlisle, Bedford, Lincoln, Littleton, Acton and Boxborough; district seven, Newton, Waltham, Watertown and Weston; district eight, Framingham, Wayland, Natick, Sherborn, Holliston, Hopkinton and Ashland; district nine, Marlborough, Hudson, Maynard, Stow and Sudbury; district ten, Ayer, Groton, Westford, Dunstable, Pepperell, Shirley, Townsend and Ashby.

Norfolk county, district one, comprising Dedham, Needham, Wellesley, Westwood, Norwood and Dover; district two, Cohasset; district three, Quincy, Milton and Randolph; district four, Weymouth, Braintree and Holbrook; district five, Avon, Stoughton, Canton, Walpole and Sharon; district six, Franklin, Foxborough and Wrentham; district seven, Medway, Medfield, Millis, Norfolk and Bellingham; and district eight, Brookline.

Plymouth county, district one, comprising Brockton, West Bridgewater, East Bridgewater, Bridgewater and Whitman; district two, Abington, Rockland, Hanover, Hanson, Norwell and Pembroke; district three, Plymouth, Halifax, Kingston, Plympton and Duxbury; district four, Middleborough, Wareham, Mattapoisett, Carver, Rochester, Lakeville and Marion; and district five, Hingham, Hull, Scituate and Marshfield.

Worcester county, district one, comprising Athol, Dana, Petersham, Phillipston and Royalston; district two, Gardner, Templeton and Winchendon; district three, Fitchburg, Ashburnham, Leominster, Lunenburg, Princeton and Westminster; district four, Berlin, Bolton, Boylston, Clinton, Harvard, Lancaster and Sterling; district five, Grafton, Northborough, Southborough and Westborough; district six, Hopedale, Mendon, Milford and Upton; district seven, Blackstone, Douglas, Millville, Northbridge and Uxbridge; district eight, Charlton, Dudley, Oxford, Southbridge, Sturbridge and Webster; district nine, Brookfield, East Brookfield, North Brookfield, Spencer, Warren and West Brookfield; district ten, Barre, Hubbardston, Hardwick, New Braintree, Oakham and Rutland; and district eleven, Worcester, Auburn, Holden, Leicester, Millbury, Paxton, Shrewsbury, Sutton and West Boylston.

SECTION 2. The associate medical examiners for Suffolk county shall, at the request of either of its medical examiners, perform the duties and have the powers of medical examiners. Each medical examiner shall in each year be entitled to two months' service in the aggregate from the associates. Associate examiners in the other counties shall, in the absence of the medical examiners or in case of their inability to act, perform in their respective districts all the duties of medical examiners.

SECTION 3. Each examiner and associate examiner, before entering upon his duties, shall be sworn and give bond for the faithful performance thereof, in the sum of five thousand dollars, to the county treasurer, with sureties by him approved. Failure for three months after appointment to give such bond shall render his appointment void. A surety or his executors or administrators may be discharged from further liability thereon in the manner provided in section six of chapter thirty-seven.

SECTION 4. Upon breach of the condition of such bond to the injury of any person, the principal may be removed from office and action brought thereon in like manner as upon the bond of a sheriff.

SECTION 5. In Suffolk county each medical examiner shall receive from the county a salary of five thousand dollars, and each associate medical examiner a salary of eight hundred and thirty-three dollars; but if either associate serves in any year more than two months, he shall for such additional service be paid at the same rate, and the amount so paid shall be deducted from the salary of the medical examiner at whose request he so serves. The medical examiners for said county shall be provided with rooms suitably furnished for the performance of their duties, the rent, furnishing and office equipment of which shall be paid for by said county upon approval of the mayor of Boston. Each of said medical examiners may, in the name of the county, contract such bills for clerical service, postage, stationery, printing, telephone, traveling, and for such other incidental expenses as may in his opinion be necessary for the proper performance of his duty, to an amount not exceeding six thousand dollars in any one year; and each associate may so contract bills for the said purposes to an amount not exceeding one thousand dollars in any one year; and all such bills shall be paid by said county, upon a certificate by the contracting examiner that they were necessarily incurred in the performance of his duty, and upon the approval of the auditor of Boston, as provided in section nineteen, and of the mayor. Medical examiners and associate medical examiners in other counties shall receive fees as follows: For a view without an autopsy, seven dollars; for a view and an autopsy, thirty dollars; and for travel, ten cents a mile to and from the place of view.

SECTION 6. Medical examiners shall make examination upon the view of the dead bodies of only such persons as are supposed to have died by violence. If a medical examiner has notice that there is within his county the body of such a person, he shall forthwith go to the place where the body lies and take charge of the same; and if, on view thereof and personal inquiry into the cause and manner of death, he considers a further examination necessary, he shall, upon written authorization of the district attorney, mayor or selectmen of the district, city or town where the body lies, make an autopsy in the presence of two or more discreet persons, whose attendance he may compel by subpœna. Before making such autopsy he shall call the attention of the witnesses to the appearance and position of the body. He shall then and there carefully record every fact and circumstance tending to show the condition of the body and the cause and manner of death, with the names and addresses of said witnesses, which record he shall subscribe. If a medical examiner or an associate examiner considers it necessary to have a physician present as a witness at an autopsy, such physician shall receive a fee of five dollars. Other witnesses, except officers named in section fifty of chapter two hundred and sixty-two, shall be allowed two dollars each. A clerk may be employed to reduce to writing the results of a medical examination or autopsy, and shall receive two dollars a day.

The medical examiner may, if he considers it necessary, employ a chemist to aid in the examination of the body or of substances supposed to have caused or contributed to the death, and he shall receive such compensation as the examiner certifies to be just and reasonable.

SECTION 7. He shall forthwith file with the district attorney for his district a report of each autopsy and view and of his personal inquiries, with a certificate that, in his judgment, the manner and cause of death could not be ascertained by view and inquiry and that an autopsy was necessary. The district attorney, if he concurs, shall so certify to the commissioners of the county where the same was held, or in Suffolk county, to the auditor of Boston. If upon such view, personal inquiry or autopsy, the medical examiner is of opinion that the death may have been caused by the act or negligence of another, he shall at once notify the district attorney and a justice of a district court or trial justice within whose jurisdiction the body was found, if the place where found and the place of the said act or negligence are within the same county, or if the latter place is unknown; otherwise, the district attorney and such a justice

[61]

within whose district or jurisdiction the said act or negligence occurred. He shall also file with the district attorney thus notified, and with the justice or in his court, an attested copy of the record of the autopsy made as provided in the preceding section. He shall in all cases certify to the town clerk or registrar in the place where the deceased died his name and residence, if known; otherwise a description as full as may be, with the cause and manner of death.

SECTION 8. The court or trial justice shall thereupon hold an inquest, from which all persons not required by law to attend may be excluded. The district attorney, or any person designated by him, may attend the inquest and examine the witnesses, who may be kept separate, so that they cannot converse with each other until they have been examined. Within sixty days after any case of death by accident upon a railroad, electric railroad, street railway or railroad for private use an inquest shall be held, and the court or justice shall give seasonable notice of the time and place thereof to the department of public utilities. Within a like period after any case of death in which a motor vehicle is involved, an inquest shall be held, and the court or justice shall give seasonable notice of the time and place thereof to the department of public works. The attorney general or the district attorney may, notwithstanding the medical examiner's report that a death was not caused by the act or negligence of another, direct an inquest to be held, and likewise in case of death by any casualty.

SECTION 9. If it appears that the place where the supposed act or negligence occurred and the place where the body was found are both without the limits of the judicial district of the court or the jurisdiction of the trial justice notified by the medical examiner under section seven, the court or justice shall nevertheless proceed with the inquest and have continuous and exclusive jurisdiction thereof if either place is within the commonwealth and within fifty rods of the boundary line of such district or jurisdiction, unless a prior and like notice shall have been issued by a medical examiner in another county in accordance with said section.

SECTION 10. A district court about to hold an inquest may appoint an officer qualified to serve criminal process to investigate the case and to summon the witnesses, and may allow him additional compensation therefor, payable in like manner as the fees of officers in criminal cases.

SECTION 11. If a magistrate believes that an inquest to be held by him relates to the accidental death of a passenger or employee upon a railroad or electric railroad or a traveler upon a public or private way at a railroad crossing, or to an accidental death connected with the operation of a street railway or of a railroad for private use, he shall cause a verbatim report of the evidence to be made and sworn to by the person making it; and the report and the bill for services, after examination and written approval by the magistrate, shall be forwarded to the department of public utilities within thirty days after the date of the inquest, and, when made, a copy of the magistrate's report on the inquest. The bill, when approved by said department, shall be forwarded to the state auditor and paid by the commonwealth, assessed on the person owning or operating such railroad or railway, and shall be collected in the same manner as taxes upon corporations. The magistrate may in his discretion refuse fees to witnesses in the employ of the person upon whose railroad or railway the accident occurred.

SECTION 12. The magistrate shall report in writing when, where and by what means the person met his death, his name, if known, and all material circumstances attending his death, and the name, if known, of any person whose unlawful act or negligence appears to have contributed thereto. He shall file his report in the superior court for the county where the inquest is held.

SECTION 13. If a person charged by the report with the commission of a crime is at large, the magistrate shall forthwith issue process for his arrest, returnable before any court or magistrate having jurisdiction. If he finds that murder, manslaughter or an assault has been committed, he may bind over, for appearance in said court, as in criminal cases, such witnesses as he considers necessary, or as the district attorney may designate.

SECTION 14. No embalming fluid, or any substitute therefor, shall be injected into the body of any person supposed to have met his death by violence, until a permit, signed by the medical examiner, has first been obtained.

SECTION 15. After an autopsy or a view or examination without an autopsy, the medical examiner shall deliver the body, upon application, to the husband or wife, to the next of kin, or to any friend of the deceased, who shall have priority in the order named. If the body is unidentified or unclaimed for forty-eight hours after the view thereof, the medical examiner shall deliver it to the overseers of the poor of the town where found, who shall bury it in accordance with section seventeen of chapter one hundred and seventeen.

SECTION 16. Medical examiners and associate examiners within their respective districts shall, on application and payment or tender of seven dollars, view the body and make personal inquiry concerning the death of any person whose body is intended for cremation, and shall authorize such cremation only when of opinion that no further examination or judicial inquiry concerning such death is necessary.

SECTION 17. The medical examiner may allow reasonable compensation, payable by the county in the manner provided in section nineteen, for services rendered in bringing to land a human body found in any of the harbors, rivers or waters of the commonwealth, but this provision shall not entitle any person to compensation for services rendered in searching for a dead body.

SECTION 18. The medical examiner shall take charge of any money or other personal property of the deceased found on or near the body, and deliver it to the person entitled to its custody or possession, or, if not claimed within

[63]

sixty days, to a public administrator. For fraudulent neglect or refusal so to deliver such property within three days after demand, a medical examiner or an associate medical examiner shall be punished by a fine of not more than five hundred dollars or by imprisonment for not more than two years.

SECTION 19. Every medical examiner shall return an account of the expenses of each view or autopsy, including his fees, to the commissioners of the county where held, or in Suffolk county to the auditor of Boston, and shall annex to his return the written authorization of the autopsy. The commissioners or auditor shall audit the same, and certify to the county treasurer what items therein are just and reasonable, and he shall pay the same to the person entitled thereto. No auditing officer shall certify any fee for an autopsy until he has received from the district attorney the certificate required by section seven.

SECTION 20. Every medical examiner and associate examiner shall annually, on or before March first, transmit to the state secretary certified copies of the records of all deaths by him investigated during the preceding year, and within sixty days after the expiration of his term shall make like returns for so much of the year as he held office. For a refusal or neglect so to do, he shall forfeit not less than ten nor more than fifty dollars.

SECTION 21. Each medical examiner and associate examiner, including those in Suffolk county, shall receive from the commonwealth twenty cents for each of the first twenty deaths recorded and returned by him in any year, as provided in the preceding section, and ten cents for each additional death so recorded and returned, as certified by the state secretary.

SECTION 22. The state secretary shall, at the expense of the commonwealth, prepare and furnish to the medical examiners blank record books and blank forms for returns, and shall cause the returns for each year to be bound together in one volume with indexes; and shall prepare therefrom such tables as will render them of utility, and shall make annual report thereof to the general court in connection with the report required by section twenty-one of chapter forty-six.

TEXT OF THE NEW YORK MEDICAL EXAMINER LAW

LAWS OF NEW YORK, 1915

Chap. 284

AN ACT to amend the Greater New York Charter, and repeal certain sections thereof and of chapter four hundred and ten of the Laws of eighteen hundred and eighty-two, in relation to the abolition of the office of Coroner and the establishment of the office of the chief medical examiner.

Became a law April 14, 1915, with the approval of the Governor. Passes, three-fifths being present.

Accepted by the City

The People of the State of New York, represented in Senate and Assembly, do enact as follows:

Section 1. The office of coroner in the City of New York shall be abolished on January first, nineteen hundred and eighteen, and after this section takes effect, a vacancy occurring in such an office in any borough shall not be filled unless by reason of the occurrence thereof, there shall be no coroner in office in such borough, in which case the vacancy in such borough last occurring shall be filled for a term to expire on January first, nineteen hundred and eighteen. If, by reason of the provisions of this section, the number of coroners in a borough be reduced, the remaining coroner or coroners in such borough shall have the powers and perform the duties conferred or imposed by law on the board of coroners in such borough.

2. Title four of chapter twenty-three, sections fifteen hundred and seventy and fifteen hundred and seventy-one of the Greater New York charter, as re-enacted by chapter four hundred and sixty-six of the laws of nineteen hundred and one is hereby repealed, and in its place is inserted a new title to be numbered four and to read as follows:

TITLE IV

Chief Medical Examiner

Section 1570.   Organization of office; officers and employees.
        1571.   Violent and suspicious deaths; procedure.
        1571a.   Autopsies; findings.
        1571b.   Report of deaths; removal of body.
        1571c.   Records.
        1571d.   Oaths and affidavits.

Organization of Office; Officers and Employees

1570. There is hereby established the office of Chief Medical Examiner of the City of New York. The head of the office shall be called the "chief medical examiner." He shall be appointed by the mayor from the classified service and be a doctor of medicine, and a skilled pathologist and microscopist.

The mayor may remove such officer upon stating in writing his reasons therefor, to be filed in the office of the municipal civil service commission and served upon such officer, and allowing him an opportunity of making a public explanation. The chief medical examiner may appoint and remove such deputies, assistant medical examiners, scientific experts, officers and employees as may be provided for pursuant to law. Such deputy medical examiners and assistant medical examiners, as may be appointed, shall possess qualifications similar to those required in the appointment of the chief medical examiner. The office shall be kept open every day in the year, including Sundays and holidays, with a clerk in constant attendance at all times during the day and night.

Violent and Suspicious Deaths; Procedure

1571. When, in the city of New York, any person shall die from criminal violence, or by a casualty, or by suicide, or suddenly when in apparent health, or when unattended by a physician, or in prison, or in any suspicious or unusual manner, the officer in charge of the station house in the police precinct in which such person died shall immediately notify the office of the chief medical examiner of the known facts, concerning the time, place, manner and circumstances of such death. Immediately upon receipt of such notification the chief medical examiner, or a deputy or assistant medical examiner, shall go to the dead body, and take charge of the same. Such examiner shall fully investigate the essential facts concerning the circumstances of the death, taking the names and address of as many witnesses thereto as it may be practical to obtain, and before leaving the premises, shall reduce all such facts to writing and file the same in his office. The police officer so detailed, shall, in the absence of the next of kin of deceased person, take possession of all property of value found on such person, make an exact inventory thereof on his report, and deliver such property to the police department, which shall surrender the same to the person entitled to its custody or possession. Such examiner shall take possession of any portable objects, which, in his opinion, may be useful in establishing the cause of death, and deliver them to the police department.

Nothing in this section contained shall effect the powers and duties of a public administrator as now provided by law.

Autopsies; Findings

1571a. If the cause of such death shall be established beyond a reasonable doubt, the medical examiner in charge shall so report to his office. If, however, in the opinion of such medical examiner, an autopsy is necessary, the same shall be performed by a medical examiner. A detailed description of the findings written during the progress of such autopsy and the conclusions drawn therefrom shall thereupon be filed in his office.

Report of Deaths; Removal of Body

1571b. It shall be the duty of any citizen who may become aware of the death of any such person to report such death forthwith to the office of the chief medical examiner and the police officer, who shall forthwith notify the officer in charge of the station house in the police precinct in which such person died. Any person who shall wilfully neglect or refuse to report such death or who, without written order from a medical examiner, shall wilfully touch, remove or disturb the body of any such person, or wilfully touch, remove or disturb the clothing, or any article upon or near such body, shall be guilty of a misdemeanor.

Records

1571c. It shall be the duty of the office of medical examiner to keep full and complete records. Such records shall be kept in the office, properly indexed, stating the name, if known, of every such person, the place where the body was found, the date of death. The record of each case shall be attached to the original report of the medical examiner and the detailed findings of the autopsy, if any. The office shall promptly deliver to the appropriate district attorney copies of all records relating to every death as to which there is, in the judgment of the medical examiner in charge, any indication of criminality. All other records shall be open to public inspection as provided in section fifteen hundred and forty-five. The appropriate district attorney and the police commissioner of the city may require, from such officer, such further records and such daily information as they may deem necessary.

Oaths and Affidavits

1571d. The chief medical examiner and all deputy or assistant medical examiners may administer oaths and take affidavits, proofs and examinations as to any matter within the jurisdiction of the office.

3. Section eleven hundred and seventy-nine of such charter is hereby amended to read as follows:

Bureaus

1179. There shall be two bureaus in the department of health. The chief officer of one bureau shall be called the sanitary superintendent, who at the time of his appointment shall have been, for at least ten years, a practicing physician, and for three years a resident of the City of New York, and he shall be the chief executive officer of said department. The chief officer of the second bureau shall be called the registrar of records, and in said bureau shall be recorded, without fees, every birth, marriage and death, which shall occur in the City of New York.

4. Section twelve hundred and three of such charter is hereby amended to read as follows:

Chief Medical Examiner's Returns

1203. The department of health, may, from time to time, make rules and regulations fixing the time of rendering, and defining the form of returns and reports to be made to said department by the office of the chief medical examiner of the city of New York, in all cases of death which shall be investigated by it, and the office of the chief medical examiner is hereby required to conform to such rules and regulations.

5. Section twelve hundred and thirty-eight of such charter is hereby amended to read as follows:

Deaths to be Reported

1238. It shall be the duty of the next of kin of any person deceased, and of each person being with such deceased person at his or her death, to file report in writing, with the department of health, within five days after such death, stating the age, color, nativity, last occupation and cause of death of such deceased person, and the borough and street the place of such person's death and last residence. Physicians who have attended deceased persons in their last illness shall, in the certificate of the deceased of such persons, specify, as near as the same ean be ascertained, the name and surname, age, occupation, term of residence in said city, place of nativity, condition of life whether single or married, widow or widower, colored, last place of residence and the cause of death of such deceased persons, and the medical examiners of the city shall, in their certificates, conform to the requirements of this section.

6. Such charter is hereby amended by inserting therein a new section to be numbered fifteen hundred and eighty-five, and to read as follows:

County Clerks to Exercise Certain Statutory Powers and Duties of Coroners

1585a. In the city of New York the powers imposed and the duties conferred upon coroners by the provisions of the title three of chapter two of the code of civil procedure shall be exercised and performed by the county clerk of the appropriate county, and said county clerk shall, in the exercise and performance thereof, be subject to the same liabilities and responsibilities as are prescribed in such title in the case of coroners.

7. Sections seventeen hundred and sixty-six to seventeen hundred and seventy-nine, both inclusive, of chapter four hundred and ten of the laws of eighteen hundred and eighty-two, entitled "An Act to consolidate into one act and to declare the special and local laws affecting public interests in the city of New York," and all acts amending such sections are hereby repealed.

8. The officers and the employees now exercising the powers and duties which by this act are abolished, or are conferred or imposed upon the office of chief medical examiner including coroner's physicians, shall be transferred to the office of chief medical examiner. Service in the office, board or body from which transferred shall count for all purposes as service in the office of the chief medical examiner.

9. All funds, property, records, books, papers and documents within the jurisdiction or control of any such coroner or such board of coroners, shall, on demand, be transferred and delivered to the office of the chief medical examiner. The board of estimate and apportionment shall transfer to the office of the chief medical examiner all unexpended appropriations made by the city to enable any coroner, or board of coroners, to exercise any of the powers and duties which by this act are abolished or are conferred or imposed upon such office of chief medical examiner.

10. Section one of this act shall take effect immediately. The remainder of the act shall take effect January first, nineteen hundred and eighteen.

LEGAL EDUCATION IN CLEVELAND

LEGAL EDUCATION IN CLEVELAND

LEGAL EDUCATION
IN CLEVELAND

BY

ALBERT M. KALES
MEMBER OF THE CHICAGO BAR

PART VI
OF THE CLEVELAND FOUNDATION SURVEY OF
CRIMINAL JUSTICE IN CLEVELAND

FOREWORD

THIS is the sixth of eight sections of the report of the Cleveland Foundation Survey of Criminal Justice in Cleveland. The survey was directed and the reports edited by Roscoe Pound and Felix Frankfurter. Sections which have been published are:

The Criminal Courts, by Reginald Heber Smith and Herbert B. Ehrmann
Prosecution, by Alfred Bettman
Police Administration, by Raymond B. Fosdick
Correctional and Penal Treatment, by Burdette G. Lewis
Medical Science and Criminal Justice, by Dr. Herman M. Adler

Other sections to be published are:

Newspapers and Criminal Justice, by M. K. Wisehart
Criminal Justice in the American City, a Summary, by Roscoe Pound

The sections are being published first in separate form, each bound in paper. About November 10 the report will be available in a single volume, cloth bound. Orders for separate sections or the bound volume may be left with book-stores or with the Cleveland Foundation, 1202 Swetland Building.

In the preparation of this report, Mr. Kales was assisted by William W. Dawson of the Cleveland bar; E. L. Findley, principal of South High School, and Miss Helen Chew of the Cleveland Foundation staff.

TABLE OF CONTENTS

LEGAL EDUCATION IN CLEVELAND

STATE REQUIREMENTS AND LOCAL FACILITIES

BEFORE taking the bar examinations in Ohio one who is not admitted to practice in another State must have studied law for three years and must have had a general education equivalent to a four-year high school course. He need not complete his high school course, or its equivalent, before commencing his legal studies. The applicant who studies in Cleveland may do so under the instruction of any attorney in Cleveland, or in any one of three law schools, viz., the Law School of Western Reserve University, the Cleveland Law School, and the John Marshall Law School.

During the past four years 58 persons who gave Cleveland as their address have been admitted to take the bar examinations upon the certificate of an attorney that the applicant had completed some period of study under his direction. Of these, the greater number are now practising in Cleveland. In some instances the period of study under the attorney was the six-month period required of those who have taken the State bar examinations and failed. In others the period of study was one year, supplementary to a law school course of two years. Probably in few instances was the entire three-year period of study under the direction of the attorney certifying. In a few well-authenticated instances men who have studied for three years at a law school, but have been refused a certificate by the law school, have secured a certificate from an attorney in Cleveland or in some other part of the State and have, on the basis thereof, been permitted to take the bar examinations. In one instance a student who had been refused a certificate by a law school was certified by an attorney outside of Cleveland. The attorney stated that the student had studied law under his direction for three years, when, as a matter of fact, the student had been for three years in attendance at a law school in Cleveland, several hours' ride by rail from the city where the certifying attorney resided and conducted his practice.

In the past four years 66 attorneys of Cleveland have certified that students under their direction have satisfactorily completed some period of legal studies as the basis for taking the bar examinations. Of these, three gave such certificates in 1917, 17 in 1918, 25 in 1919 (one certifying to two applicants and one to four), and 22 in 1920 (two certifying each to two applicants and one certifying who had also certified in 1918).

Inquiry among these attorneys as to the course of study pursued under their direction resulted in the following information: In one instance an attempt was made to give a review course of six months for those who failed in the bar examinations. In one instance the attorney conducted an informal school for business men and certified two students who had done sufficient work to warrant, in his judgment, the certification. In one instance the student had taken a correspondence school course and also done bona fide work under the direction of the attorney certifying for three years. But it seems to be the view of many that an attorney is justified in certifying if he has personal knowledge that the student has actually pursued legal studies, and if the attorney has quizzed him at least once in regard to the subjects studied. It is the exception that a definite course is laid out by the attorney and the student pursues it under his immediate personal direction and is quizzed from week to week, or even from month to month.

At least one attempt has been made by a correspondence school to secure for its students the certificate of an attorney that its students have (on the basis of the correspondence school course alone) satisfactorily completed a three-year course of legal study. In this instance the Supreme Court intimated that it would be improper for the attorney to give the certification, and he refused to do so.

The Law School of Western Reserve University has been established since 1892. It now has 609 graduates, of which approximately 280 are practising law in Cleveland. It is at present contributing from 35 to 50 graduates a year, 75 per cent. of whom, it is estimated, remain in Cleveland for the practice of the law.

The Cleveland Law School has been established since 1897, and during that time has been under the direction of Judge Willis Vickery. It has approximately 1,000 graduates, of which about one-third are estimated by Judge Vickery to be in practice, and of these by far the larger portion are engaged in practice in Cleveland. This school for the past two or three years has been graduating yearly between 70 and 80 students, by far the larger portion of whom remain in Cleveland for the practice of the law.

The John Marshall Law School has been established since 1916 and has graduated 35 students, of whom about two-thirds are estimated to be in practice, and of these, all but two are in practice in Cleveland.

In 1921 it graduated 21 students, by far the larger portion of whom remained in Cleveland to practise.

Of the members of the bar of Cleveland who have acted as prosecutors in the past twenty years in Cleveland, 27 are graduates of the Cleveland Law School, 11 of the Law School of Western Reserve University, none of the John Marshall Law School, and 11 of other law schools, including one from Harvard, five from Michigan, one from Cornell, and two from Ohio State.

In the current lawyers' directory of Cleveland about 1,400 persons are listed. Of these, it may be inferred, 280 are graduates of the Western Reserve Law School, about 300 of the Cleveland Law School, and about 20 of the John Marshall Law School.

THE LAW SCHOOL OF WESTERN RESERVE UNIVERSITY

Students entering this school must have completed a four-year college course in an approved college and have obtained a degree; or they must have satisfactorily completed three years of college work in Adelbert College (the Liberal Arts Department of Western Reserve University), thereby becoming candidates for a degree at Adelbert College after the first year in the Law School.

Of the 154 students now in this school, all but three answer these requirements. The school has admitted three persons as special students. The vote of the faculty is based, in all but one of these cases, upon the fact that the special student has probably had the equivalent of a college course, but in an institution about whose standards exact information is not readily obtainable. The special students are not candidates for a degree.

Four students now in the school were foreign born—two in Austria-Hungary, one in Finland, and one in Russia. Three-fourths of the students are engaged in supporting themselves partially by work outside of the school, and 10 per cent. are supporting themselves wholly in this way. The work engaged in by these students occurs for the most part in the heart of the city, about thirty minutes' ride on the street-cars from the university.

The hours devoted to recitations are from 8 A. M. to 12 noon. These hours accommodate the men who earn a livelihood, wholly or in part, while at the same time taking their law course.

FACULTY AND CURRICULUM

Resident teachers, viz., those who give all their time to teaching at the school, receive salaries ranging from $4,500 to $6,000 a year. Members of the bar in Cleveland who do a slight amount of teaching receive compensation at the rate of five dollars an hour, but this is in practically all cases turned back to the school, so that the services of these men are donated.

Following is a list of the resident teachers with some facts as to the teachers and the courses they conduct:

Archibald Hall Throckmorton: A.B., Roanoke College, 1896; A.M., Princeton University, 1897; LL.B., Washington and Lee University, 1900. Resident professor. Not in active practice. Teaches Constitutional Law, Insurance, Pleading, and Torts. Uses Hall's *Cases in Constitutional Law;* lectures and Hinton's *Cases in Pleading;* Wambaugh's *Cases in Insurance;* lectures and Hepburn's *Cases in Torts.* Inspection of examination papers in the above courses shows 10 problem questions in each. These questions appear to be in accordance with the standard of questions used by the best law schools.

Walter Thomas Dunmore: A.B., Oberlin College, 1900; A.M., Oberlin College, 1905; LL.B., Western Reserve University, 1904. Resident professor. Not in active practice. Teaches Property, Evidence, and Conflict of Laws. Uses Bigelow's *Cases,* Volumes I and II, and Gray's *Cases in Property,* Volumes III and IV; Thayer's *Cases in Evidence* and Beale's *Cases in Conflict of Laws.* Inspection of examination papers in the above courses shows 10 problem questions in each. These questions appear to be in accordance with the standard of questions used by the best law schools.

Alvin Collins Brightman: A.B., Oberlin College, 1900; LL.B., Western Reserve University, 1909. Resident professor. Not in active practice. Teaches Contracts, Quasi-Contracts, Sales, Partnership, and Damages. Uses Williston's *Cases in Contracts;* Woodruff's *Cases in Quasi-Contracts;* Williston's *Cases in Sales;* Mechem's *Cases in Partnership,* and Mechem and Gilbert's *Cases in Damages.* Inspection of examination papers in the above courses shows 10 problem questions in each. These questions appear to be in accordance with the standard of questions used by the best law schools.

Clarence Millard Finfrock: A.B., Ohio Wesleyan University, 1902; A.M., 1907; LL.B., Western Reserve University, 1907. Resident professor. Not in active practice. Teaches Equity Jurisdiction, Trusts, Negotiable Instruments, and Domestic Relations. Uses Woodruff's *Cases in Domestic Relations;* Smith and Moore's *Cases in Bills and Notes;* Ames' *Cases in Equity Jurisdiction;* Scott's *Cases in Trusts.* An inspection of examination papers in the above courses shows 10 problem questions in each. These questions appear to be in accordance with the standard of questions used by the best law schools.

Alexander Hadden: A.B., Oberlin College, 1873. Practised law until he became Probate Judge in 1905. Teaches Crimes and Criminal Procedure. Uses lectures and Rood's *Cases.* Examination paper for 1920 shows 5 problem questions and 5 questions calling for definitions and conventional distinctions. Examination paper of February, 1921, shows 4 problem questions and the balance calling for definitions and distinctions.

Frank MacMillan Cobb: A.B., Yale University, 1897; LL.B., Western Reserve University, 1899. In active practice. Teaches Public Service Corporations two hours each week for half the year. Uses Wyman's *Cases*. Specimen examination paper shows 10 problem questions. These questions appear to be in accordance with the standard of questions used in the best law schools.

Richard Inglis: A.B., Harvard University, 1903; LL.B., 1906. Teaches Private Corporations. In active practice. Uses Warren's *Cases*. Specimen examination paper shows 10 problem questions. These questions appear to be in accordance with the standard of questions used by the best law schools.

Clinton DeWitt: A.B., Adelbert College, 1910; LL.B., Western Reserve University, 1912. In active practice. Teaches Suretyship and Mortgages. Uses DeWitt's *Cases in Suretyship;* Durfee's *Cases in Mortgages.* Specimen examination paper shows 10 problem questions. These questions appear to be in accordance with the standard of questions used in the best law schools.

Austin V. Cannon: B.S., Buchtel College, 1892. In practice since 1894. Teaches Bankruptcy. Lectures and selected decisions used. No examination paper submitted.

William Cullen Keough: A.B., Harvard University, 1904; A.M., 1905; LL.B., Western Reserve University, 1909. In practice since 1909. Teaches Municipal Corporations. Uses Beale's *Cases*. Specimen examination paper shows 10 problem questions. These questions appear to be in accordance with the standard of questions used in the best law schools.

James Cooper Logue: A.B., Adelbert College, 1907; LL.B., Western Reserve University, 1909. In practice since 1909. Teaches Agency. Uses Wambaugh's *Cases*. Specimen examination paper shows 10 problem questions. These questions appear to be in accordance with the standard of questions used in the best law schools.

John Frederic Oberlin: Gives special lectures on Patents, Trade-mark, and Copyright Law.

Physical characteristics of the school: The school occupies an entire building adjoining the campus of Western Reserve University, with adequate class-rooms, teachers' offices, library, reading-room, and library stacks. The library consists of upward of 15,000 volumes. They include the English and American reports, statutes, and leading text-books. The library reading-room seats 90. It is open from 8 A. M. to 9.30 P. M., and is used by the students as a place of study.

The school has a special endowment, yielding at the present time about $7,000 per annum. The policy is to pay out of tuition fees the difference between its endowment income and its overhead expenses (not including the interest on the investment in the land and buildings which it occupies). In fact, it is now operating with an annual deficit of about $4,000, which is made up by the trustees of Western Reserve University. The school hopes to eliminate this by an increased special endowment.

THE CLEVELAND LAW SCHOOL

Without attempting to analyze the published entrance requirements, the fact is that anyone, regardless of his preliminary education, may become a student of law at the school. From the students' registration cards the following facts appear as to the preliminary education upon entering the school of the 419 students now enrolled:

	Number
College graduates	25
Those having some college training, from one semester to three years	74
Those having apparently a full four-year high school course	226
Those who have not completed a full four-year high school course, but have had some high school work	47
Those who have had no high school work at all before entering the law school	24
Those about whom no information could be obtained from the registration cards	23

Whenever the registration card contained the general statement that the student had had a preliminary education designated as "high school," it was assumed that he had completed the high school course. The test of a number of such answers by inquiry of the student makes it probable that some who wrote on their cards "high school" had not completed the high school course. Judge Vickery, the dean of the school, made an estimate of those who had not completed a high school course as somewhat more than 94.

Of the 25 college graduates, one was foreign born, having been born in Hungary. Of the 74 who had some college training, 11 were foreign born—four in Russia, three in Austria-Hungary, one in Germany, one in Croatia, one in Canada, one in Transylvania. Of the 226 who appear to have completed a high school course, 42 were foreign born—15 in Russia, four in Austria-Hungary, three in Hungary, three in Poland, four in Czecho-Slovakia, three in Italy, one in Croatia, one in Jugo-Slavia, two in Scotland, one in Ireland, one in England, one in Canada, one in New South Wales, one in Jamaica, one in Barbados (British West Indies). Of the 47 who had done some high school work, nine were foreign born—three in Russia, two in Italy, two in Austria-Hungary, one in Rumania, one in Hungary. Of the 24 who had received no high school education or its equivalent, eight were foreign born—two in Russia, one in Poland, one in Austria, one in Sicily, one in England, one in Ireland, one in Norway. Of the 23 as to whose preliminary education no information appears on the registration cards, only three gave information as to their place of birth—one native born, one born in Russia, and one in Ireland.

All the students with a few exceptions, not exceeding five, were, upon entering the school, earning their livelihood in regular occupations, such as clerk, salesman, insurance, real estate, accountant, stenographer, and private secretary.

Classes are held from 5 to 7 and 7 to 9 P. M., Mondays, Wednesdays, and Fridays, each of two sections having each two hours of class-room work.

FACULTY AND CURRICULUM

All the teachers are lawyers practising in Cleveland, who perform their duties as teachers in addition to their professional efforts as lawyers. They receive compensation in cash at a rate which causes practising attorneys to seek places on the teaching staff.

Following is a list of the teachers now actually teaching at the school, with some facts concerning the teachers and the courses they give:

Willis Vickery: Boston University Law School, 1884. In active practice twenty-one years; on the Common Pleas Bench ten years, and two and one-half years on the Circuit Court of Appeals. Gives Contracts, seventy hours, using Clark's text-book; Constitutional Law, twenty-six hours, using Black's text-book; Criminal Law, forty hours, using Clark and Marshall; Partnership, thirty-six hours, using Gilmore; Legal Ethics, ten hours, using lectures. From 10 to 12 per cent. of the entire class fail to receive degrees. Each year three or four men are denied a certificate of satisfactory completion of studies for the bar examiners. This year about five will fail to get such a certificate. Examination paper in Contracts shows about 10 problem questions out of 20, the rest calling for definitions and distinctions. Examination paper in Constitutional Law shows 10 questions, of which only one appears to be a problem question, the rest calling for discussion of general rules or the doctrine of particular cases. Examination paper in Partnership shows 10 questions, of which three are problem questions, the rest calling for definitions or precise information. Examination paper in Criminal Law shows 12 questions, of which four are problem questions.

[7]

Melville W. Vickery: Graduate of Cleveland Law School. Admitted to the bar in 1914. In active practice. Teaches Domestic Relations, twenty hours, using Schouler's text-book. Covers the course by lectures on the text. About three or four out of a class of 60 failed. Examination paper shows 10 questions, six of which are problem questions and the other four call for definitions.

James Lind: Western Reserve Law School, 1912. In active practice as much as possible since 1912. Teaches Criminal Law, thirty hours, using Clark and Marshall's text-book. Examination paper shows 10 questions, of which five are problem questions and five call for definitions.

William Fish Marsteller: Graduate of University of Michigan Law School. In active practice. Employed by a firm as trial lawyer. Admitted to the bar, 1918. Teaches Contracts, seventy hours, using Clark's text-book; Partnership, thirty-five hours, using Gilmore's text-book; Contracts, one semester, using Huffcutt and Woodruff's *Cases;* Negotiable Instruments, one semester, using Bunker. No examination paper submitted.

Alfred Clum: Graduate of George Washington University Law School. General practice since 1890. Gives Equity, five weeks, using Merwin's text-book; Evidence, five weeks, using McKelvey. Examination paper shows five questions in Evidence, all of which call for statement of rules and none of which are problem questions. Another examination paper in Evidence shows 10 questions, none of which are problem questions, but all call for statement of rules. Examination paper in Equity shows six questions, three of which appear to be problem questions and the rest call for definitions or information as to particular rules. Another examination paper in Equity shows 10 questions, none of which are problem questions.

L. Q. Rawson: Graduate of Cincinnati Law School. Entire time given to practice. Admitted to bar twenty-nine years. Gives Negotiable Instruments, twenty-six hours, using Bigelow on *Bills and Notes;* Suretyship, twenty-six hours, using Stearns on *Suretyship.* Examination paper in Negotiable Instruments shows 10 questions, of which five are problem questions and the rest call for statement of rules or definitions. Examination paper in Suretyship shows 10 questions, of which eight are problem questions and the rest call for definitions.

Howard D. Burnett: Graduate of Y. M. C. A. Law School of Cincinnati. In general practice since 1906. Gives Wills, forty-two hours, using Gardner; Agency, thirty-six hours, using Mechem; Sales and Personal Property, fifty-two hours, using Benjamin on *Sales.* Examination paper in Wills shows 10 questions, of which three appear to be problem questions and the rest call for definitions or statement of rules. Another examination paper in Wills shows five questions, of which one appears to be a problem. Examination paper in Agency shows five questions, of which four appear to be problems and one calls for definitions. Examination paper on Sales shows five questions, of which two appear to be problem questions. Another examination paper in Agency shows

[8]

10 questions, of which six appear to be problem questions. Another examination paper in Sales and Personal Property shows 10 questions, of which eight appear to be problem questions and the others call for definitions.

Harry Lewis Beibel: Graduate of Western Reserve Law School. In general practice. Admitted to the bar in 1914. Gives Wills, forty hours, using Gardner; Torts, thirty-eight hours, using Cooley. Examination paper in Wills shows 10 questions, of which five appear to be problems and the rest call for definitions or statement of particular rules. Another examination paper in Wills shows five questions, of which two are problem questions. Examination paper in Torts shows five questions, of which three appear to be problems. Another examination paper in Torts shows 10 questions, of which four appear to be problems.

Samuel H. Silbert: Graduate of Baldwin-Wallace University and Cleveland Law School. In active practice for eight years and six years on the bench. Teaches Bailments, twenty-six hours, using Dobie's text-book; Domestic Relations, twenty hours, using Schouler. Examination paper in Domestic Relations shows 10 questions and contains a mixture of slight problem questions and a test as to definitions and statement of particular rules. Examination paper in Bailments shows 10 questions, each with from two to five subdivisions, calling for a mixture of slight problems and definitions and statement of particular rules.

Arthur E. Rowley: Graduate of University of Michigan and the Chicago College of Law. Admitted to the bar in 1892. In practice since that time. Gives a short course of lectures on Statutory Law.

Physical characteristics of the school: Its rooms are situated on the top floor of a modern office building, within a block of the public square, and have the appearance of being well kept up. It has three class-rooms and adequate seating capacity, a general office room, and Judge Vickery's private office. Its library is kept in the office room and consists of the Ohio reports, digests, and statutes, a few text-books and encyclopedias of law. Judge Vickery said he had at one time paid a sum to secure the use, by his students, of the County Law Library which is used by the lawyers and judges of Cleveland, but that since the students did not avail themselves of the privilege he had ceased to provide it.

The school is the private enterprise of Judge Vickery. It is run for private profit, but it is fair to state that while he has sought to make the school a profitable investment, he has also sought to provide as good a legal education for his students as the conditions under which they were taught permitted. He has been insistent upon requiring full time of his teachers.

[9]

THE JOHN MARSHALL LAW SCHOOL

Again, without attempting to analyze the published statement of entrance requirements, the fact is that anyone, regardless of his preliminary education, may become a student of law at this school. The following facts concerning the preliminary education of the students in this school appear from their answers to a questionnaire filled out by the students themselves:

	Number
College graduates	17
Those having some college training, from one semester to three years	30
Those who have completed a four-year high school course	58
Those who have had some high school work only	36
Those who have had no high school training	6
Those from whom no information was obtained	5

Of the 17 college graduates, one was foreign born, having been born in Germany. In two instances where the student was native born both parents were foreign born—in one instance they were English and in the other German. Of the 30 who had had some college work, five were foreign born: three in Russia, one in Jugo-Slavia, one in Germany. In five instances where the student was native born both parents were foreign born—three Irish, one Russian, one Holland-Swiss. Of the 58 who had completed the high school course, 17 were foreign born: nine in Russia, two in Poland, two in Hungary, two in Czecho-Slovakia, one in Austria, one in England. In 10 instances where the student was native born both parents were foreign born—five Russian, two German, one Hungarian, one Czecho-Slovakian, one Syrian. Of the 36 who had had some high school training, six were foreign born—three in Russia, one in Austria, one in Ireland, one in Netherlands. In 12 instances where the student was native born both parents were foreign born—four Russian, two German, one Polish, one Austrian, one Italian, one English, one Irish. Of the six who had received no high school education at all, one was foreign born, having been born in Italy. In two instances where the student was native born both parents were foreign born—one German and one Irish.

All the students in the school, with the exception of not to exceed five, were earning their livelihood in regular occupations while pursuing their studies.

Classes are held from 4 to 6 and 7 to 9 P. M. on Mondays, Wednesdays, and Fridays, which provides two hours of class-room work for each of two sections.

All the teachers in the school except two are lawyers practising at the bar in Cleveland. Their teaching is in addition to their regular duties as practitioners. Their rate of compensation ranges from $5 to $10 per each double section hour of teaching.

Following is a list of the teachers actually teaching at the school, together with some facts about the teachers and the courses which they give:

Robert Parsons Abbey: Graduate of Cleveland Law School. In active practice eleven years. Teaches Bills and Notes two hours five days a week, running for three months. Uses text-book by Tilden with Brannan as auxiliary. Fails on an average of three men out of 20. No specimen examination paper given.

Cary R. Alburn: A.B., Adelbert College. Attended Western Reserve University Law School and Oxford University, England; B.C.L. (Oxford). In active practice twelve and one-half years. Teaches Private Corporations. Uses Clark's text-book and Wormser's *Cases*. Average of 7 per cent. of those taking the course fail. None, however, have failed to receive a degree in two years. One was denied a certificate of satisfactory completion of studies. Specimen examination paper submitted shows 10 questions, none of which were problems; many called for definitions and a few for general answers as to extent of liability.

John C. Barkley: Western Reserve University Law School, 1906. In active practice fourteen years. Teaches Bills and Notes twenty-six hours. Course is based upon Ohio Negotiable Instruments Code and Ohio decisions. An average of eight out of 41 students fail to pass the examination. A specimen examination paper shows 12 questions, one-half of which call for definitions and the other one-half are to a considerable extent problem questions.

Kenneth D. Carter: Attended the University of Wisconsin. Graduate of Ohio State University Law School. In active practice full time. Admitted to the bar four years. Teaches Partnership eighteen hours, using Mechem's *Elements*, second edition, which he completes and thereafter discusses the Ohio cases. Also teaches Constitutional Law twenty hours, using text-book by Black, third edition. Covers about five-sevenths of the text-book, with the Ohio and Federal Constitutions. Has taught the course only one year and has no record of the number of men failed. Specimen examination paper in Partnership shows a series of 10 substantial and rather ambitious problem questions.

Norton McGiffin: Graduate of University of Michigan Law School. In general practice since December, 1912. Has given Suretyship, September 15 to December 1, three hours a week, using Stearns' text-book, second edition, of which he covers all. Also taught Equity three hours a week, September 15 to December 15, using Pomeroy, students' edition, of which he omits Rights and

Interests of Married Women, Probate Law and Wills, and Mortgages. An average of from 5 to 15 per cent. of his men fail to pass the examination. Specimen examination paper shows in one case 10 ambitious problem questions and in two instances in another, a series of questions calling for definitions with but two problem questions.

Ralph T. Hisey: Western Reserve Law School, 1915. Secretary of the Pyramid Savings Co. Not in active practice. Teaches Personal Property thirty hours, using Childs' *Personal Property,* of which he covers all. First year as an instructor and presents no specimen examination paper and makes no report as to number of students failed.

C. T. Kirkbride: Graduate of Western Reserve Law School. In practice for fifteen years. Teaches Domestic Relations about twenty hours, using Long, *Domestic Relations.* Covers entire volume. Fails from 5 to 10 per cent. of men taking examination. Specimen examination paper attached shows six questions calling for definitions and four problem questions.

Dean Lawrence: Graduate of the John Marshall Law School. In practice two years, mostly office work. Teaches Torts forty hours, using text-book by Chapin, all of which is covered. Also teaches Suretyship thirty hours, using Stearns, all of which is covered. An average of from 20 to 30 per cent. of his pupils fail to pass the examination, but none fail to receive a degree and none are denied a certificate of satisfactory completion of studies for bar examination. Specimen examination paper attached shows a series of 20 questions, practically all of which are problems.

Cyrus Locher: Graduate of Western Reserve Law School. In active practice since 1907. Teaches Mortgages twelve hours. Uses no text-book. An average of 5 per cent. of his men fail to pass examination. Gives no specimen examination paper.

Dean B. Meck: Graduate of John Marshall Law School. Assistant to the Director of Law of the National Lamp Works of the General Electric Company. Admitted to the bar five years. Teaches Agency thirty hours, using Huffcutt on Agency, covering the entire volume. An average of about 15 per cent. of the men in his course fail to pass, and about 5 per cent. of these fail to receive a degree. About 10 per cent. fail to receive a certificate of satisfactory completion of studies for the bar examination. Specimen examination paper shows about 20 questions, of which about eight are problem questions and about 12 call for definitions or discussion of general principles.

David C. Meck: Dean of the John Marshall Law School. Graduate of the Cleveland Law School. Not in practice. Admitted to the bar eight years. Teaches Contracts one-half year, using Clark's text-book, of which he covers all, together with Throckmorton's case book and Ohio State reports. Also teaches Bailments and Carriers one-third of year, using Dobie's text-book, of which he covers all, together with 60 cases from the Ohio State and Federal reports. Fails to pass on an average of 15 per cent. of his students. Of those taught by him who are candidates for a degree, 5 per cent. fail to receive a degree and the same number are refused a certificate of satistfacory completion of studies for the bar examination. A specimen examination paper shows 24 questions, all of them calling for definitions or the drawing of distinctions.

Edwin E. Miller: Graduate of Western Reserve Law School. In active general practice to the fullest extent. Admitted to the bar twelve years. Gives the course on Evidence thirty-five hours, using Hughes on *Evidence*, covering every page, including the illustrations in the back of the book. Also teaches Wills forty-three hours, covering all the text of Gardner on *Wills*. In addition students draw at least four wills and other papers for the Probate Court and go over a series of 40 problems formulated by the instructor. Also teaches Practical Conveyancing thirteen hours. This course is taught with a series of 11 problems. A series of these problems submitted show them to cover many of the practical details relating to Abstracts in Cleveland. Examination of a specimen paper in Evidence shows 20 to 30 questions calling for definitions or statement of particular rules of evidence for the most part; three or four were in the form of problems. A specimen examination paper in Wills shows a series of 10 questions, seven of which are problem questions. In 1920 no one failed to pass the examination in Wills and only one failed in Evidence. In 1921 there were two who failed in Evidence.

Sterling Parks: A.B., University of Michigan, 1888; LL.B., George Washington, 1894. In active practice twenty-seven years. Gives course on Real Estate, three lectures a week, four and one-half months, using Burdick's text-book. Covers practically the entire work. One specimen examination paper shows about 20 questions, practically all definitions. Another paper shows 10 questions, practically all of which are problems. Out of a class of 40 students, five failed to pass the examination given.

James B. Ruhl: Graduate of Ohio Northern Law School. Degrees B.S. M.S., LL.B., LL.M. Active practice in Cleveland since 1891. Teaches Pleading forty hours, using Phillips' text-book and covering all of the text; also Stephen's *Common Law Pleading* in part and Ohio decisions and statutes. Not yet had a student who did not pass. Specimen examination paper shows eight questions calling for definitions and statement of rules and one question calling for the drafting of papers.

K. T. Siddall: Graduate of Harvard Law School. In active practice eight years. Teaches course on Real Property three hours a week for six months. Uses text-book by Burdick and covers subject as treated by Burdick. None have failed to pass his examinations. Specimen examination paper shows five problem questions out of nine.

J. W. Woods: Graduate of University of Michigan Law School. Very active practice. Admitted to the bar in 1909. Teaches Criminal Law thirty hours, using Clark's text-book, and covers entire text and procedure. Specimen examination paper shows 10 problems.

The following have been instructors at the John Marshall Law School, but are not now teaching:

Howard A. Couse: Graduate of the Yale Law School. In practice since 1894.

John H. Schultz: Graduate of Western Reserve Law School. Admitted to the bar in 1918.

E. J. Hopple: Attended Western Reserve Law School but did not graduate. In active practice sixteen years.

Edward H. Tracy: Graduate of Yale Law School. In practice since 1895. Taught Domestic Relations.

Physical surroundings of the school: Its rooms are situated on the third floor of the old court-house building facing the public square. They consist of three lecture rooms, a library and study room, office of the dean, and law fraternity room. Its library consists of the Ohio reports, United States reports, *Cyc.*, *Corpus Juris*, *Ohio Digest*, *Federal Digest*, Ohio Statutes, and 50 reference text-books. No access to any other library is provided.

The school is a corporation for pecuniary profit. David C. Meck holds the largest amount of stock held by any one individual. Other stockholders are, with a few exceptions, teachers in the school. The school has only graduated one class—that of the year 1920.

HOURS OF TEACHING IN LAW SCHOOLS IN CLEVELAND

Table 1 is a comparative study of the number of hours of teaching given to the different subjects at Western Reserve University Law School, Cleveland Law School, and John Marshall Law School, and other well-known law schools throughout the country.

The only subjects offered in the Cleveland Law School and the John Marshall Law School are those prescribed by the bar examiners for admission to the bar. Courses on Bankruptcy, Damages, Insurance, Quasi-Contracts, Conflict of Laws, Municipal Corporations, Mortgages, and Trusts offered at other law schools are not offered at the Cleveland Law School or the John Marshall Law School. These subjects are not in the list of subjects required to be studied to qualify the applicant for taking the Ohio State bar examinations.

TABLE 1.—COMPARATIVE STUDY OF HOURS OF TEACHING IN LAW SCHOOLS

Subject	Cleveland Law	John Marshall	Western Reserve University	Cincinnati	Ohio State	Northwestern	Michigan	Yale	Chicago	Illinois	Indiana	Minneapolis	Missouri	Wisconsin	Pennsylvania
Agency	36	42	72	72	36	54	72	36	72	54	72	36	36	36	72
Contracts	70	54	108	108	108	108	108	84	108	108	108	108	96	108	108
Criminal Law and Procedure	26	30	90	72	72	108	90	36	60	54	54	48	36	72	108
Domestic Relations	12	18	36	36	36	54	36	24	48	54	..	36	36	36	..
Common Law and Code Pleading	40	36	108	72	90	90	108	60	84	54	72	36	72	108	108
Property, Personal	..	24	36	54*	36	54	54	36	24	54	36	132	36	36	36
Property, Real	42†	54	90	90*	144	102	198	108	156	162	108	198	108	108	144
Torts	40	42	90	72	108	72	90	108	90	90	108	108	72	108	108
Bailments and Public Service	26	30	36	72	72	72	72	108	36	54	..	36	60	36	72
Equity	30	30	108	72	108	108	108	120	120	128	108	72	48	90	108
Evidence	33	42	72	72	72	72	72	72	54	72	72	72	60	72	72
Negotiable Instruments	26	36	72	72	54	54	54	36	72	54	72	48	36	54	72
Sales	52	12	54	72	36	36	36	36	60	54	36	48	36	54	72
Wills	42	42	36	36	36	36	54	36	48	54	36	48	36	54	36
Constitutional Law	26	36	72	72	90	72	108	72	48	90	54	72	60	108	108
Private Corporations	40	36	72	72	72	72	72	72	72	54	72	72	48	126‡	90†
Partnership	30	18	36	36	36	36	54	24	60	36	..	36	..	36	72
Suretyship	26	24	36	36	36	72	36	72	36	54	36	48	36	27	36
Bankruptcy	..	..	18	36	18	18	36	24	36	36	36	24	24	36	12
Damages	..	..	36	..	36	36	36	24	48	36	36	36	36	36	..
Insurance	..	..	36	..	36	36	36	24	36	36	36	36	36	54	..
Quasi-Contracts	..	..	54	36	36	54	36	24	48	36	36	48	36	54	72
Conflict of Laws	..	..	72	36	36	72	54	72	72	54	..	72	36	54	72
Municipal Corporations	..	..	36	36	36	18	36	36	48	36	72	36	24	36	..
Mortgages	..	..	36	27	36	54	36	36	36	54	36	24	36	27	36
Trusts	..	..	54	54	36	72	72	72	72	54	72	48	36	72	54

* Cincinnati combines Property and Damages in first year.
† All Property that is given.
‡ Includes Partnership.

[15]

In 1915–16 the Cleveland Law School was the only night law school in Cleveland. It had been in operation about twenty years and had a large body of alumni in Cleveland. Judge Vickery felt that it was strong enough to raise the standard of night-law-school education. He therefore proposed to put into effect a four-year course and to require the completion of this course before giving a certificate enabling students to take the State bar examinations. But a new night law school was started on the basis of providing the student with a certificate after three years of study. A considerable number of students were deflected to the new law school, and the plan for a four-year course was given up.

NIGHT HIGH SCHOOLS

The bar examiners require as a condition of taking examinations that the applicant shall have had four years of high school work in a Class 1 high school, or its equivalent, in addition to the required study of law. It is permissible, however, that the high school and the law course be taken at the same time. In the Cleveland Law School and the John Marshall Law School together at least 141 students have not completed a high school course. Of these, 30, at least, have had no part of a high school course.

Those who have not completed a high school course, or its equivalent, may do so by attending one of two night high schools, the Baldwin-Wallace (Night) Preparatory School, affiliated with the Baldwin-Wallace College, and the John Marshall Night High School, affiliated with Ohio Northern University. These night high schools are operated in convenient proximity to the night law schools. Their classes are held on Tuesday and Thursday evenings.

Of the 47 students at the John Marshall Law School who have not had any high school work or who have not completed a high school course, 21 were taking a night high school course. Of these, 15 were taking the night high school course at the John Marshall Night High School. Of the 94 students of the Cleveland Law School who had not completed a high school course or had any high school training, 20 were taking a night high school course at the Baldwin-Wallace Preparatory Night High School. How many other students in the Cleveland Law School were taking night high school work at other night high schools could not be ascertained.

A report upon the night high schools was made under our direction by E. L. Findley, a principal in a Cleveland public high school. From his report it appears that these schools have a competent corps of teachers and give a four-year high school course which meets the requirements of the course for Class 1 high schools in Ohio. By adding a summer high school term these schools enable a student to do one and one-half years of high school work in each twelve months. It appears also that the principals of the night high schools, except in rare and special cases, do not permit men who have had less than two years of high school to take the night high school course at the same time they are taking the night law school course.

The John Marshall Night High School has an enrollment of 90, of whom only 15 are taking a night law course. The Baldwin-Wallace has an enrollment of 122, of whom only 20 are taking a night law course. Both the night high schools accommodate a considerable majority of students who are not taking any law course.

The principal in each school has full discretion in determining what credits he will allow for work done at other schools or in bookkeeping and typewriting, and may admit students to any year of the night high school work on such showing. When students so admitted have graduated from the night high school they receive a certificate that they have completed the equivalent of a four-year high school course. This certificate enables the student, in the case of the Baldwin-Wallace Night Preparatory School, to matriculate at the Baldwin-Wallace College, and in the case of the John Marshall Night High School, to matriculate at Ohio Northern University, and these matriculations enable the student to fulfil the requirements of the bar examiners as to their general education. The principals of the schools in question reported to Mr. Findley that, in this matter of allowing credits to students who had studied in other schools or done work outside of school, they followed the usual practice which obtains in the Ohio public high schools of the first class, and this statement has been accepted as correct without investigation.

BAR EXAMINATION CRAMMERS

There are at least two quiz courses conducted in Cleveland for the purpose of cramming candidates for the bar examinations. Both of these draw from the Cleveland Law School. They are conducted by the following:

Melville W. Vickery (a son of Judge Vickery): Has about 20 students. He charges one dollar an hour and conducts the course three hours a week for about six weeks.

Howard D. Burnett: Received his training in Judge Guswiler's quiz in Cincinnati. He has over 100 students, divided into classes which meet in his office three times a week. He charges one dollar an hour.

OHIO BAR EXAMINATIONS

During the past five years an average of 85 per cent. of all those taking the bar examinations have passed them. We have no data as to what proportion, if any, of those who failed come from law schools in Cleveland. The percentage of failures in the years 1910–1919 of those taking the bar examinations in New York is as follows:

1910	57 per cent.
1911	57 per cent.
1912	48 per cent.
1913	40 per cent.
1914	50 per cent.
1915	41 per cent.
1916	44 per cent.
1917	38 per cent.
1918	44 per cent.
1919	43 per cent.

The percentage of failures in the years 1912–1920 of those taking the bar examinations in Illinois is as follows:

1912	28 per cent.
1913	48 per cent.
1914	35 per cent.
1915	23 per cent.
1916	27 per cent.
1917	37 per cent.
1918	72 per cent.
1919	55 per cent.
1920	58 per cent.

CONCLUSIONS

1. The privilege of qualifying for the bar examinations by presenting a certificate of a member of the bar does not result to any substantial extent in providing an adequate means of legal education. Its principal use appears to be to enable to qualify for the bar examinations those who have not completed a three-year course of legal study in a law school; or who have taken the bar examinations and failed and are required to study for at least six months before taking the bar examinations again; or who have attempted to prepare by means of a correspondence school course, which is not accepted by the State bar examiners as a satisfactory course of legal study; or who have taken a three-year course in a regularly organized law school, but have failed to receive a certificate of satisfactory work from the authorities of such school.

2. The Cleveland Law School and the John Marshall Law School succeed in giving to their students at least the minimum amount of legal education which will enable them to pass the bar examinations. It is, therefore, proper to conclude that those schools give such legal education as the public authorities having control thereof in Ohio regard as sufficient for admission to the bar.

No effort has been made to reach a conclusion as to the comparative merits of the several law schools or to make a complete analysis of the standard of legal education which each respectively maintains. It is fair, however, to point out that the night law schools of Cleveland give only six hours a week of class-room work for a period not to exceed thirty-six weeks in each year, or six hundred and forty-eight class-room hours in three years. In admittedly first-class law schools the number of class-room hours in a three-year course is, on the same basis of calculation, one thousand and eighty hours. As students in the night law schools are earning their own living in occupations out of school hours, as a large proportion have a very meager preliminary education, and as they receive only six hundred and forty-eight hours of class-room teaching in three years, a good deal of which, as evidenced by the examination questions, has to do with definitions of legal conceptions and conventional distinctions, it is evident that the standard of legal education in the night law schools should be raised. In this conclusion Judge Vickery, the dean of the Cleveland Law School, and Mr. Meck, the dean of the John Marshall Law School, concur.

3. So long as the standard of legal education set by the State board of bar examiners remains what it is, it is futile to make a purely destructive attack upon the existence or standard of education of night law schools run for pecuniary profit. If it were conceivable—which it is not—that such schools should be prohibited, the result would not be to throw the 500 or 600 men who wish to study law into schools with a higher standard, but would be to throw them into the hands of attorneys under whose direction they would study, or purport to study, for the purpose of qualifying themselves to take the State bar examinations.

Nor is it practicable to call upon the night law schools run for profit to adopt a higher standard. It is an economic fact that so long as law schools run for private profit may freely enter the field of legal education, no such school can raise its standard above the minimum which will enable applicants for admission to the bar to pass the bar examinations. If one attempts to do so by requiring a longer period of study or more hours of study a week, it will at once lose patronage to a school which keeps to the minimum standard, or it will call into existence a school which will secure students on the basis of the minimum standard. This has already been demonstrated in Cleveland.

The only way to defeat the economic effect of free competition in night law schools run for profit is to organize a night law school, regardless of profit, which in the same time of study and with the same convenient hours for students earning a livelihood, and for a smaller price, will offer a better course and by this means draw students from the present night law schools, or force them to raise their standards. Experience, however, indicates that up to the present time the limit of altruistic effort by law teachers and others interested in higher standards of legal education has been reached.

4. The practical course to pursue in raising the standard of legal education in night law schools run for profit is to raise the standards for admission to the bar. By this means the increased standard must be met by all alike, and one school cannot cut in on another with a lower standard. Such a move would receive the support of proprietors of the present night law schools in Cleveland.

5. In asking for stricter requirements for admission to the bar it must be borne in mind that such requests defeat their own ends if they go too far, for the temper of those in authority is still strong that entrance into the legal profession shall not be more difficult than is necessary to insure the minimum capacity and talent required for the less exacting and important positions in the profession.

6. The public is entitled to demand at least a bona fide general elementary education equivalent to four years of high school, *completed before the student commences his legal studies*, so that he is not in the position of earning his own living, attending a night high school and a night school of law all at the same time.

7. The gap between the amount of class-room teaching in admittedly first-class law schools and that given in the night law schools of Cleveland is too wide. The former provide a period of from thirty-two to thirty-six weeks each year, with a minimum of class-room work of ten hours per week. This equals approximately one thousand and eighty class-room hours in the three-year course. The latter, with a maximum of six hours a week for thirty-six weeks each year, give only six hundred and forty-eight hours. This difference should be cut down by requiring of the night schools that they give at least eight hundred and sixty-four class-room hours of instruction. This can be done if the night law school work is continued for thirty-six weeks each year with six class-room hours a week for four years. At the same time the curriculum of the night law schools should be enlarged so as to include at least the greater part

of the following subjects: Bankruptcy, Damages, Insurance, Quasi-Contracts, Conflict of Laws, Municipal Corporations, Mortgages and Trusts, and a considerable addition of Real Property.

It should be kept in mind, however, that there is no use in advancing the requirements for study in night law schools if study with an attorney is to be permitted with no guaranty that instruction by him will be maintained at the level required of the night law school, and if the standard of the bar examinations be not also advanced to keep pace with the advanced standard required of the law schools. With bar examinations conducted as at present and the power of students to obtain certificates from attorneys that they studied three years, increased requirements of the law school would be futile. The student would study at a law school long enough to prepare for the bar examinations as at present conducted, and then would seek the certificate of a practising attorney. The net result would be that students taking the night-law-school course would, in fact, spend but three years at the night law school, just as they do at present.

8. The public is entitled to the exercise of visitorial powers by the board of bar examiners, or by committees of the bar acting under their direction, over all law schools and all persons giving instruction in law whose certificates are accepted by the board. The public is equally entitled to the exercise of visitorial powers by the board of bar examiners, or committees of lawyers acting under their direction, over all schools (other than the public high schools) whose certificate that a student has completed the equivalent of a four-year high school course is accepted by the board.

9. The public is entitled to ask for a rigid inquiry into the moral character of applicants to take bar examinations, especially those elements of moral character which, when lacking in a member of the legal profession, are most disastrous to the public administration of justice and to the interests of clients—such elements as his conception of the code of legal ethics and of the oath of attorney which he takes, and his appreciation of the meaning of his oath to support the Constitution and the laws of the State and the United States.

RECOMMENDATIONS

1. No certificate of an attorney that a student has completed a satisfactory course of study under him should be accepted by the State board of bar examiners unless—(1) The attorney giving the certificate shall have registered with the board before the commencement of such

course his desire to give a course of legal study, and (2) at the same time outlined the course which he proposes to give and show his means for giving adequate and regular instruction equivalent to that given by schools giving at least six hours a week of class-room instruction for thirty-six weeks during the year. The attorney should submit also to the visitorial powers of the State board of bar examiners or of a committee of lawyers acting under their direction. The student desiring to study under the direction of such attorney should obtain a certificate from him at the completion of each period of study of one year or less, and the attorney's certificate should state the fact to be that he has personally given to the student the course of study as outlined in his application to the bar examiners.

2. It should be required that a four-year high school course, or its equivalent, shall have been completed by the student before he commences his three-year course of legal study, and that where the certificate showing the completion of the four-year high school course is given by the principal of a school run for private profit, such school be subject to visitorial powers by the bar examiners, or by a committee of lawyers acting under their direction, with power in the bar examiners, on cause shown, to refuse to recognize its certificate.

3. The character of the period of legal study should be specified more in detail, both as to the subjects which the law school should offer and the amount of time that must be spent in recitation each week by the student and the number of weeks in each year that classes shall be held. Thus, candidates for the bar examinations should be required to have completed a course of legal study extending over a period equivalent to thirty-six weeks in each year for three years, with a minimum of eight class-room exercises a week of at least fifty minutes each, or eight hundred and sixty-four class-room hours. This would mean that a night law school giving six hours a week for thirty-six weeks each year would complete the required course in four years instead of three.

The standard of the bar examinations should be raised to meet the standard of study involved in the requirement of eight hundred and sixty-four class-room hours of teaching, as against the present requirement of six hundred and forty-eight class-room hours—that is to say, the bar examination questions should cover more subjects and with an increased proportion of problem questions which test the student's power of legal reasoning and grasp of legal principles as distinguished from his mere knowledge of definitions of legal conceptions, conventional distinctions, and fixed rules.

4. A committee of the bar should be appointed by the State bar ex-

aminers to act under their direction to examine into the moral fitness of all applicants for permission to take the bar examinations; each candidate should come before the committee personally for direct oral examination, and the scrutiny of the candidate's moral character should be broadened so as to include not only his conduct and reputation for honesty, but his conception of the fiduciary relation, his knowledge of legal ethics, and his general training and conduct as throwing light upon his willingness to live up to the oath of attorney. To this committee also might well be turned over the conduct of the written examination of the student on the subject of legal ethics.

CRIMINAL JUSTICE IN THE AMERICAN CITY—A SUMMARY

THE CLEVELAND FOUNDATION
1202 Swetland Building, Cleveland, Ohio

COMMITTEE

J. D. Williamson, Chairman
Thomas G. Fitzsimons
Malcolm L. McBride
W. H. Prescott
Belle Sherwin

Leonard P. Ayres, Secretary
James R. Garfield, Counsel

———

Raymond Moley, Director

———

THE SURVEY OF CRIMINAL JUSTICE

Roscoe Pound }
Felix Frankfurter } Directors

Amos Burt Thompson, Chairman of the
Advisory Committee

CRIMINAL JUSTICE IN
THE AMERICAN CITY—
A SUMMARY

BY

ROSCOE POUND

DEAN OF THE LAW SCHOOL OF HARVARD UNIVERSITY

PART VII

OF THE CLEVELAND FOUNDATION SURVEY OF

CRIMINAL JUSTICE IN CLEVELAND

FOREWORD

THIS is the summary section of the report of the Cleveland Foundation Survey of Criminal Justice in Cleveland. The survey was directed and the reports edited by Roscoe Pound, who is the author of this report, and Felix Frankfurter. Sections which have been published are:

The Criminal Courts, by Reginald Heber Smith and Herbert B. Ehrmann

Prosecution, by Alfred Bettman

Police Administration, by Raymond B. Fosdick

Correctional and Penal Treatment, by Burdette G. Lewis

Medical Science and Criminal Justice, by Dr. Herman M. Adler

Legal Education in Cleveland, by Albert M. Kales

The sections are published first in separate form, each bound in paper, and are to be consolidated in a single volume, entitled "Criminal Justice in Cleveland."

TABLE OF CONTENTS

CRIMINAL JUSTICE IN THE AMERICAN CITY—A SUMMARY

CHAPTER I

THE NATURE OF THE PROBLEM

Men, Machinery, and Environment

PRIMITIVE man interprets all things in terms of benevolent or malevolent powers whom he must placate and to whose caprices he is subjected. His laws are gifts or revelations of the gods. The need for obeying them is to avoid the wrath of the gods, which will fall indiscriminately upon the community which harbors those who do not walk in the divinely dictated path. He seeks to understand things in terms of personalities, with wants and desires and wills like his own. This interpretation of the occurrences of nature in terms of personality is closely connected with a primitive instinct to hurt somebody or be avenged on something when things go wrong or one is crossed in his purposes or meets with some injury. The fundamental instinct of pugnacity reacts at once to such situations. In the Mosaic Law, if an ox gored a man, the ox must be surrendered for vengeance. In Athens, when a man was killed by the falling of a branch from a tree, the kinsmen of the dead man solemnly chopped down the tree. At Rome, if a domestic animal did any injury, the owner must surrender the animal to the vengeance of the injured person or pay a penalty for standing between the latter and his vengeance. When Huckleberry Finn's father stumbled over the barrel, he promptly kicked it in response to the same instinct. So when things go wrong in the conduct of government or in the administration of justice, the instinct of pugnacity is aroused and the public cries out for some one to be hurt. The general assumption is that legal and political miscarriages resolve themselves into a matter of good men and bad men, and that the task is a simple one of discovery and elimination of the bad.

In truth, the matter is much more complicated than the bad-man interpretation of social and political difficulties assumes. Formerly men sought to understand history by means of a great-man interpretation. History was the record of the actions of great men and of the effects of those actions upon social life. Just now there is a certain tendency to revive this interpretation, and we need not ignore the rôle of great men while insisting that much else needs to be taken into account in order to understand history. In the same way we need not ignore the importance of good men in public life in insisting that much beside individual character needs to be considered in order to understand the shortcomings of legal administration. For good men, if we get them, must work in the social and political and legal environment, and with the legal and administrative tools of the time and place. Often the best of men are the victims of bad or inadequate machinery which impedes their earnest efforts to do right, and may even constrain them to do what they would not do freely. Easy-going men of the best intentions become caught in the machinery and unconsciously become part of it. Moreover, bad men, who commonly make their livelihood by their wits, are unceasingly vigilant to take advantage of the opportunities which outworn or inadequate machinery affords. Where the good are impeded by the instruments with which they must work, the easy-going give up the effort to do things in the face of the impediments and let the machinery take its own course. Thus the well-intentioned drift. It may be that the ill-intentioned secretly give direction to the drift; but quite as likely the drift is to their profit because they are watchful to make it so. We may not expect that any political or legal machinery may be conceived which will eliminate wholly these opportunities for the ill-intentioned to warp the administration of justice to their desires. Yet some machinery increases them both in number and in possibilities, and it must be our study to devise political and legal apparatus which will reduce them to a minimum in both respects.

Along with the bad-man interpretation there commonly goes a faith in legal and political machinery in and of itself: a belief that when anything goes wrong we should appeal at once to the legislature to put a law upon the statute book in order to meet the special case, and that if this law is but abstractly just and reasonable, it will in some way enforce itself and set things to rights. We must enact the one perfect law for each special situation and put out of office the one bad man who perverts its operation. Then all will go well of itself. This faith in legal and political machinery is inherited and deep rooted. Our Puritan forbears abhorred subordination of one man's will to another's, and sought rather a "consociation" in which men should be "with one another, not over one another." They conceived of laws as guides to the conscience of the upright man, and believed that if laws were inherently just and reasonable, they would appeal to his conscience as such, and secure obedience by their own moral weight. This mode of political thought, well suited to the needs of a small group of God-fearing men founding a commonwealth in a new world, is ill suited to the needs of the enormous groups of men of all sorts and conditions who jostle each other in the city of today. There, law must be more than a guide to conscience. There, men will not take time to consider how the intrinsic right and justice of the law appeal to their consciences, but in the rush and turmoil of a busy, crowded life, will consider offhand how far the law may be made an instrument of achieving their desires. There, good laws will not enforce themselves, and the problem of enforcement becomes no less urgent than the problem of providing just laws. The administrative element in justice, the work of adjusting the application of law to individual cases with an eye to their unique features, becomes increasingly important as we become more crowded and division of labor becomes more minute, and individual wants and desires and claims come in contact or conflict at more points. In this administrative element of justice men count for more than machinery. And yet even here men must work with machinery. The output is a joint product of man and of machine, and it often happens that what the man does is dictated by the capacity or the exigencies of the machine quite as much as that what the machine does is dictated by the will of the man.

Not the least significant discoveries of modern psychology are the extent to which what we have called free will is a product, not a cause, and the extent to which what we take to be reasons for actions are but rationalizings of what we desire to do and do on different grounds. In the administration of justice there are many subtle forces at work of which we are but partially conscious. Tradition, education, physical surroundings, race, class and professional solidarity, and economic, political, and social influence of, all sorts and degrees make up a complex environment in which men endeavor to reach certain results by means of legal machinery. No discussion simply in terms of men or of legal and political machinery, or of both, ignoring this complex environment, will serve. At whatever cost in loss of dramatic interest or satisfying simplicity of plan, we must insist on plurality of causes and plurality and relativity of remedies.

Both the bad-man interpretation and the faith in legislation and new laws as remedies illustrate a common mode of thinking which seeks to explain everything by some one cause and to cure every ill by some one sovereign remedy. It is not hard for an ordinary person to toss up one ball so as to keep it in motion continually. With practice one may learn to keep two going at once. But only a skilful juggler can so handle three or more at once. In the same way the ordinary man may think of one cause or one remedy at a time, but finds difficulty in bearing two in mind at once and leaves consideration of larger numbers to the expert. All branches of knowledge, theoretical and practical, have had to contend with this difficulty of holding all the factors of problems in mind at once. In all ages men have sought to avoid this difficulty by searching for some solving word or phrase or some ultimate idea or some universal cure-all, whereby to escape the hard task of thinking of many things in one connection. The several sciences have struggled with the desire for a simplification that covers up difficulties instead of overcoming them and the assumption of one cause for each phenomenon and one remedy for each ill. Neither the science of law nor the science of politics has escaped this struggle to master complex facts by giving them a fictitious appearance of simplicity. Nor has the quest for the simple and easy been more successful in these sciences than elsewhere. There was no easy royal road to learning, and there is no simple and easy popular road to an understanding of law and government and mastery of the difficult problems which each presents. The citizen who seeks such understanding must expect to study hard and think critically and to keep many things in mind at once while framing his judgments. He must expect those judgments to be largely tentative and relative to time, place, and circumstances. Much as he might like to rest in some formula and to believe in the efficacy of some one specific applied once for all, he will find such hope as futile as the quest for the philosopher's stone or the fountain of youth or the one cure for all bodily ills in which men formerly engaged in a like hope of achieving an easy simplicity. At the very outset we must give up the search for a single explanation of the inadequacy to its purposes of punitive justice in action, and hence must give up the search for any single simple remedy.

We may say that the three chief factors in the administration of justice are—(1) the men by whom it is administered; (2) the machinery of legal and political institutions by means of which they administer justice; and (3) the environment in which they do so. One who surveys the workings of a legal system with these three things in mind will not go far wrong. Yet his picture will not be complete nor wholly accurate. He must take account also of certain practical limitations and practical difficulties inherent in the legal ordering of human relations, at least by any legal institutions thus far devised. The purposes of law, as we know them, and the very nature of legal institutions as we have received and fashioned them, involve certain obstacles to our doing everything which we should like to do by means thereof, and even to our doing well many things which we have been trying to do thereby for generations. These practical limitations on effective legal action explain much that, on a superficial view, is ascribed to bad men or bad legal machinery. Hence a fourth factor must be added, namely, (4) the bounds within which the law may function effectively as a practical system.

THE FUNCTION OF LAW

We look to the physical and biological sciences to augment the means of satisfying human wants and to teach us to conserve those means. We look to the social sciences to teach us how we may apply those means to the purpose of satisfying human wants with a minimum of friction and waste. Thus we may think of the legal order as a piece of social engineering; as a human attempt to conserve values and eliminate friction and preclude waste in the process of satisfying human wants. That part of the whole process of social engineering which has to do with the ordering of human relations and of human conduct through applying to men the force of politically organized society is the domain of law.

To illustrate the function of law we may consider the common case where large numbers of persons seek admission to a baseball game or seek to buy tickets at a theater. If each individual is left to himself, and in his desire to get to the ticket window first and procure the best seat pushes and shoves his individual way thereto as his strength and disposition dictate, it is not unlikely that few will be served in any reasonable time. When all seek to be served at once, no one may be served. In the endeavor of each to secure his individual desire in a crowd of fellow-men seeking likewise to secure their individual desires, he and they are sure to lose much of what they seek through the friction of a disorderly scramble, the waste of time and temper in trials of individual strength and persistence, and the inability to do business at the window in the push and shove of an unregulated crowd after they get there. On the other hand, if the crowd is "lined up," is ordered, and is required or persuaded to pursue an orderly course to the window and await each his turn, friction is done away with, time is conserved, waste of effort is eliminated, and each may secure freely and with comparative speed what he seeks to the extent that there are accommodations available. If there are not enough for all, yet all are satisfied so far as may be with a minimum of waste. The task of the law is similar. It is one of making the goods of existence` go as far as possible in the satisfaction of human wants by preventing friction in the use of them and waste in the enjoyment of them, so that where each may not have everything that he wants or all that he claims, he may at least have all that is reasonably possible.

[5]

In this process of adjusting and ordering human relations and ordering human conduct in order to eliminate friction and waste, the legal order deals, on the one hand, with controversies between individuals. Where their claims or wants or desires overlap, it seeks to harmonize and reconcile those claims or wants or desires by a system of rules and principles administered in tribunals. On the other hand, it has to deal with certain acts or courses of conduct which run counter to the interests involved in the existence and functioning of civilized society. Civilized society rests upon the general security, including the general safety, the general health, peace, and good order, and the security of the economic order. It is maintained through social institutions, domestic, religious and political. It involves a moral life and hence calls for protection of the general morals. In a crowded world it presupposes conservation of social resources. It is a society of individual human beings, and hence its proper functioning presupposes the moral and social life of each individual therein according to its standards. These social interests, as they may be called, namely, the general security, the security of social institutions, the general morals, the conservation of social resources, and the individual moral or social life, are threatened by the anti-social acts or anti-social conduct or even anti-social mode of life of particular individuals. To restrain these persons, to deter others who might follow their example, to correct such anti-social mode of life as far as possible, and to give effect to these social interests, the law imposes a system of duties upon all persons in society, enforced through administrative and police supervision, through prosecution and through penal treatment. The part of the legal system that defines these duties and prescribes how they shall be enforced by means of prosecutions and penal treatment is the criminal law.

It is important to bear in mind that the law is only one of many regulative agencies whereby human conduct is ordered for the securing of social interests. The household, religious organizations, fraternal organizations, social, professional, and trade organizations may operate also, through their internal discipline, to order the conduct of their members and to restrain them from anti-social conduct. In the past these organizations, whereby the force of the opinions of one's fellow-members may be brought to bear upon him, have played a large part in maintaining civilized society. When the law seems to break down in whole or in part we may well inquire, among other things, how far it is supported or is interfered with by some or all of these organizations, and how far they also or some of them must bear the blame. Obviously the number and vitality of these organizations in any society and the manner in which and ends for which they are conducted are important items in the environment of the administration of justice.

To think of the legal order functionally, in terms of engineering, is especially important in such a survey as the present. Here we are not concerned with legal rules in their abstract nature, but in their concrete workings. We are not seeking to know what the law is. We seek to know what the legal system does and how what it does measures up to the requirements of the ends for which it is done. Hence the purpose of the law must be before us as a critique of its achievements in action, not some criterion drawn from the law itself. When the growth of a city makes the old mechanical structures, set up by the engineers of the past, inadequate to the wants or needs of the present, and calls for newer and larger and better structures of mechanical engineering, we do not judge the old structures by their conformity to some ideal plan, conceived before they were built, but by their results in action. We do not abuse the men who devised nor those who, for the time being, are operating the old structures. We set out to plan and build new and better structures. No less science, no less preliminary study, no less thorough preparation, no less intelligently directed effort, is required when the growth of a city calls for new structures in the way of social engineering. In each case the question is one of achieving certain practical ends in view of the means at hand, the structures of the past, the ingenuity of the engineers, the limitations of science, and the strength or feebleness of the public desire that those ends be met. In each case, also, the preliminary survey must take account, in the first instance, of the difficulties to be overcome.

DIFFICULTIES INVOLVED IN THE ADMINISTRATION OF JUSTICE

Difficulties in the administration of justice, with which we must reckon in order to appraise intelligently the workings of any particular legal or judicial organization, are partly in the very subject matter. That is, they are wider than time and place and inhere in all attempts to order human conduct and human relations by the force of politically organized society—at least through any legal or administrative machinery which thus far the wit of man has been able to devise. Also they are partly in the times in which justice is administering. That is, they are wider than the place which we may be investigating and are involved in the general condition of legal science in the civilized world, in a particular time, the ideas as to the purpose of law entertained generally in that time, and the general attitude of the time toward law and government. Again, they are partly in the system that has come down to us from a past in which it was constructed under and to cope with different conditions

[7]

and hence is ill-adapted to the social, economic, and political environment in which it must operate.   Finally they may be partly in purely local conditions.   Accordingly, I shall consider these difficulties under four heads: (1) Inherent difficulties; (2) general difficulties; (3) American difficulties; (4) local difficulties.

CHAPTER II

INHERENT DIFFICULTIES

DISSATISFACTION WITH THE ADMINISTRATION OF JUSTICE

DISSATISFACTION with the administration of justice is as old as law. As long as there have been laws and lawyers conscientious men have believed that laws were but arbitrary technicalities, and that the attempt to govern the relations of men in accordance with them resulted largely in injustice. From the beginning others have asserted that, so far as laws were good, they were perverted in their application, and that the actual administration of justice was unequal or inefficient or corrupt. In the first stage of legal development one of the Greek Seven Sages said that "laws are like spiders' webs, wherein small flies are caught, while the great break through." In the history of Anglo-American law discontent has an ancient and unbroken pedigree from Anglo-Saxon times to the present. The Anglo-Saxon law books are full of complaint that the king's peace is not well kept, that justice is not done equally, and that great men do not readily submit to the law which is appropriate to them. Later the Mirror of Justices contains a list of 155 abuses in legal administration. Still later Wyclif complains that lawyers try causes "by subtlety and cavilations of law," and not by the gospel, "as if the gospel were not so good as pagan's law." In the reign of Henry VIII it was complained that good laws were obstructed in their operation by interpretations in the courts in which "everyone that can color reason maketh a stop to the best law that is beforetime devised." James I sent for the judges on complaint of the Archbishop of Canterbury, and argued to them that "the law was founded upon reason and that he and others had reason as well as the judges." In the eighteenth century there was complaint that the bench was occupied by "legal monks," utterly ignorant of human nature and of the affairs of men. After the Revolution the administration of justice in America was the subject of bitter attacks. Many judges were impeached, not for any crimes or misdemeanors, but because the whole administration of justice was suspected or objected to. The movement for an elective bench which swept over the United States about the middle of the last century grew out of these attacks. In England in the first half of the nineteenth century attacks on the courts were hardly less bitter, as the reader of Dickens may readily verify. In our own time the agitation for recall of judges and recall of judicial decisions was strong less than a decade ago. We must not allow this perennial and perhaps inevitable discontent with all law to blind us to serious and well-founded complaints as to the actual operation of the legal system today. But it may give us a needed warning that some discontent is unavoidable, that we may not hope to obviate all grounds of complaint, and that we must begin by taking account of the inherent difficulties, because of which a certain amount of dissatisfaction must always be discounted.

INHERENT DIFFICULTIES IN ALL JUSTICE ACCORDING TO LAW

1. The Mechanical Operation of Legal Rules

To a certain extent legal rules must operate mechanically and the most important and most constant cause of dissatisfaction with all law in all times grows out of this circumstance. A proper balance between strict rule and magisterial discretion is one of the most difficult problems of the science of law. Throughout the history of law men have turned from an extreme of the one to an extreme of the other and then back again, without being able to attain a satisfactory administration of justice through either. Sometimes, as in the strict law of the late medieval courts in England, or as in the maturity of American law in the last half of the nineteenth century, men put their faith in strict confinement of the magistrate by minute and detailed rules or by a mechanical process of application of law through logical deduction from fixed principles. By way of reaction at other times men pin their faith in a wide magisterial power to fit justice to the facts of the particular case through judicial discretion, as in the administrative tribunals of sixteenth- and seventeenth-century England, the executive and legislative justice of the American colonies, and the executive boards and commissions which are setting up in this country today on every hand. But these reactions are followed by new periods of fixed rules. Thus experience seems to show that the mechanical action of law may be tempered but may not be obviated.

We seek to administer justice according to law. That is, we seek just results by means of a machinery of legal rules. But a certain sacrifice of justice is involved in the very attainment of it through rules, which yet are, on the whole, the best and most certain method of attaining it which we have discovered. Legal rules are general rules. In order to make them general we must eliminate what by and large are the immaterial elements of particular controversies. This would be of no consequence if all cases were alike, or if it were possible to foresee or to reckon precisely the degree in which actual cases approach or depart from the types which the law defines. In practice they approximate to these types in endless gradations, the one often shading into the next, so that in difficult cases choice of the proper type is not easy and often gives rise to judicial disagreement. As a result, when the law eliminates what are taken to be immaterial factors in order to frame a general rule, it can never avoid entirely elimination of factors which may have an important bearing upon some particular controversy.

There are three ways of meeting this difficulty: One is to provide a judicial or magisterial dispensing power, or even a series of devices for introducing discretion into the administration of justice. In American administration of criminal justice today there is a long series of such devices, one imposed upon the other. There is the discretion of the police as to who and what shall be brought before the tribunals. There are wide and substantially uncontrolled powers in prosecuting attorneys to ignore offenses or offenders, to dismiss proceedings in their earlier stages, to present them to grand juries in such a way that no indictment follows, to decline to prosecute after indictment, or to agree to accept a plea of guilty of a lesser offense. There is the power of the grand jury to ignore the charge. There is the power of the trial jury to exercise a dispensing power through a general verdict of not guilty. Next comes judicial discretion as to sentence or suspension of sentence or mitigation of sentence. Finally there is administrative parole or probation, and in the last resort executive pardon. All these involve uncertainty—opportunity for perversion of the device intended to meet exceptional cases into a means of enabling the typical offender to escape, and a sometimes intolerable scope for the personal equation of the official.

A second way of meeting this difficulty is to eliminate all discretion and seek to meet exceptional cases by an elaborate series of legal exceptions and qualifications and detailed provisos. But human foresight has not proved equal to foreseeing all the varieties of exception for which provision must be made, and the attempt to cover everything by special provisions makes the legal system cumbrous and unworkable.

Hence the law usually ends by adopting a third method of compromising between wide discretion and over-minute law making. But in order to reach a middle ground between rule and discretion some sacrifice of flexibility of application to individual cases is necessary. And this sacrifice cannot go far without a danger of occasional injustice. Moreover, the slightest sacrifice, necessary as it is, makes legal rules appear arbitrary and brings the application of them more or less into conflict with the moral ideas of individual citizens. Whenever, in a complex and crowded society containing heterogeneous elements, groups and classes and interests have conflicting ideas of justice, this cause of dissatisfaction is likely to become acute. The individual citizen looks only at single cases, and measures them by his individual sense of right and wrong. The courts must look at cases by types or classes and must measure them by what is necessarily to some extent an artificial standard. If discretion is given the judge, his exercise of it may reflect the view of the element of society from which he comes or with which he associates. If his hands are tied by law, he may be forced to apply the ethical ideas of the past as formulated in common law and legislation. In either event there are many chances that judicial standards and the ethical standards of individual critics will diverge. Herein lies a fruitful cause of popular dissatisfaction with the administration of justice.

2. *Difference in Rate of Progress Between Law and Public Opinion*

In seeking to maintain the interests of civilized society through public administration of justice we risk a certain sacrifice of those interests through corruption or the personal prejudices of magistrates or individual incompetency of those to whom administration is committed. To make this risk as small as possible, to preclude corruption, restrain personal prejudices, and minimize the scope of incompetency, the law formulates the moral ideas of the community in rules and requires the tribunals to apply those rules. So far as they are formulations of public opinion, legal rules cannot exist until public opinion has become fixed and settled, and cannot well change until public opinion has definitely changed. It follows that law is likely to lag somewhat behind public opinion whenever the latter is active and growing.

Many devices have been resorted to in order to make the law more immediately sensitive and responsive to public opinion. Some of these are frequent and copious legislation upon legal subjects, deprofessionalizing the practice of law by opening it to all, regardless of education and special training, putting of the courts into politics through making judges elective for short terms, conferring wide powers upon juries at the expense of courts, setting up of administrative tribunals with large jurisdiction, to be exercised in a non-technical fashion, and recall of judges or of judicial decisions. The first four of these expedients were tried in the fore part of the last century, and many jurisdictions carried some or even all of them to extremes. The last three have been urged in the present century, and a tendency to commit enforcement of law to administrative agencies and tribunals has gone far. But none of them has succeeded in its purpose, and many of them in action have subjected the administration of justice not to public opinion, but to influences destructive of the interests which law seeks to maintain. We must recognize that this difficulty in justice according to law may be minimized, but not wholly obviated. We must make a practical compromise. Experience has shown that public opinion must affect the administration of justice through the rules by which justice is administered rather than through direct pressure upon those who apply them. Interference with the uniform and scientific application of them, when actual controversies arise, introduces elements of uncertainty, caprice, and deference to aggressive interests which defeat the general security. But if public opinion affects tribunals through the rules by which they decide, as these rules, once established, stand till abrogated or altered, it follows that the law will not respond quickly to new conditions. It will not change until ill effects are felt—often not until they are felt acutely. The economic or political or moral change must come first. While it is coming and until it is so definite and complete as to affect the law and formulate itself therein, divergence between law and a growing public opinion is likely to be acute and to create much dissatisfaction. We must pay this price for the certainty and uniformity demanded by the general security. It should be said, however, that consciousness of this inherent difficulty easily leads lawyers to neglect the importance of reducing this difference in rate of growth between law and public opinion so far as possible.

3. Popular Underestimation of the Difficulties in Administering Justice

Much popular dissatisfaction with justice according to law arises from a popular assumption that the administration of justice is an easy task to which anyone is competent. If the task of law may be described in terms of social engineering, laws may be compared to the formulas of engineers. They sum up the experience of many courts with many cases and enable the magistrate to apply that experience without being aware of it. In the same way the formula enables the engineer to utilize the accumulated experience of past builders even though he could not of himself work out a step in its evolution. The lay public are no more competent to construct and apply the one formula than the other. Each requires special knowledge and special preparation. But the notion that any one is competent to understand what justice requires in the intricate controversies and complicated relations of a modern urban community leads to all manner of obstacles to proper standards of training for the bar, to low standards of qualification for judicial office, and to impatience of scientific methods and a high measure of technical skill. This notion was especially strong in pioneer America, and its influence may be seen in extravagant powers of juries, lay judges of probate, and legislative or judicial attacks upon the authority of precedents in most of the States of the South and West. In criminal law it is usually manifest in legislation committing the fixing of penalties to trial juries, not perceiving that the trier, in order to determine the facts fairly, ought not to know certain things without which, on the other hand, the penalty cannot be fixed intelligently. Popular judgments are reached by labeling acts according to certain obvious characteristics. A judge, on the other hand, must examine carefully into all the details of the act, the conditions, internal and external, under which it was done, its motive and its consequences. Hence his judgment may well differ from that of the man in the street, although they apply the same moral standard. The man in the street is likely to regard this disagreement as proof of defects in the administration of justice. Yet courts do not sit to register his judgment on such data as he has but to do what the sober judgment of the community would dictate upon the basis of all the facts.

It is not generally realized how much the public is interested in maintaining the highest scientific standards in the administration of justice. It is the most certain protection against corruption, prejudice, class feeling, and incompetence. Publicity is important, but it is impossible to invoke public indignation in every case, nor is it always evoked in the right cases. Our main reliance must be put in the training of bench and bar, whereby the judges form habits of seeking and applying principles when called upon to act, and the lawyers are able to subject their decisions to expert criticism. The latter is especially important. The daily criticism of trained minds, the knowledge that nothing which does not conform to the principles and received doctrines of scientific law will escape notice, will do more than any other agency for the every-day purity and efficiency of courts of justice. But as things are today the best trained element of the bar more and more does its chief work out of court, and wholly avoids criminal cases. Thus in our large cities the most effective check upon the administration of justice becomes inoperative, and this special difficulty is added to the inherent difficulty involved in public reluctance to admit the necessity of scientific justice and the training of bench and bar which it presupposes.

4. Popular Impatience of Restraint

Law involves restraint and regulation with the sheriff and his posse or the police force in the background to enforce it. As a society becomes more complex, as it carries further the division of labor, as it becomes more crowded and more diversified in race and in habits of life and thought, the amount of restraint and regulation must increase enormously. But however necessary and salutary this restraint, men have never been reconciled to it entirely; and most American communities are still so close to the frontier that pioneer hostility toward discipline, good order, and obedience is still often a latent instinct in the better class of citizens. The very fact that the restraint of the legal order is in some sort a compromise between the individual and his fellows makes the individual, who must abate some part of his activities in the interest of his fellows, more or less restive. In a time of absolute democratic theories this restiveness may be acute. The feeling that each individual, as an organ of the sovereign democracy, is above the law which he helps to make, fosters disrespect for legal methods and legal institutions and a spirit of resistance to them. Thus the administration of justice according to law is made more difficult. Whether the law is enforced or is not enforced, dissatisfaction will result.

Popular impatience of restraint is aggravated in the United States by political and legal theories of "natural law." As a political doctrine, they lead individuals to put into action a conviction that conformity to the dictates of the individual conscience is a test of the validity of a law. Accordingly, jurors will disregard statutes in perfect good faith, as in the Sunday-closing prosecutions in Chicago in 1908. In the same spirit a well-known preacher wrote not long since that a prime cause of lawlessness was enactment of legislation at variance with the law of nature. In the same spirit a sincere and, as he believed, a law-abiding labor leader declared in a Labor Day address that he would not obey mandates of the courts which deprived him of his natural "rights." In the same spirit the business man may regard evasion of statutes which interfere with his carrying on business as he chooses as something entirely legitimate. In the same spirit public officials in recent addresses have commended administrative violation of the legal rights of certain obnoxious persons, and one of the law officers of the federal government has publicly approved of mob violence toward such persons. Such examples at the top of the social scale do not make for respect for law at the bottom.

[15]

5. Inherent Limitations on Effective Legal Action

There are certain limitations inherent in the administration of justice through legal machinery—at least, through any of which we have knowledge—which prevent the law from securing all interests which ethical considerations or social ideals indicate as proper or even desirable to be secured. Five such limitations are of much importance in connection with the criminal law. These are: (1) Difficulties involved in ascertainment of the facts to which legal rules are to be applied, so that, especially in certain types of case, it is difficult to discover the offender or there is danger of convicting the innocent; (2) the intangibleness of certain duties which morally are of much moment but legally defy enforcement, as, for instance, many duties involved in the family relation to which courts of domestic relations or juvenile courts seek to give effect; (3) the subtlety of certain modes of inflicting injury and of modes of infringing important interests which the legal order would be glad to secure effectively if it might; (4) the inapplicability of the legal machinery of rule and sanction to many human relations and to some serious wrongs, and (5) the necessity of relying upon individuals to set the law in motion.

Three of the limitations just enumerated call for some notice. Intrigue may seriously disturb the peace of a household. The subtle methods by which grievous wrongs may be done in this way have been the theme of playwright and novelist for generations. One court, indeed, has tried the experiment of enjoining a defendant from flirting with a plaintiff's wife. But the futility of legal interference in such cases is obvious and is generally recognized. In no other cases is self-redress so persistently resorted to nor so commonly approved by the public. Again, many cases are too small for the ponderous machinery of prosecution and yet may involve undoubted and serious wrongs to individuals. How to deal with the small annoyances and neighborhood quarrels and petty depredations and small-scale predatory activities which irritate the mass of an urban population but do not seem to involve enough to justify the expensive process of the law is by no means the least of the problems of the legal order in the modern city. Here as elsewhere we must make a practical compromise, and whatever the compromise, many will needs be dissatisfied. Finally, law will not enforce itself. We must in some way stimulate individuals to go to the trouble of vindicating it; and yet we must not suffer them to use it as a means of extortion or of gratifying spite. Our rules must obtain in action, not merely lie dormant in the books. But if they are to obtain in action, the authority which prescribes them must be so backed by social-psychological power as to be in a position to give them effect as motives for action in spite of countervailing

[16]

individual motives. Hence the notorious futility of two sorts of lawmaking which are very common: (1) Lawmaking which has nothing behind it but the sovereign imperative, in which the mere words "be it enacted" are relied upon to accomplish the end sought, and (2) lawmaking which is intended to "educate"—to set up an ideal of what men ought to do rather than a rule of what they shall do. To a large extent law depends for its enforcement upon the extent to which it can identify social interests with individual interests, and can give rise to or rely upon individual desire to enforce its rules. In criminal law the desire of the offender to escape and the desire of his friends and relatives that he escape, are strong and active. Unless the desires of other individuals may be enlisted in the service of the law, administrative machinery is likely to fall into an easy-going routine, readily manipulated in the interest of offenders, and the law in the books to become wholly academic, while something quite different obtains in action.

Few appreciate the far-reaching operation of the foregoing limitations upon legal action. There is constant pressure upon the law to "do something," whether it may do anything worth while or not. In periods of expansion the tendency to call upon law to do more than it is adapted to do is especially strong. The result is sure to be failure and the failure affects the whole legal order injuriously.

INHERENT DIFFICULTIES IN ALL CRIMINAL JUSTICE

1. Public Desire for Vengeance

Historically, one of the origins of criminal law is in summary community self-help, in offhand public vengeance by a more or less orderly mob. Regulation of this public vengeance, giving rise to a sort of orderly lynch law, is one of the earliest forms of criminal law. The spirit which gave rise to this institution of summary mob self-help in primitive society is still active. It has its roots in a deep-seated instinct, and must be reckoned with in all administration of criminal justice. Moralists and sociologists no longer regard revenge or satisfaction of a desire for vengeance as a legitimate end of penal treatment. But jurists are not agreed. Many insist upon the retributive theory in one form or another, and Anglo-American lawyers commonly regard satisfaction of public desire for vengeance as both a legitimate and a practically necessary end. This disagreement is reflected in all our criminal legislation. Statutes enacted at different times proceed upon different theories. Indeed, the usual course is that adherents of one theory of penal treatment will procure one measure, and adherents of a different theory another, from law-

3   [17]

makers who have no theory of their own. For nothing is done with so little of scientific or orderly method as the legislative making of laws.

Administration is necessarily affected by the fundamental conflict with respect to aims and purposes which pervades our penal legislation. But apart from this, the conflicting theories are also at work in administration. One magistrate paroles freely; another may condemn the system of parole. One executive pardons freely, another not at all. One jury is stern and as like as not acts upon the revenge theory; another jury is soft-hearted. One judge is systematically severe and holds that crime must inevitably be followed by retribution; another is systematically lenient, and many others have no system or policy whatever. Thus the fact that we are not all agreed, nor are we ourselves agreed in all our moods, infects both legislation and administration with uncertainty, inconsistency, and in consequence inefficiency. All attempts to better this situation must reckon with a deep-seated popular desire for vengeance in crimes appealing to the emotions, or in times when crimes against the general security are numerous. Lawyers know well that the average client is apt to be eager to begin a criminal prosecution. He is not satisfied to sue civilly and obtain compensation for an injury. He insists upon something that will hurt the wrongdoer, and is willing to pay liberally to that end. It has taken a long time to eliminate the revenge element from the civil side of the law. Indeed, traces still remain there. On the criminal side this element is still vigorous. The general security requires us to repress self-help, especially mob or mass self-help. Also we must strive to meet the demands of the moral sentiment of the community. These considerations constrain us to keep many things in the criminal law which are purely retributive, and thus serve to preserve a condition of fundamental conflict between different parts of the system. Undoubtedly the law and its administration should reflect the sober views of the community, not its views when momentarily inflamed. But the sober views of the average citizen are by no means so advanced on this subject as to make a wholly scientific system possible.

2. A Condition of Internal Opposition in Criminal Law Due to Historical Causes

As has been said, criminal law exists to maintain social interests as such; but the social interest in the general security and the social interest in the individual life continually come into conflict, and in criminal law, as everywhere else in law, the problem is one of compromise; of balancing conflicting interests and of securing as much as may be with the least sacrifice of other interests. The most insistent and fundamental of social interests are involved in criminal law. Civilized society presupposes peace and good order, security of social institutions, security of the general morals, and conservation and intelligent use of social resources. But it demands no less that free individual initiative which is the basis of economic progress, that freedom of criticism without which political progress is impossible, and that free mental activity which is a prerequisite of cultural progress. Above all it demands that the individual be able to live a moral and social life as a human being. These claims, which may be put broadly as a social interest in the individual life, continually trench upon the interest in the security of social institutions, and often, in appearance at least, run counter to the paramount interest in the general security. Compromise of such claims for the purpose of securing as much as we may is peculiarly difficult. For historical reasons this difficulty has taken the form of a condition of internal opposition in criminal law which has always impaired its efficiency. As a result there has been a continual movement back and forth between an extreme solicitude for the general security, leading to a minimum of regard for the individual accused and reliance upon summary, unhampered, arbitrary, administrative punitive justice, and at the other extreme excessive solicitude for the social interest in the individual life, leading to a minimum of regard for the general security and security of social institutions and reliance upon strictly regulated judicial punitive justice, hampered at all points by checks and balances and technical obstacles. In England the medieval legal checks upon punitive justice were followed by the rise of the Star Chamber and other forms of executive criminal administration. This was followed by the exaggerated legalism of a common-law prosecution. The latter, carried to an extreme in nineteenth-century America, is being followed hard today by the rise of administrative justice·through boards and commissions. The over-technical tenderness for the offender in our criminal law of the last century is giving way to carelessness of violation of the constitutional rights of accused persons and callousness as to administrative methods of dealing with criminals, real or supposed, in the supposed interest of efficient enforcement of penal laws. It happens that within the present century Cleveland has seen both sentimental tenderness toward accused persons and Draconian judicial severity in action. In this contrast, familiar to the citizens of Cleveland, may be seen a picture in miniature of what has always gone on in the history of criminal law.

Criminal law has its origin, historically, in legal regulation of certain crude forms of social control. Thus it has two sides from the beginning. On the one hand, it is made up of prohibitions addressed to the individual in order to secure social interests. On the other hand, it is made up of limitations upon the enforcement of these prohibitions in order to secure the social interest in the individual life. In Anglo-American criminal law, as a result of the contests between courts and king in seventeenth-century England, the accused came to be thought of not as an offender pursued by the justice of society, but as a presumably innocent person pursued by the potentially oppressive power of the king. The common law, declared in bills of rights, came to be thought of as standing between the individual and the state, and as protecting the individual from oppression by the agents of the state. No efficient administration of criminal law in a large urban population is possible under the reign of such a theory. But we have abandoned it in places only. Despite an obvious reaction, it still determines many features of American criminal prosecution. Moreover, we must not forget that it is but a historical form of one of the two elements of which criminal law is made up.

3. The Close Connection of Criminal Law and Administration with Politics

Criminal law has a much closer connection with politics than the civil side of the law, and this operates to its disadvantage, particularly in respect of administration. There is relatively little danger of oppression through civil litigation. On the other hand, there has been constant fear of oppression through the criminal law. In history drastic enforcement of severe penal laws has been employed notoriously to keep a people or a class in subjection. Not only is one class suspicious of attempts by another to force its ideas upon the community under penalty of prosecution, but the power of a majority or even a plurality to visit with punishment practices which a strong minority consider in no way objectionable is liable to abuse. Whether rightly or wrongly used, this power puts a strain upon criminal law and administration. Also criminal prosecutions are possible weapons of offense and defense in class and industrial conflicts. Hence suspicion arises that one side or the other may get an advantage through abuse of the prosecuting machinery, giving rise to political struggles to get control of that machinery. Thus considerations of efficient securing of social interests are pushed into the background, and the atmosphere in which prosecutions are conducted becomes political. In practice the result is, when the public conscience is active or public indignation is roused, to be spectacular at the expense of efficiency. When the public conscience is sluggish and public attention is focused elsewhere, the temptation is to be lax for fear of offending dominant or militant political groups.

4. *The Inherent Unreliability of Evidence in Criminal Cases*

Inherent unreliability of evidence upon which tribunals must proceed affects all departments of judicial administration of justice. But in criminal law, where passions are aroused, where the consequences are so serious, where unscrupulous persons are so apt to be arrayed on one side or the other, the difficulties growing out of the necessity of relying upon human testimony are grave. Psychologists have demonstrated abundantly the extent to which errors of observation and unsuspected suggestion affect the testimony of the most conscientious. Undoubtedly there is much practical psychology and trained intuition behind the common-law rules of evidence; but they are based largely on the psychology of the jury rather than on that of the witness. The problem of lying witnesses, defective observation, and suggestion, as affecting proof in criminal cases, has yet to be studied scientifically by American lawyers. The maxims and presumptions in which we express our practical experience in these connections are too much of the rule-of-thumb type, and are apt to be merely pieces to move in the procedural game between prosecutor and accused.

Moreover, in the administration of criminal law the inherent unreliability of oral evidence of witnesses is aggravated by three circumstances. On the one hand there is the bad influence of police *esprit de corps*. The unfortunate convictions of Beck and Edalji in England, which will long remain classical examples of convictions of the innocent in modern times, were clearly traceable to determination of the police to convict innocent men whom they had erroneously assumed to be guilty. The testimony of experienced trial lawyers who have written memoirs or reminiscences is uniform to the effect that the testimony upon which prosecutors must chiefly rely is apt to be so colored and warped as to be subject to grave doubt. Serjeant Ballantine, whose long experience in prosecuting and defending entitled him to speak with authority, says that *esprit de corps*, antipathy toward the criminal classes, the habit of testifying so that it ceases to be regarded as a serious matter, and the temptation which besets police officers to communicate opinions or theories to the press, thus "pledging themselves to views which it is damaging to their sagacity to retract," so operate as to cause serious and even fatal miscarriages of justice. The student of criminology may verify this abundantly by study of American criminal trials. Yet from the nature of the case such testimony is the best available.

In some part police *esprit de corps* is counteracted by the activity of habitual defenders of criminals and activity of friends and relatives of the accused. But these are often more available and more efficacious in the service of the guilty than of the innocent. Getting witnesses out of the way or silencing them or modifying their testimony by importunity, social pressure, intimidation, appeals to race solidarity, or sympathy are thoroughly familiar matters to the observer of criminal justice in action, and the memoirs and reminiscences of criminal trial lawyers show that nothing new in these respects has been devised in the modern American city. Caleb Quirk, Esq., of Alibi House, in the early part of the last century, would be quite at home in any of our cities today.

We are dealing here with an inherent difficulty. Yet much may be done to mitigate it which we are not doing. (1) If scientific methods of criminal investigation were employed at the very beginning and the preparation of the general run of criminal cases in the prosecutor's office were as thorough and systematic as the preparation of the civil cases, for example, of a public service company, the opportunities for subornation that have made the alibi notorious and the opportunity for suppression of evidence would be much lessened. (2) If the administration of oaths and the formalities of reception of evidence in all stages of a criminal proceeding and before all tribunals were such as to impress those who take part with the seriousness of what is going on, some part of the notorious perjury which attends the administration of justice might be precluded. (3) A better organized and better trained and better disciplined bar might eliminate the type of practitioner that promotes subornation and grows rich on systematic and scientific suppression of evidence and silencing of witnesses. It is noteworthy that incorporation of the lower branch of the legal profession in England had the effect of driving out a low type of solicitor which still thrives in large numbers with us. But for the most part we must hope that study of the psychology of testimony will reveal better methods of ascertaining facts in criminal prosecutions than those which are now available. Until such methods come we must reckon with unreliability of evidence as a formidable inherent difficulty.

5. The Wider Scope for Administrative Discretion Required in Criminal Law

As compared with the adjustment of civil relations, criminal law involves a much greater scope for discretion. Much that may be done mechanically in matters of property and contract, and hence with assurance that improper influences are excluded by the perfection of the machinery, must be done by the individual judgment of judges or public officers when we are dealing with human conduct, and hence is open to all the disturbing influences that may be brought to bear upon the individual human being. It is one of the difficult problems of all law to maintain a due proportion between detailed rules and judicial or administrative discretion. In criminal law the dangers involved in such discretion are obvious. The power which it involves is large and is peculiarly liable to abuse. Moreover, the consequences of abuse are serious, involving life and liberty, where on the civil side of the law the effects extend rather to property. But there are two circumstances in criminal law that require a wide discretion on the part of prosecutors and magistrates: (1) In the administration of criminal law the moral or ethical element plays a large part, and purely moral or ethical matters do not lend themselves to strict rules. (2) As we now think, penal treatment is to fit the criminal rather than punishment to fit the crime. Hence whether there shall be a prosecution and what shall be done to and with the convicted offender after prosecution must be left largely to the discretion of someone. Even when we sought to make the punishment fit the crime the impossibility of a mathematically constructed system of penalties became manifest, and sentence, within wide limits, was a matter for the discretion of the trial judge. In those days notorious inequalities in sentences bore constant witness to the liability of unfettered discretion to abuse, even in the best of hands. In England, review of sentences by the Court of Criminal Appeal is relied upon to meet this particular danger. In the United States the tendency is to entrust the nature and duration of penal treatment to some administrative board. But whichever course is taken the beginning and continuation as well as the details of the ultimate result of a criminal prosecution must be left largely to the discretion of someone, with all which that may imply.

6. Inherent Inadequacy of Penal Methods

On the civil side of the law the modes of enforcement have become very efficacious. If A dispossesses B of land, the sheriff may put A out and B back in possession. If A dispossesses B of a chattel, the sheriff may take it from A and give it back to B. If A does not convey to B as he promised, an officer of the court may make a deed to which the law gives the effect of the promised conveyance. If A does not pay a debt he owes B, the sheriff may sell A's goods and pay B out of the proceeds. No such thoroughgoing remedies are available in criminal law. To guard against further harm from a particular offender, and to guard against others who might repeat the offense, society relies upon fear as a deterrent. It attempts to create a wide-spread fear of punishment and to bring this fear home to the particular offender. Preventive justice, in such matters as are dealt with by the criminal law, must be confined within narrow limits, since it involves undue interference with the freedom of action of individuals. Accordingly, in the great mass of cases the criminal law can only step in after an offense has been committed. But the system of protecting society by creating a general fear of punishment encounters two inherent difficulties: (1) Experience has shown that fear is never a complete deterrent. The venturesome will believe they can escape. The fearless will be indifferent whether they escape. The crafty will believe they can evade, and enough will succeed to encourage others. (2) Threats of punishment are often likely to defeat themselves. The zeal of lawmakers frequently imposes penalties to which juries will not agree that offenders should be subjected. It sometimes defines acts as criminal for which juries will not agree to see men punished. Thus we get so-called dead-letter laws, which weaken the authority of law and destroy the efficacy of fear as a deterrent. Sometimes, indeed, it has happened that courts did not have sympathy with over-severe laws or extreme penalties and warped the law to prevent conviction. Our criminal procedure still suffers from the astuteness of judges in the past to avoid convictions at a time when all felonies were punishable with death. However efficient the administration of criminal law, it will be necessary to make some allowance for this inherent difficulty.

7. The Tendency to Put Too Great a Burden on the Criminal Law

It is a great disadvantage to the criminal law that it is so interesting in action to the layman. Criminal law is the type of law which figures chiefly in the morning papers; hence when the layman thinks of law, he is almost certain to think of criminal law. Moreover, because of a well-known human instinct, the layman's short and simple cure for all ills is to hurt somebody. Hence every lay lawmaker turns instinctively to the criminal law when he comes to provide a sanction for his new measure, and every new statute adds one more to the mass of prescribed penalties for which a criminal prosecution may be invoked. It is impossible for any legal machinery to do all which our voluminous penal legislation expects of it. Serious study of how to make our huge annual output of legislation effective for its purpose without prosecutions and giving up the naïve faith that finds expression in the common phrase, "there ought to be a law against it," as an article in the legislative creed, would do much for the efficiency of criminal law.

CHAPTER III

GENERAL DIFFICULTIES

PREVALENCE OF DISSATISFACTION WITH CRIMINAL LAW AND ITS ADMINISTRATION

D ISSATISFACTION with criminal law and its administration is neither a local nor an American phenomenon. It was world wide at the beginning of the second decade of the present century. For the past seven years other matters have occupied men's thoughts. But there are signs already that agitation for improvement is breaking out again or will soon break out again in many lands. In Italy a commission is now at work upon a new criminal code and promises a thoroughgoing reform, especially in procedure. Certain causes operating throughout the civilized world, and affecting all administration of criminal justice in the present generation, must be taken into account in any critical appraisal of the workings of the criminal law in a particular locality.

NEW DEMANDS UPON LAW

Law, it has been said, "is but the skeleton of social order." It must be "clothed upon with the flesh and blood of morality." In a time of unrest and doubt as to the very foundations of belief and of conduct, when absolute theories of morals and supernatural sanctions have much less hold upon the mass of the people than when our institutions were formative, and as a consequence conscience and individual responsibility are relaxed, law is strained to do double duty, and much more is expected of it than in a time when morals as a regulating agency were more efficacious. In an era of secularization in which the law is looked to for much that was formerly conceived as in the domain of the church and the home, in an urban, industrial society in which, for example, truancy and incorrigibility of children may be matters for a court rather than for household discipline, we must expect that the legal administration of justice will be affected sensibly.

1. The Problem of Enforcement

In the present century new demands upon law and new social conditions involved in our urban, industrial civilization have made enforcement of law a conspicuous problem in legal science. In a simpler, more homogeneous, less crowded society it was assumed that the enforcing machinery and the efficiency of its operation were not matters of concern to the lawyer. He might think of law as the declared will of the State. In that event he would say that his business was to know and interpret and apply the declaration of the State's will. If the precepts in which that will was declared were not enforced, the trouble lay, not in the law, but in the supineness or incompetency or corruption of the executive officials whose duty it was to execute the law. Or he might think of law as a body of principles of justice, discovered by human experience of conduct and decision, and only formulated by legislator or court or jurist. In that event, if they were not enforced, he was inclined to say that it was because they ought not to be enforced; because they were not sound or accurate formulations of the principles revealed by history and tested by experience. Or, again, he might think of law as a formulation of moral or ethical principles, deriving their real authority from their inherent justice. In that case he was likely to think that they would largely enforce themselves because of their appeal to the conscience of the individual. Nor was this wholly untrue at a time when the program of law was relatively simple and the reasons behind the relatively few laws were apparent on the surface to almost any thoughtful man. But when the area of legal interference becomes greatly enlarged, as it must be in the complex urban industrial society of today; when law has an ambitious program of interposing in almost every field of human activity and regulating human conduct in all its forms and relations, the reasons behind the multitude of legal precepts contained in our voluminous criminal codes and administrative regulations are not readily apparent, and often may well be disputed by those who are able to perceive them. The lawyer, trained in ideas which were appropriate to the simple legal program of the past, is likely to assume today that enforcement of the law is nothing of which he need think. Accordingly, when in the endeavor to secure newly pressing interests ambitious but inexpert reformers turn to penal legislation and add new sections to the overburdened penal code, or the public become alarmed in a time of reconstruction and unrest and threaten an orgy of drastic penal legislation, the lawyer whose habit has been to study the justice of rules, rather than the enforcement of them, is in no position to give effective assistance. Much of popular distrust of the legal profession is due to this change in the conditions to which legal theories are to be applied, while the theories still obtain.

2. The Demand for Concrete Justice

In the nineteenth century, with a simple program of preserving the general security in a primarily rural agricultural society, we were wont to think of justice in terms of the abstract claims of abstract human beings. Today emphasis is put rather upon concrete justice in the individual case. We are not so ready to admit, as an excuse for failure of justice in particular cases, that "John Doe must suffer for the commonwealth's sake." It is felt that abstractly just rules do not justify results that fall short of justice, and that injury to John Doe may be avoided if we bestir ourselves to find more effective legal and administrative devices. Hence today legal proceedings are judged by their results in action, not by their conformity to some abstract, ideal scheme. Features of the administration of justice which were regarded patiently in the middle of the nineteenth century are spoken of now with impatience in a community in which conservation of time and effort has become important, and men have learned from modern business and industrial engineering to think in terms of results. The lawyer has been trained to think of the general or average result reached in a type or class of cases, and the demand of the present century for results in individual cases conflicts with his traditional ideas. Adjustment of legal thinking and judicial methods to this demand for concrete justice—to a large extent a legitimate demand in the conditions of today—must go forward slowly in the nature of things, and will long contribute to an unsatisfactory administration of law in certain types of case in which the demand is particularly insistent and the legal tradition is specially averse thereto.

3. The Demand for Individualization

One of the most insistent demands of today is for individualization of criminal justice—for a criminal justice that will not turn recidivists through the mill of justice periodically at regular intervals, nor, on the other hand, divert the youthful occasional offender into a habitual criminal by treating the crime, in his person, rather than the criminal. The nineteenth century was hostile to individualization and to administrative discretion, which is the chief agency of individualization, seeking to reduce the whole administration of justice to abstractly just, formal, rigid rules, mechanically administered. This was true the world over. It was specially true, and true to an exaggerated degree, in America, because of the political ideas of the Puritan, who believed men should be "with one another, not over one another," of politico-legal ideas that grew out of contests between courts and crown in seventeenth-century England, of experience of the American colonists with executive and legislative justice, and of pioneer jealousy of administrative and governmental action. The result was to impose shackles of detailed rules and rigid procedure upon every sort of judicial, administrative, and governmental activity. In practice there was a general policy of "can't." No agency of government was to be allowed to do anything beyond a necessary minimum. Hence we got rigid, detailed procedure and hard and fast schemes of penal treatment, lest prosecutor or court or prison authorities do something spontaneously in view of the exigencies of a particular case—we got a procedure governed by a code, rather than by rule and custom of the court, as at common law; we got in some states a police discipline shackled by checks that deprived it of all real efficacy, and we got in many states constitutional obstacles to legislation in the form of detailed requirements as to the generality of laws, as to what should appear in legislative journals, and as to title and repeal. It should be emphasized that this spirit, which hampers effective criminal justice so seriously, has no necessary connection with an economic policy of *laissez faire*. Whatever the policy of a society may be as to interference with or regulation of men's general activities or economic activities or business relations, it is no part of a *laissez faire* policy to leave individual criminal activity as free as possible to follow its own course. The spirit of hampering judicial and administrative agencies was due rather to faith in abstract rules and in machinery as inherently efficacious, and to lack of faith in official action as such for *any* purpose, than to any economic policy. Without regulating many things, the law may yet set out to deal effectively with what it does attempt to regulate or to prevent.

CHANGED IDEAS AS TO THE END OF CRIMINAL LAW

1. The Passing of the Retributive Theory

Our traditional criminal law thinks of the offender as a free moral agent who, having before him the choice whether to do right or wrong, intentionally chose to do wrong. In the nineteenth century we believed that justice consisted in imposing upon this wilful wrongdoer a penalty exactly corresponding to his crime. It was not a question of treatment of this offender, but of the exact retribution appropriate to this crime. We know today that the matter is much more complicated than this simple theory assumes. We know that criminals must be classified as well as crimes. We know that the old analysis of act and intent can stand only as an artificial legal analysis and that the mental element in crime presents a series of difficult problems. We recognize that in order to deal with crime in an intelligent and practical manner we must give up the

[28]

retributive theory. But this means that we must largely make over our whole criminal law, which was rebuilt around that theory in the last two centuries, and that work is going on slowly all over the world. The condition of criminal law calls for continuous intelligent bringing to bear upon the problem of securing social interests by law and upon the detailed applications of that problem—for the bringing to bear upon them of every resource of legal and social and medical science. We shall achieve lasting results neither by some analytical scheme or rigid system worked out logically in libraries on the sole basis of books and law reports, as some lawyers seem to hope, nor by abandoning the experience of the past, preserved in the law reports, and turning exclusively to administrative, non-legal, expert agencies, which is the hope of many laymen. Pending this making over of criminal law we must expect that many features of the administration of criminal justice will remain unsatisfactory.

2. Increased Regard for Human Personality

Today we feel that when the law confers or exercises a power of control the legal order should safeguard the human existence of the person controlled. Thus the old-time sea law, with its absolute power of the master over the sailor, described in action by Dana in *Two Years Before the Mast*, the old-time ignominious punishments that treated the human offender like a brute, that did not save his human dignity—all such things have been disappearing as we come to take account of the social interest in the individual human life and to weigh that interest against the social interest in the general security on which the last century insisted so exclusively. This feeling for the human dignity, the human life, of the offender is somewhat different from the feeling for abstract individual liberty and consequent system of checks upon prosecution and safeguards of accused persons and loopholes for escape which developed in Anglo-American criminal law for historical reasons from the seventeenth to the nineteenth century. Until it crystallizes in well-settled and well-understood legal and administrative policies, until proper compromises between the interest in the individual human life and the general security, security of social institutions, and general morals are worked out at many points, there is likely to be vacillation, uncertainty, and inefficiency in the administration of criminal justice. This will be true especially at the two extremes of a prosecution—the beginning in police discretion when an offense has been committed, and the end in penal treatment of the convicted offender. Cleveland has seen in somewhat acute form a phenomenon that is to be seen in criminal justice throughout the

[29]

world, and is merely an incident of changing ideas as to what we are doing through the criminal law and why we are doing it. The effect in unsettling the administration of criminal law is unfortunate. Discontent with the results of some of the newer methods of penal treatment is not unlikely to lead to temporary reaction to older methods, which will but aggravate the difficulty. Partly these newer methods and their results have been misunderstood and misrepresented. Partly results which are justly objected to are due to the inevitable crude fumblings involved in all application of new methods. Naturally the public is impatient. But we can no more return to the old methods than we can return to horse-cars or ox-teams or flails or sickles. We must go forward scientifically and not vacillate between extreme experiments along new lines and reactionary reversions to methods that belong wholly to the past.

3. New Developments in Psychology and Psychopathology

Medical science has all but undergone a rebirth within a generation. Within a generation psychology has risen to a practical science of the first importance, with far-reaching applications on every side. Psychopathology has overturned much that the criminal law of the past had built upon. Indeed, the fundamental theory of our orthodox criminal law has gone down before modern psychology and psychopathology. The results are only beginning to be felt. One result is a just dissatisfaction on the part of the medical profession with what they observe in judicial administration of justice and legal treatment of criminals. In prevention, in criminal investigation as a preliminary to prosecution, in the trial of issues of fact and in penal treatment we have much to learn from the physician and psychologist and psychopathologist. But during the period of transition in which we are learning it and are learning how to use it there will be much experimenting and some fumbling and much dissatisfaction.

THE PRESENT CONDITION OF CRIMINAL LAW

As a result of the several causes suggested above, the criminal law of today, throughout the world, is made up more or less of successive strata of rules, institutions, traditional modes of thought, and legislative provisions representing different and inconsistent ideas of the end of criminal law, the purpose of penal treatment, and the nature of crime. This is true especially in Anglo-American criminal law. With us all stages of development and all theories and all manner of combinations of them are represented in rules and doctrines which the courts are called upon to administer. Indeed, all or many of them may be represented in legislative acts bearing the same date. The result is that our criminal law is not internally consistent, much less homogeneous and well organized. Even if the administrative machinery were all that it should be and the personnel of administration were all that it should be, the condition of criminal law of itself would impede satisfactory administration.

Unfortunately, criminal law never attained the systematic perfection that marks the civil side of the law in Roman law, and is beginning to be found on the civil side of Anglo-American law. Until the criminal law is studied as zealously and scientifically and is regarded by teachers, students, lawyers, and judges as being as worthy of their best and most intelligent efforts as is the civil side of the law, the administration of criminal justice will continue to fall short of public expectation.

CHAPTER IV

AMERICAN DIFFICULTIES

CONDITIONS FOR WHICH AMERICAN CRIMINAL LAW AND PROCEDURE WERE SHAPED

TO UNDERSTAND the administration of criminal justice in American cities today we must first perceive the problems of administration of justice in a homogeneous, pioneer, primarily agricultural community of the first half of the nineteenth century, and the difficulties involved in meeting those problems with the legal institutions and legal doctrines inherited or received from seventeenth-century England. We must then perceive the problems of administration of justice in a modern heterogeneous, urban, industrial community and the difficulties involved in meeting those problems with the legal and judicial machinery inherited or received from England and adapted and given new and fixed shape for pioneer rural America.

Professor Sumner called attention to the importance of an understanding of frontier or pioneer conditions in the study of American politics. "Some of our worst political abuses," he said, "come from transferring to our now large and crowded cities maxims and usages which were convenient and harmless in backwoods country towns." This is no less true of our most serious legal abuses. It must be remembered that our judicial organization and the great body of our legal institutions and common law are the work of the last quarter of the eighteenth century and the first half of the nineteenth century. For practical purposes American legal and judicial history begins after the Revolution. In colonial America the administration of justice was at first executive and legislative. American law reports begin at the end of the eighteenth century. The America for which seventeenth-century English legal institutions and eighteenth-century English law were received and made over was not at all the America in which those institutions and that law must function today. Our great cities and the social and legal problems to which they give rise are of the last half of the nineteenth century. Many are of the last quarter of that century. Our largest city now contains in 326 square miles a larger and infinitely more diversified population than the whole 13 States when the federal judicial organization which has served so generally as a model was adopted. The last State of the Union was opened to settlement by the white man within a generation. Except perhaps in the narrow fringe of original settlements along the Atlantic coast, rural conditions prevailed everywhere within the memory of those now living, and in any part of the country one need do little more than scratch the surface in order to come upon the pioneer. Thus our law and our legal institutions got the stamp of the pioneer while they were formative.

Our Anglo-American judicial and prosecuting organization, criminal law and criminal procedure, as they grew up and took shape in the fore part of the last century, presuppose a homogeneous people, jealous of its rights, zealous to keep order, and in sympathy with institutions of government which it understands and in which it believes—a people which, in all matters of moment, will conform to the precepts of law when they are ascertained and made known, which may be relied upon to set the machinery of the law in motion of its own initiative when wrong has been done, and to enforce the law intelligently and steadfastly in the jury-box. In other words, they presuppose an American farming community of the first half of the nineteenth century. We are employing them to do justice in a heterogeneous, diversified, crowded city population, containing elements used to being trodden on by those in authority, ignorant of our institutions, at least in all but form, with good reason suspicious of government as they have known it, and hence often imbued with distrust of all government, loth to invoke legal machinery, of which they think in terms of the social conditions in another part of the world, and inclined to think of a jury trial as some sort of man hunt, not knowing the nature of the proceedings that have gone before nor appreciating the manifold guarantees by which at common law an accused person is assured every facility for a full defense.

THE ADMINISTRATION OF CRIMINAL JUSTICE IN THE FIRST HALF OF THE NINETEENTH CENTURY

1. The Criminals and Conditions of Crime

At the outset we must notice the different type of criminal and different conditions of crime for which our formative institutions were shaped. The occasional criminal, the criminal of passion, and the mentally defective, were the chief concern of the criminal law, and its task was to restrain them in a homogeneous community under pioneer or rural conditions, in a society little diversified economically and for the most

4

part restrained already by deep religious conviction and strict moral training. So far as it was necessary to deal with vice it was the rough, virile vice of a vigorous stock that lived out-of-doors. Organised professional criminality on a large scale, operating over the whole country, was unknown. The occasional band of robbers or of cattle thieves could be dealt with by a sheriff and a posse. Commercialized vice on a large scale, extending its operations over many localities, was unknown. Large cities with a diversified, shifting industrial population, with extreme divergencies of economic condition, with rapid and easy communications with other like centers, with a population moving back and forth daily in swarms to a business center and crowding a great volume of business into a few hours, did not afford opportunities for specialized professional crime. Such conditions have come upon us slowly in some parts of the country, but with extreme rapidity in others, as in Cleveland. In either event they have come upon an administrative and judicial machinery made for rural communities and simply added to or patched from time to time to meet special emergencies. The professional criminal and his advisers have learned readily to use this machinery and to make devices intended to temper the application of criminal law to the occasional offender a means of escape for the habitual offender. Experience has shown this in all our cities. But the "Mortality Tables" in the report on Prosecution[1] and the examples of the facility with which old offenders take advantage of the series of mitigating agencies, set forth in Chapter II of the report on Criminal Courts, tell the story eloquently.

2. Administrative Machinery

We inherited from England a medieval system of sheriffs, coroners, and constables, devised originally for a rural society and easily adapted to pioneer rural conditions. The town marshal was a constable with no civil functions and some added powers and duties. He went out of office with every political change. He kept order and did an occasional bit of detection in the event of a sensational crime. A police force, as we now know it, is an institution of the nineteenth century, and, unhappily, our police organization and administration have been affected to no small extent by ideas derived from the older, pre-urban régime. What is particularly noticeable about the nineteenth-century Anglo-American administrative system is its lack of organization, decentralized responsibility, and abundant facilities for obstruction in comparison with means for effective achievement of results. As a rule, none of these officials was

---

[1] Pp. 7, 9, and 11.

answerable to any one but the electorate. He coöperated with other officials or thwarted them as his fancy or the exigencies of politics might dictate. Each locality had its own administrative officer, acting on his own judgment, and responsible to no superior, and the execution or non-execution of laws therein was its own affair.

This decentralization, division of power, and hampering of administration was part of the system of checks and balances to which we pinned our faith in the last century. It has been said that our institutions were the work of men who believed in original sin and were unwilling to leave open any door for the intrinsically sinful official which they could possibly close. To this Puritan jealousy of administration we added a pioneer jealousy of administration. "The unthinking sons of the sagebrush," says Owen Wister, "ill tolerate anything which stands for discipline, good order, and obedience; and the man who lets another command him they despise." Such has always been the spirit of the pioneer, and institutions shaped by that spirit are well adapted to a pioneer society. But in a crowded urban society, in holding down the potentially sinful administrative official we give the actually sinful professional criminal his opportunity, and in insuring a latitude of free individual self-assertion beyond what they require for the upright, we give a dangerous scope to the corrupt. The local conditions of cities demand centralization and organization of administrative agencies, coördination of responsibility with power, and reliance upon personality rather than upon checks and balances as emphatically as a pioneer, rural community demands decentralization, division of power, independent magistracies, and checks upon administration.

3. English Criminal Law at the Revolution

When, at the end of the eighteenth century and in the early nineteenth century, we began to build an American criminal law with received English materials, the memory of the contests between courts and crown in seventeenth-century England, of the abuse of prosecutions by Stuart kings, and of the extent to which criminal law might be used as an agency of religious persecution and political subjection, was still fresh. Hence a hundred years ago the problem seemed to be how to hold down the administration of punitive justice and protect the individual from oppression under the guise thereof, rather than how to make criminal law an effective agency for securing social interests. English criminal law had grown out of royal regulations of summary local self-redress and had been developed by judicial experience to meet violent crimes in an age of force and violence. Later the necessities of more civilized times had led to the development in the court of Star Chamber of what is now the common law as to misdemeanors. Thus one part of the English law of crimes as we found it at the Revolution was harsh and brutal, as befitted a law made to put down murder by violence, robbery, rape, and cattle-stealing in a rough and ready community. The legislation in New York at the end of the eighteenth century which abolished the death penalty for felonies other than murder, and the English legislation of the legislative reform movement in the fore part of the nineteenth century, was chiefly concerned in doing away with the brutalities of the old law as to felonies. Another part of the English law of crimes at the Revolution seemed to involve dangerous magisterial discretion, as might have been expected of a body of law made in the council of Tudor and Stuart kings in an age of absolute government and extreme theories of royal prerogative. Puritan jealousy of subordination and administration, pioneer self-reliance, and inherited fear of political oppression by governmental agencies, since the colonists had had experience of the close connection of law with politics, were decisive of our shaping of this body of criminal law at the time when it was formative. In particular these things had three important results:

(1) They led nineteenth-century American law to exaggerate the complicated, expensive, and time-consuming machinery of a common-law prosecution, lest some safeguard of individual liberty be overlooked. It is only thus that we may understand the many steps set forth in Chapter III of the report upon the Criminal Courts.

(2) They led to curtailings of the power of the judge to control the trial and hold the jury to its province, and to conferring of excessive power upon juries. These had their origin in colonial America, before true courts and judicial justice had developed, when juries were a needed check upon the executive justice of royal governors. They were added to through the need of checks upon royal judges. They were carried still further during the hostility to courts and lawyers and English legal institutions that prevailed immediately after the Revolution. Finally, they got their fullest development in frontier communities in the nineteenth century.

(3) Both had the result of enfeebling the administration of criminal law. But these enfeeblings did not work much evil in a time when crime was relatively rare and abnormal; when the community did not require the swift-moving punitive justice adjusted to the task of enforcing a voluminous criminal code against a multitude of offenders which we demand today. How they affect the enforcement of law today is shown strikingly in Table 2 of the report on Criminal Courts, and Tables 1, 2,

and 3 in the report on Prosecution. Unfortunately, when the conditions that call for a more effective criminal justice became acute, we had ceased to take the same interest in criminal law that had been taken early in the nineteenth century, when the leaders of the legal profession achieved their most conspicuous triumphs in criminal cases, and in consequence there has been no such systematic expert consideration of how to give efficacy to criminal justice in the present as was devoted to the work of enfeebling it in the past.

4. English Criminal Procedure at the Revolution

As the substantive criminal law had been brutal in the spirit of a substitute for lynch law, so English criminal procedure had been brutal and unfair to the accused. The trial methods of seventeenth-century prosecutors and the conduct of seventeenth-century trial judges, imitated by some royal judges in eighteenth-century America, led to stringent provisions in our bills of rights for the protection of accused persons and for securing them a fair trial. Except in political prosecutions, criminal prosecutions in the English polity were privately conducted. Also there was no review of convictions except for error on the face of the formal record and no granting of new trials to the convicted. Both of these conditions were changed in American law. A local public prosecutor was set up in each locality. The practice of review of administrative convictions before colonial legislatures and granting of new trials by colonial legislatures after judicial judgments made us familiar with review of criminal proceedings and led to a system of criminal appellate procedure. But the local prosecutor, the model whereof is the federal district attorney of the Judiciary Act of 1789, while suggested by the French *procureur du roi*, was not made part of an organized administrative system, but instead was given complete independence as a sort of attorney general *in petto*. In the federal system a certain control is had through the federal department of justice. In the States there is no such power. The local prosecutor and the attorney general may coöperate or may ignore each other or may clash as their dispositions or their politics lead them. The wide powers of local prosecutors, the lack of control over them, and the extent to which they may determine the whole course of law enforcement, without leaving a tangible record of what they have done and what they have undone, are beginning to attract attention.

No officer in our large cities has so much real power with so little ostensible power. The easiest path to improper influence upon criminal justice is through the office of the public prosecutor, and there is much evidence that professional defenders of professional criminals and professional extortioners from occasional offenders in more than one American city understand this thoroughly. In a rural pioneer community with a small local bar, a small criminal docket, and only occasional terms of court, the public prosecutor had relatively little power. Grand juries had ample time to deliberate and did their work critically. What the public prosecutor did or failed to do was evident to and subject to criticism by alert and expert critics actively engaged in the courts. In the modern city, with congested criminal dockets, a crowded bar, the leaders of which seldom or never go into the criminal courts, and continuous sessions of court almost throughout the year, he is watched only by alert and expert professional defenders who often know the game of criminal justice better than he does. There is no effective check upon him. The series of mitigating agencies which were introduced into our criminal justice under different conditions offer abundant opportunity to cover up his tracks, and the pressure of judicial business makes the common-law check of judicial approval, when required, a perfunctory ceremony. The chief pressure upon him is political, and this sort of pressure is easily exerted by politician-criminal-law practitioners as a means of defeating enforcement of the law. No feature of our administration of criminal justice calls for thoroughgoing study so urgently as the public prosecutor. Mr. Bettman's pioneer study of a prosecutor's office in action in an urban community should be pondered by every thoughtful lawyer.

Review of convictions and granting of new trials by appellate courts were called for especially in America because of the need for judicial finding and shaping of the law which we were receiving from England and adapting to our conditions. When James Kent went upon the bench in New York in 1791 he tells us that there were no State law reports and nobody knew what was the law. Later there was need of judicial interpretation of the criminal codes which became common in the United States after the model of the French penal code of 1810. But this institution had the effect of enfeebling the administration of criminal law in that settlement of the law was then more important than punishment of the individual offender. Thus, in the second half of the nineteenth century, when the law had become settled, new trials were granted constantly on academic legal points although no doubt of guilt could exist. There has been a marked change in this respect in the past two decades. Yet the function of finding the law for a pioneer community whose criminal law is formative, as the real function of a criminal appellate tribunal rather than reviewing guilt or innocence of the accused, has impressed its spirit upon our whole system of review of convictions. How much it still affects our administration of justice may be seen by comparing the reported decisions of an American supreme court with those of the English Court of Criminal Appeal.

It will have been noted that all three of our American innovations upon seventeenth-century English criminal procedure were in the direction of mitigation and afforded additional incidental opportunities for the guilty to escape. Accordingly, as English criminal justice is notoriously more feeble than criminal justice upon the Continent, American criminal justice is more feeble than English. What this means to the habitual offender is suggested by the statistics in Chapter I of the report on Police Administration.

5. The System of Courts at the Revolution

English judicial organization at the time of the Revolution was too arbitrary and involved to be taken as a model to be followed in detail in this country. Yet by eliminating the more obvious anomalies, a general outline could be perceived which was the model of our system of courts. For the purposes of criminal justice, beginning at the bottom, this was: (1) Local peace magistrates and local inferior courts with jurisdiction to examine and bind over for felonies and a petty jurisdiction over misdemeanors, subject to appeal to and retrial in the court of general jurisdiction; (2) a central court of general jurisdiction at law and over crimes, with provision for local trial of causes at circuit; (3) a supreme court of review. The defect in that scheme that appealed to the formative period of judicial organization was not its lack of unity, the multiplicity of courts or the double appeals, but its over-centralization for the needs of a sparsely settled community that sought to bring justice to every man. In a community of long distances in a time of slow communication and expensive travel central courts entailed intolerable expense upon litigants. Judicial organizations were devised with a view to bringing justice to every man's door. But the model was English at a time when English judicial organization was at its worst. For in the eighteenth century the English had not yet overhauled their system of courts. It had grown up by successive creation or evolution of new courts when new types of work arose or old tribunals ceased to function efficiently, so that some 74 courts existed, 17 of which did the work now done in England by three. Thus we took an archaic system for our model, and the circumstances of the time in which our courts were organized tended to foster a policy of multiplication. As a result, we go on creating new courts at a time when the conditions of our large cities call for unification.

A contributing factor in this decentralized judicial organization was the need of judicial ascertainment of the law in a new community already adverted to. We had to devise a body of substantive criminal law in a time of rapid expansion. For more than a century the main energies of our judicial system were devoted to the working out of a consistent, logical, minutely precise body of precedents. To us the important part of the system was not the trial judge who tried and sentenced the accused, but the judge of the appellate court who availed himself of the occasion given by the prosecution to develop the law. We judged the judicial system rather by the written opinions filed in its highest court than by the efficient functioning of its prosecuting machinery. Our eyes were fixed upon the task of providing rules. It is no wonder that our failure to devote equal attention to application and enforcement of rules too often allowed the machinery designed to give effect to the rules to defeat the purposes of law in their actual operation. If one reads the report upon the courts in Cleveland with this historical background in mind, he will understand many things. The rise of special problems, such as those which come before juvenile courts and our urban courts of domestic relations, the great increase in police regulations, especially of traffic regulations since the advent of the automobile, the increased opportunities for professional crime and consequent large-scale organization of criminal enterprises, the presence in our cities of large groups of aliens, as well as of citizens of foreign birth and no little race solidarity, the resulting colonies in our cities of large numbers of persons not trained in the ideas which our legal polity presupposes, and the complex economic organization, with its incidental results of recurring times of unemployment and continual inflow and outflow of laborers—all these things affect court organization as well as police and prosecutor. They call for strong peace magistrates, well organized and provided with ample facilities. They call for a single court of criminal jurisdiction, in which the steps in a prosecution may be reduced to a minimum—a court well organized and continually in session. All this is very far from the system we inherited from the nineteenth century.

6. The Bench at the Revolution and in the Nineteenth Century

As has been said, the administration of justice in colonial America was at first executive and legislative, rather than judicial. Legislative new trials persisted until the end of the eighteenth century, legislative appellate jurisdiction until the middle of the nineteenth century, and legislative divorces until the last quarter of the nineteenth century. Judicial justice was only just establishing itself at the time of the Revolution, and came to its own in the last decades of the eighteenth century and the beginning of the nineteenth. In the colonies the courts were manned by laymen, with the occasional exception of the chief justice, and in some of the colonies the royal chief justices did not so conduct themselves as to inspire confidence in lawyers as judicial magistrates. At the time of the Revolution it was beginning to be thought advisable to have judges learned in the law. But many of the States relied upon judges without legal training until well into the nineteenth century. Thus, two of the three justices in New Hampshire after the Revolution were laymen, and the Chief Justice of Rhode Island from 1819 to 1826 was a farmer.

Three factors brought about a wholly different attitude toward the bench from that which has obtained in England since 1688. Here, as in so many cases in American legal and political institutions, we derive from seventeenth-century rather than from eighteenth-century England. The politics-ridden bench of the Stuarts rather than the independent judiciary of modern England was the original model. The federal constitution and the federal judiciary act of 1789 set a better model and, on the whole, the federal courts have kept to the best traditions of a common-law bench. Also the appointive State courts, with permanent tenure, at the end of the eighteenth century and in the first half of the nineteenth century, were manned by judges of the highest type, who made that period a classical one in the history of Anglo-American law. But the hostility to courts and lawyers due to economic causes after the Revolution, and the radical democratic movement of the next generation, with its leveling tendencies, its tendency to carry out abstract political theory to its logical conclusions, and its cult of incompetency, which is so often a by-product of democracy, combined to work a gradual change. Hostility to Federalist judges, some of whom, it must be admitted, followed the example of political judges in England too closely, had much to do with the first experiments with an elective bench. Thus a complete change took place in the mode of choice and tenure of judges which became general after 1850.

In rural pioneer America the elective short-term judge did not work badly, although it is significant that the great names which are the ornaments of American judicial history belong, with scarcely an exception, to the era of appointed judges with permanent tenure. Today judges in rural jurisdictions chosen at the polls and for relatively short terms are, on the whole, reasonably satisfactory. But the elected short term bench has not achieved what its adherents expected of it, and has achieved some other things which have a bad influence upon the administration of justice.

It may be shown from the debates in constitutional conventions by which elective judges were provided for that the advocates of that system expected to put the judges into the closest touch with the people, to make them responsive to public opinion, to subject them to the pressure of popular criticism and to liberalize the administration of justice. English law, which we were receiving and making over, was looked upon with suspicion by a large part of the community and it was thought that a permanent judiciary was over-technical. This feeling had some justification in the obstinacy with which some strong judges adhered to English rules and practices simply as such, and in the impossibility of administering justice in the nineteenth century by the formal, involved, artificial common-law procedure of the eighteenth century. But what the new system of choosing judges actually did was to subject the bench to professional political pressure, to make judges responsive to political considerations rather than to public opinion, and, in the long run, to insure at most a mediocre bench which has proved more narrowly technical and, on the whole, less liberal in practice than appointed judges with permanent tenure in the few jurisdictions which retained that system. On the other hand, the judges elected for short terms soon lost effective control over the administration of justice, and common-law traditions of legal proceeding became seriously impaired. Lack of control over the trial bar on the part of judges who cannot afford to antagonize and cannot insist upon expedition and high ethical forensic standards of conduct without imperiling their positions is a chief cause of the unnecessary continuances and postponements, the difficulties in obtaining juries, the wranglings of counsel and the ill treatment of witnesses which have cast discredit upon American criminal trials. It is significant that these things are almost unknown in jurisdictions in which judicial tenure is permanent and secure.

Moreover, the putting of the bench into politics and the modes of thought of the pioneer resulted in breaking down the common-law standards of decorum and of judicial propriety. How far this decadence of dignity and decorum may go is strikingly illustrated in the report on Criminal Courts. The habitual presence of the higher type of lawyer in the civil courts has prevented such things as are of common occurrence in inferior criminal tribunals. But the judicial Barnum and even the judicial mountebank are well-known characters in most American jurisdictions today, and they are fostered by a system under which, in the large city, a magistrate must keep in the public eye in order to hold his place. Even more serious is the careless, slip-shod despatch of business which develops in courts conducted without regard for decorum—a method which lends itself to such things as are described in Chapter III of the report on Prosecution, and Chapter V of the report on Criminal Courts. The nadir is reached when campaign funds for judges are raised by subscription from those who practise or have litigation before them.

That the public should see and feel that justice is done is scarcely less important than the actual doing of justice. Order, decorum, and judicial dignity, in fact, promote the despatch of business. More than this, they promote respect for law and confidence in the work of the courts. No one should wonder at the prevalence of perjury in courts so conducted as to make the administration of oaths and the giving of testimony perfunctory acts, done offhand in the midst of Babel. No one should wonder at the lack of public confidence in the administration of justice by courts which appear to be conducted by whispered confidential communications with politicians and criminal-law practitioners of doubtful repute, rather than by solemn public proceedings in open court. All these things are natural results of putting the bench into politics under the conditions of the modern city. One of the chief items in any program of improvement must be to free the court-rooms of our lower tribunals from the atmosphere of crudity and coarseness given them by the "Jefferson Brick" era of American politics, confirmed in them by the pioneer, and accentuated by the press of work, mixed population, and crowd of low-grade lawyers in the large city.

7. *The Bar At and After the Revolution*

At the Revolution the bar was hardly more than beginning in this country. The colonies had little need of lawyers until after the middle of the eighteenth century. With the rise of judicial justice administered by courts in place of executive justice and legislative justice which prevailed during the greater part of the colonial period, a tendency to go to England for legal education began to appear, and there were a few good lawyers in more than one colony at the Revolution. After the Revolution law and lawyers were in much disfavor; the law, because it could not escape the odium of its English origin in the period of bitter feelings after the war, lawyers, because they alone seemed to thrive in the economic disorganization and disturbed conditions that followed peace. These circumstances and the radical democratic notions of the Jeffersonian era determined our professional organization.

In England, as now, the legal profession was organized in two branches. The upper branch, barristers or counselors, were alone eligible for judicial office and had exclusive exercise of the function of advocacy. This branch was well organized in societies coming down from the Middle Ages, had high professional traditions, professional discipline, control of admission to its ranks, and a decayed system of legal education which, nevertheless, was capable of being modernized and made effective. The lower branch, attorneys, solicitors, did the work of client-caretaking and acted as agents for their clients in litigation. Although some American jurisdictions made a distinction between counselors and attorneys, it soon came to little in practice, and "attorney and counselor" became the American rule. But the attorney furnished the model rather than the counselor. The profession was not organized in any real sense. As in the case of attorneys and solicitors in England, each court had its roll of practitioners, there was no professional discipline, the power of the courts to remove from the roll was exercised in flagrant cases only, and the training was wholly by apprenticeship. Thus the bar was largely deprofessionalized. In rural circuits the close daily contact of a small bar, each well known to his fellows, served to maintain traditional professional standards. But with the obsolescence of the practice of going circuit and the rise of large urban bars, containing numbers who are wholly unknown to their fellow practitioners, it ceased to be possible to keep up traditional standards in this way. Gradually also a differentiation took place and three well-defined groups became set off from the main body of the bar, namely, a well-educated, well-trained stratum at the top, an uneducated, untrained, or ill-trained stratum at the bottom, and a small group of none too scrupulous politician-lawyers. The practice of criminal law came to be almost exclusively the domain of the two last.

Readers of English fiction of the fore part of the last century will remember the condition of the lower branch of the profession in England at that time as there portrayed. Sampson Brass, Dodson & Fogg, and Quirk, Gammon & Snap are types that we recognize perfectly today. In England incorporation of the lower branch of the profession, with the consequent introduction of discipline, professional feeling, and requirements of education and professional training, have effected a reform. We have moved more slowly. In the last quarter of the nineteenth century the rise of bar associations was the beginning of better things. These associations have done much for professional organization, professional ethics, and professional discipline. But they are voluntary organizations, and it has happened in some cities, and may happen anywhere, that the lower strata of the bar, seeing the advantages of voluntary organization, have formed organizations and exercised a sinister influence upon the administration of justice.

Three stages may be perceived in the development of the American bar. The first stage is marked by the leadership of the trial lawyer. The great achievements of the bar were in the forum, and the most conspicuous success was success before juries in the trial of criminal cases. The bench and the legislature were recruited from the trial bar. The law was largely fashioned to be a body of rules for use in the trial of causes. This stage lasted until the Civil War and still persists in some rural communities. In a second stage leadership passed to the railroad lawyer. The proof of professional success was to represent a railroad company. The leaders of the bar were permanently employed as defenders in civil causes and their energies, their ingenuity, and their learning were exercised in defeating or thwarting those who sought relief against public service companies in the courts. But where the bench was elective, because of popular suspicion of those companies, judges and legislators were seldom chosen from these leaders. Hence criminal law became the almost exclusive field of the lower stratum of the bar, and the recognized leaders in ability and learning ceased to be the official leaders as judges, prosecutors, and lawmakers. Today leadership seems to have passed to the client-caretaker. The office of a leader of the bar is a huge business organization. Its function is to advise, to organize, to reorganize, and direct busines enterprises, to point out dangers and mark safe channels and chart reefs for the business adventurer, and in our older communities to act, as one might say, as a steward for the absentee owners of our industries. The actual administration of justice in the courts interests him only as it discloses reefs or bars or currents to be avoided by the pilot of business men. Thus the leaders of the bar in the cities are coming to be divorced not only from the administration of criminal justice, but from the whole work of the courts, and the most effective check upon judicial administration of justice is ceasing to be operative.

It may be conceded that the economic causes which have turned the energies of the ablest and best trained in the profession into client-caretaking are inexorable, and that we may not hope to divert the leaders to less remunerative work and work of less magnitude with respect to the economic interests involved. But it does not follow that those who practise chiefly in the courts, and especially those who do the bulk of the work in criminal cases, should be uneducated, ill trained, and undisciplined.

Corporate organization of the bar, as at common law, and as both branches of the legal profession are now organized in England, and proper educational standards, both preliminary and professional, are items of the first moment in any plan for improving the administration of justice in our large cities. In such cities there must be many lawyers of foreign birth or foreign parentage. To confine the practice of law to any group, racial or linguistic or economic, would be to exclude other groups from their just share in making, interpreting, and applying the law, and thus to deprive them of their just share in a polity which is primarily legal. But it is vital that these lawyers should know the spirit of our polity; and that is the spirit of our common law. The mere rule-of-thumb training in local law and procedure or in meager generalities of definition and abstract principle which most of them now get in night law schools gives no adequate conception of our law nor of our legal institutions. However good their intentions, they cannot use the machinery of a common-law prosecution intelligently with such training, and it is no wonder that our legal system functions badly in their hands. Chapter III of the report on Prosecution, disclosing methods at variance not only with justice, but with the whole spirit of our institutions, should be read with these things in mind.

8. Penal Treatment at the End of the Eighteenth Century

Modern criminal science begins in the second half of the eighteenth century, after the classical treatise of Beccaria on crimes and punishments. But the movement for a rational and humane penal treatment which that treatise began did not affect our law till the end of the eighteenth century, when legislation began to provide imprisonment rather than death as a punishment for all but a few felonies. Thus our penal treatment was grafted on a system that proceeded on radically different ideas. The jail system, inherited from England, did not work badly in small country county-seats in the fore part of the nineteenth century, but became intolerable in the large city of the present century. The American Prison Congress was not organized till 1870, and the American Institute of Criminal Law and Criminology not until 1910. In other words, our system of penal treatment, experimental in its inception and grafted on a bad system, has had not much more than a century in which to develop, has been studied scientifically for not much more than a generation, and before it was much more than worked out for the conditions of agricultural America has had to be applied, as well as we might, to the predominantly urban America of today. These facts explain much.

THE PROBLEMS OF CRIMINAL JUSTICE IN THE AMERICAN CITY OF TODAY

1. Reshaping of the Substantive Criminal Law

From the foregoing discussion it will have been seen that before our criminal justice may function satisfactorily the chaotic, internally inconsistent, to a large extent anachronistic, condition of our substantive criminal law must be taken in hand. Both the report on Prosecution and the report on the Criminal Courts bring out the relative disproportion in the time devoted to civil as compared with criminal litigation. It is not that the former receives too much judicial attention, but that we have acquired a habit of neglecting the latter. This is true no less of the substance of the law. We have made great strides in the civil side of the law in a generation. Much has been done in civil procedure in the last two decades. But criminal law has stood still, and with a few notable exceptions in one or two localities criminal procedure remains what it was fifty years ago. Thus the neglect of the criminal law by the leaders of the bar, reflected in neglect of it in our law schools, bears fruit in a backward condition which is full of advantage to the law breaker and to those who make their livelihood by representing him. What we have to do is nothing less than to reshape the substantive criminal law so as to maintain the general security and the security of social institutions, and at the same time maintain the social interest in the human life of every individual, under the circumstances of the modern city; and we must do this upon the basis of traditional rules and principles in which the latter was chiefly regarded, and yet were warped in their application by those who regarded only the former.

This is too large a subject for the city. As things are it calls for nothing less than a ministry of justice, at least in each of our larger States; for our so-called departments of justice are but offices for legal advice to State officers, for representation of the State in its civil litigation, and for advocacy in the courts of review in criminal causes. In the federal government the Department of Justice is more. There it is a well-organized prosecuting bureau. But nowhere is it organized to study the functioning of our legal institutions, the application and enforcement of law, the cases in which and reasons for which it fails to do justice or to do complete justice, the new situations which arise continually and the means of meeting them, what legislation achieves its purpose and what not and why, and thus to give expert and intelligent guidance to those who frame and those who administer our laws. In the rural, agricultural society of the past, the judiciary committees of the two houses of the legislature could do efficiently so much of this as was needed. Today, even if our crowded legislative sessions allowed the time, no legislative committee is competent to the highly specialized work required. In consequence, commissions are provided from time to time to study particular subjects. But their work is not coördinated, there is no continuity in what they do nor in what successive legislatures do, and the whole process is wasteful, expensive and ineffective. A ministry of justice in the foregoing sense was proposed by Jeremy Bentham during the English legislative reform movement of the last century. It was approved by the Conference of Bar Association Delegates at the meeting of the American Bar Association in 1917. It was recommended in 1918 by a Parliamentary Commission headed by Lord Haldane as one of the chief items in a plan for reconstruction of the British administrative system.[1] It deserves to be kept in mind by American lawyers as one of the things to be provided in the inevitable reconstruction of our administrative system in a country in which the center of gravity has definitely shifted to the city.

2. Organization of the Administration of Justice

It is no less urgent, and more immediately practicable, to organize the administration of justice as a whole and in all its branches, to prune the accumulation of checks and mitigating agencies which discourage prosecuting witnesses and afford opportunity of escape to the guilty without profiting the innocent (see, for example, the manner in which preliminary examinations are conducted in the Municipal Court, as disclosed in the report on Prosecution), to coördinate responsibility and power, putting both in a few conspicuous officials charged with authority to supervise and direct and plan and enforce their policies, and with responsibility for the due functioning of criminal justice, and to correlate the judicial and administrative agencies, so that, instead of acting independently, and sometimes in conflict, they will operate with one known policy in all things and will not be able to shift responsibility from one to the other or let it fall down between them, as in the Raleigh prosecution. Only in this way is it possible to insure an efficient machine to dispose of the great volume of prosecution required in the modern city and enforce the great mass of police regulation demanded by the conditions of urban life.

Specifically, three points are to be urged:

(i) Unification of Courts

The system of courts should be unified. An administrative head should be provided with large powers of organizing judicial business, of systematizing the assignment of cases to judges and judges to types of work, of applying the judicial force where the exigencies of the work demand, and of applying it upon that work to the best advantage. Thus, in place of rotation of judges dictated by political exigencies, the personnel of the bench would be employed systematically and intelligently, as the size and importance of the work demand. Also he should have power,

---

[1] See Judge Cardozo's "Ministry of Justice," 35 Harv. L. Rev. 113.

in connection with a council of judges, to initiate and determine policies so that the unseemly spectacle of two judges of coördinate jurisdiction applying the same law in two wholly different ways in two adjoining rooms shall come to an end, and he should be responsible for the due functioning of the judicial system in all these respects.

(ii) Organization of the Prosecuting System

The prosecuting system should be unified. The administrative head of the system should have full power to control and responsibility for the acts of his subordinates. He should be required to keep proper records of all that goes on in the course of a prosecution from the beginning, with recorded reasons for his action in types of proceeding where the law, made for simpler conditions, now requires what has become a perfunctory approval by the court. He should be a part of an organized general prosecuting system of the State, not a wholly independent functionary. Note, for example, in the report on Prosecution the extent to which the public prosecutor may, if he chooses, neglect to assist the court of review with proper briefs or arguments. No publicity attends his neglect of that duty, and he has it in his power to present the State's side of a criminal appeal or not, wholly as he likes. In the same way he may coöperate with or operate independently or even thwart the police, and they are in a like position with respect to him. Criminal investigation and preparation of causes for trial have reached a high degree of development. But our prosecuting system is not adapted to the one, and except in sensational cases, its methods with respect to the other are usually crude in comparison with those employed in civil litigation. If nothing else were to be considered, the mere waste of energy involved in an unorganized prosecuting system ought not to be tolerated in view of the volume of criminal business in the courts of a modern city. To no small extent the effectiveness of English criminal justice is due to the centralized administrative supervision exercised by the Director of Public Prosecutions. His vigilant scrutiny of what is done and what is not done by local prosecuting agencies has no parallel in our State prosecuting organization.

(iii) Organization of Administrative Agencies

All administrative agencies, including the work now done in connection with the administration of justice by sheriffs, coroners, clerks, bailiffs, and probation officers, should be unified and organized under a responsible head, put in proper relation to the head of the judicial system, so as to eliminate friction and insure uniform policies in judicial and administrative action. This administrative head should have the power to determine the details of organization as circumstances require, to systematize and supervise, to initiate and enforce policies, and to set up such technical and expert adjuncts to the court as the business before it may require. He should be responsible for the proper functioning of this part of the administration of justice. He could easily save enough by proper organization and improved administrative methods to justify his position on that score alone. If for no other reasons, organization of the administrative agencies of our judicial system is demanded by considerations of expense. The cost of administering criminal justice in the modern city by methods devised for wholly different conditions precludes doing many things as they should be done, while wasting money in doing other things that need not be done, or in doing them in clumsy and expensive fashion. The enormous sums of money which we spend each year in the judicial administration of justice and its administrative incidents must eventually invite scrutiny of the mode in which those sums are employed. Through the fault of no person, but because of the system made for other times and different conditions, they are not employed to the best advantage. Nor can they be so long as city and county administration of justice go on parallel and independent in the same urban area, overlapping in many things, duplicating machinery unnecessarily, and without effective correlation of activities. Other functions of government are requiring and will continue to require increased expenditures and exacting taxation. Every source of expense that competes with them must justify itself by economy and efficiency. Here as elsewhere these things are not to be had through a decentralized congeries of independent functionaries, but by organization, system, supervision, and concentrated responsible authority.

3. Adequate Provision for Petty Prosecutions

Comparison of the facilities provided for and time spent upon small civil causes as compared with small criminal causes calls for serious reflection. The statistics on this head in the report on Prosecution and the report on Criminal Courts may be duplicated in almost any metropolitan area, and are a reproach to American administration of justice. It is at this point that the administration of criminal justice touches immediately the greatest number of people. It is at this point that the great mass of an urban population, whose experience of law is too likely to have been only an experience of arbitrary discretion of police officers and off-hand action of magistrates, tempered by political influence, might be taught the spirit of our institutions and made to feel that the law was a living force for securing their interests. Such extra-legal proceedings as those by summons in the municipal prosecutor's office, proceedings with no warrant in law and hence no legal safeguards that may easily degenerate into violation of constitutional rights under color of legal authority, should give way to a proper administrative organization whereby the courts in our large cities could function legally as bureaus of justice. The legal profession as a whole has little interest in petty prosecutions. But for the very reason that these proceedings are in consequence withdrawn from the field of active scrutiny by the bulk of the profession our bar associations should be zealous to see that adequate provision is made for them. Few of the leaders of the profession are aware of the actual situation, and when the facts are stated publicly, some of the best, most public-spirited, and most respected members of the bar are not unlikely to assume that such things cannot be true and to denounce those who reveal them as agitators or muck-rakers.

4. Preventive Methods

Preventive justice is no less important than preventive medicine. If we think of the legal order in terms of social engineering, it must be evident that sanitary engineering is not the least important feature. Prevention at the source rather than penal treatment afterward must be a large item in dealing with crime. Cleveland is well awake to this, and has well-organized institutions for social work. But no survey would be complete that did not emphasize the importance of correlating these institutions and agencies with police, prosecution, judicial organization, and agencies of penal treatment. There ought to be no possibility of misunderstanding, friction, or cross-purposes. And this requires that the administrative agencies connected with the administration of justice be unified and organized under a responsible head.

5. Justice in Family Relations

Conditions of crowded urban life, periodical unemployment, shifting of labor from city to city, and economic pressure threaten the security of the social institutions of marriage and the family and call for special consideration in organizing the courts of our large cities. Administration of justice in relations of family life is difficult for two reasons: one is that it involves questions on the borderline between law and morals, where, from its very nature, law is least efficacious; the other is that proper judicial adjustment of controversies involving those relations calls for wide discretion and yet they involve matters more tender than any that can come before tribunals. Such questions must be dealt with as a whole, not piecemeal, partly in criminal prosecutions, partly in juvenile courts, partly in petty proceedings before magistrates, and partly in courts having jurisdiction to appoint guardians. They must be dealt with by strong judges with large experience and trained intuitions. Anything less is a denial of justice to the mass of the population which cannot afford protracted legal proceedings in many courts. Anything less is a menace to the most fundamental of social institutions. To achieve these things the courts and administrative agencies connected therewith must be unified so that causes may be disposed of as a whole, without repeated partial threshings over of the same straw in separate proceedings, and so that causes that call for strong judges may receive the treatment they deserve without regard to the sums of money involved.

6. Unshackling of Administration

Above all, effective administration of criminal justice in the modern American city calls for an unshackling of administration from the bonds imposed when men who had little experience of popular government and much experience of royal government sought to make rules do the whole work of the legal order. The principle involved in the constitutional separation of powers is really no more than the principle involved in all specialization. Certain things which involve special training or special competency or special attention are done better by those who devote thereto their whole time or their whole attention for the time being. Hence if the officers of a court may best gather and study statistics of judicial administration to the end that such administration be improved; if they may best conduct psychological laboratories or psychopathological examinations or laboratories for the study of criminals, there is really nothing in the nature of a court to prevent. There is no reason why the courts in metropolitan areas may not be so organized as to permit these things, although they are not needed or are less needed in rural areas and hence are not provided for therein. The nineteenth-century political idea of uniformity over geographic areas, thinking in feudal terms of soil rather than of human beings peopling the soil, is not applicable to States of today in which populations greater than those in whole States when this idea took root in our State constitutions are compressed within a few square miles of municipal jurisdiction. A unification of administrative agencies with power to adapt administration to the peculiar needs of particular localities must supersede rigid uniformity over areas laid out according to the exigencies of the map. Regulation of public utilities, factory inspection, tenement house inspection, building laws, and a score of things of the sort have accustomed us to administrative boards and commissions with wide powers to organize their business and large administrative discretion. There are no such checks upon these boards and commissions as are operative in the case of courts. And yet, for historical reasons, we are loth to confer upon judicial administrative agencies the latitude which we freely concede to newly created executive agencies. Undoubtedly one of the tasks of American law today is to work out an adequate system of administrative law. But there is no reason to suppose that judicial administration is not as adequate to this task as executive administration.

STATE AND CITY

For the larger part of what it needs in the way of machinery to cope with crime the city must depend upon action by the State legislature or even amendments of the State constitution. The State may do anything not prohibited by the federal constitution. The State legislature may do anything not prohibited by federal and State constitutions. The city may do only what the State empowers it to do. Hence in order to adapt the institutions devised for rural conditions of the past to the rapidly changing urban conditions of today, it must first induce action by those who live under quite different conditions, to whom the methods and agencies developed for rural communities of the last century seem entirely adequate. When there are several large cities in a State, each with its own problems, and a large agricultural population with preponderant political power, proper provision for the special needs of criminal justice in the city becomes a matter of much difficulty. Here again a unified judicial organization for the whole State and organization of the administrative agencies of justice for the whole State, under a head responsible for insuring an adequate functioning of the legal system in each locality, and clothed with power to make the proper adjustments to that end, may bring about the right compromises between urban and rural needs from time to time as occasion requires, and preserve the balance as changes take place, without disturbance of the fundamental organization.

CHAPTER V

LOCAL AND TEMPORARY DIFFICULTIES

EXCEPTIONALLY RAPID GROWTH

FEATURES of the administration of criminal justice which may be found in large cities throughout the country and difficulties which operate in all American cities to a greater or less degree are exaggerated in Cleveland because of exceptionally rapid growth in population and rapid industrial expansion. A city which has increased in population so rapidly and in so large a proportion within the past decade may not expect that its legal institutions will keep pace with such expansion.

INSTABILITY OF THE INDUSTRIAL POPULATION

Another factor of importance is the mobile population due to the rapidity of industrial expansion in recent years. In May, 1920, there were 127,285 children in the public schools of Cleveland. Between June, 1920, and April, 1921, 40,300 children in the public schools changed their residence. Of these, 5,063 moved out of the city. The figures at hand indicate that a little more than 63,000, or more than 40 per cent. of the whole number of children in the public schools, moved during the past year. In some instances the same child moved twice or oftener during that time. These figures show a high degree of mobility among the relatively stable part of the industrial population represented by children in the schools. Data from the census of 1920 as to the mobility of the population of Cleveland are not yet available and will not be published for some time to come. The census of 1910 showed that 52.8 per cent. of the population was born in Ohio, 11.9 per cent. in other States, and 35 per cent. in foreign countries. Since that time the city population has increased nearly a quarter of a million.

Some studies made during the war indicate that the moral implications of an increasingly migratory laboring population call for serious consideration. Our institutions presuppose a stable, home-owning, tax-paying population, of which each individual has and feels a personal interest in its legal and political institutions and bears his share in the

[54]

conduct of them. Irregularity and discontinuity of employment and consequent migration from city to city, or back and forth between city and country, preclude the sort of society for which our institutions were shaped. That these things must make for crime and for the bad functioning of criminal justice in a large urban population is self-evident, and is shown abundantly by the facts disclosed by this survey. A survey of the industrial situation with reference to these things would no doubt disclose much that might be used with effect in preventing crime.

POST-WAR CONDITIONS

Finally, a temporary difficulty of some moment is to be seen in the conditions following the war. Legal history shows us that crime has always increased notably for a time after a long or hard war. In this country the increase of crime after the Revolution and after the Civil War was marked. In England it was especially notable after the Napoleonic wars. It is well marked in Europe today. The economic and social conditions which contribute to this phenomenon are especially pronounced in the large city. Moreover, the circumstances of the late war, during which laborers were highly paid and all members of the family were employed, leading to habits and modes of life which do not readily readjust, coöperate with the habits of rough and ready action and callousness toward life and limb and property, which every war has developed for a time. Thus the conditions arose which came to be known as "crime waves." These things belong to a social and economic survey rather than to a survey of criminal justice. Yet we must take account of them in any appraisal of the functioning of criminal justice during the past three years.

Thus far I have considered the difficulties involved in the administration of criminal justice in an American city of today, seeking to connect the conditions found in Cleveland with those that exist to some degree in all our cities, and have considered the ultimate remedies. This is a necessary background. It shows also that remedying many of the clear evils involved must be a slow process, and that the remedies immediately available may not be expected to achieve permanent results. Yet they may improve the administration of criminal justice in Cleveland a great deal. These immediate measures of improvement will be considered in the following pages.

CHAPTER VI

POLICE

IN reading Mr. Fosdick's study of police administration in Cleveland one must be struck with the relation of the points which he brings out to those which are disclosed in the studies of courts, of prosecutors, and of penal treatment. In each case the primary difficulties arise from "transient administration," suitable enough in a rural community of the nineteenth century, and from trying to meet the needs of an urban community of today by merely adding numbers to the administrative force or by adding further incoördinated administrative agencies to a system which was devised originally for a small town.

Seven points in connection with the report upon police, most of which will recur in one form or another in each of the other reports, deserve to be noted. These are: (1) The transition from rural to urban and thence to metropolitan conditions has been met not by intelligent reconstruction, but by patching and addition of numbers; (2) lack of continuity in administration; (3) rigidity of organization, making adjustment to the exigencies of rapid growth and exceptional diversity of population impossible; (4) a tendency to perfunctory routine growing out of the foregoing circumstances; (5) division of power and diffused, ill-defined responsibility, making it difficult to hold any one to account for unsatisfactory results; (6) an assumption of versatility on the part of the officials and subordinates, whereby they are expected to do specialized work offhand in a system of frequent rotation without any adequate provision for the specialization involved in the large undertaking of enforcing the criminal law in a modern city; (7) want of provision for intelligent study of the functioning of administrative machinery, either by those who operate it or by others.

(1) As growth in population takes place the staple resource of our lawmakers has been to provide more offices, more officials to each office, and more administrative machinery of the same sort as that already existing. Hence no student of American legal and political institutions need be surprised to learn from Mr. Fosdick's report that Cleveland's police force of 1921 is little more than the police department of 1866 magnified. We shall not appreciate what this means if we say merely

that the population now is more than eight times what it was before. For the difference between the Cleveland of that day and the Cleveland of today is one of kind, not merely one of degree. The change has been treated as if it were but one of degree. A few examples discussed in the report on police will bring this out.

Thus it appears that the patrol force is distributed and managed exactly as it was thirty years ago, and the patrol routine is determined by a tradition coming down from a time when demands upon and conditions of the patrol service were wholly different. The complete change in these demands and conditions in recent years has brought little change in the method of distribution of the patrol force or in the supervision of its operations. Again, we are told that the radical change in the population of Cleveland and the consequences thereof for police administration have brought about nothing new in the detective service except new faces and a few meager records. In Cleveland, as everywhere else, it has been assumed that given a certain number of officers, administrative machinery would somehow run of its own motion. Nor will it do to say that money is lacking or has been lacking to do more. A system of patching and of adding more men to an organization made for different circumstances consumes money in doing needless things. See, for instance, the reports on 16 cases of burglary in January, 1921, set out in Chapter VIII of Mr. Fosdick's report. Such expenditure of time and money in perfunctory routine is worse than useless. A system that allows such things to go on indefinitely without scrutiny and with provision of more of the same sort as a staple remedial device cannot be expected to leave money available for needed facilities in a metropolitan community.

(2) "Transient administration," as Mr. Fosdick well puts it, "is fatal to success in any complex technical enterprise." The public business is the only sort of business in which it is tolerated in the United States of today. Every part of the administration of criminal justice suffers from it. It is one of the legacies of pioneer America. It results in almost complete want of continuity in administration, leading to want of settled policy, conflict of policy between successive incumbents, and waste of time and effort by each incumbent in learning what ought to be a known body of organized experience handed down from official to official, continually added to and continually adapted by trained intelligence to the newer conditions as they arise. But such things are impossible unless the head of the police is a permanent official, chosen without regard to politics or to geography. The pioneer notion of short tenure and selection from among the voters of a politico-geographical area is out of place in the city of today.

(3) Rigid organization applied to the entire force regardless of the differences in the types of work appropriate to the different branches of police service and regardless of the shiftings of population, changes in the character of localities, and rise of new sorts of crime and instruments of wrongdoing, is an obstacle to police efficiency, just as rigidity of organization impedes efficiency of the courts and, indeed, of all the administrative agencies of criminal justice. A striking example may be seen in the organization of patrolling. The city is divided into precincts, which are in effect so many separate police departments with their own records, their own hierarchy of rank, their own complement of men, and an organized system of commanding and of supervising officers. The occasion of this precinct organization is to be found in old-time conditions of transportation and of the attempt to solve the problem of police distribution in view of those conditions. When policemen had to go on foot or on horseback to their posts and to the station where they reported, it was necessary to set up substations where they could meet and report and from which they could be sent out. Motor cycles and motor cars have obviated the conditions for which the organization grew up. But the hard and fast geographical lines and precinct organization remain and are unaffected by continual changes in the character of the several districts and in the problem they present to police administration. Mr. Fosdick's recommendations in this respect deserve thorough consideration, not only in themselves, but because the condition of rigid organization on which he comments is not confined to the police but pervades the whole administration of criminal justice.

(4) Lack of continuity, rigid organization, and division of responsibility result in administrative lethargy. Officials become caught, as it were, in the cogs of the machinery and cease to bestir themselves to effect results or to take advantage of the opportunities of their positions. They easily fall into a perfunctory routine and work in a rut, laborious and conscientious it may be, but without intelligence or constructive policy. The poor work of the detective bureau shown in Chapter VIII of the report on Police Administration, the poor development of crime prevention shown in Chapter IX, the circumstance that Cleveland was the only city of over half a million population at the date of this survey which was without policewomen, the want of adequate provision for use of motors in patrolling and in police work generally, as set forth in Chapter VII, and the stereotyped, unelastic work of the civil service commission set forth in Chapter IV, will be found paralleled by a like failure to rise to the opportunities of administration disclosed in the report on prosecution. These things are not to be attributed to the de-

ficiencies of persons holding office for the time being. They are deep seated in our administrative system. The development of police training schools in Cleveland, a notable administrative achievement, shows that, in spite of the system, individual ingenuity and capacity will do things. Yet by their very contrast such achievements serve to emphasize the condition of drift which must go with lack of continuous policy, rigid organization, and divided or undefined or non-located responsibility.

(5) Division of power, diffused, ill-defined, and non-located responsibility, are obstacles to efficient working of the administration of criminal justice in every department. In police administration in Cleveland we find a conspicuous example in the undefined line between the authority of the chief of police and the authority of the director of public safety, (discussed in Chapter III of Mr. Fosdick's report), the curious situation in which the chief of police is responsible to the mayor for incompetency, but to the director of public safety for the conduct of his work, the falling down of responsibility for discipline between the chief and the director, and the system of two officials with much power to check and thwart each other, but with little power of assured initiative and with indefinite responsibility. Another example may be seen in the divided power with respect to discipline, discussed in Chapter IV. Still another may be seen in the lack of coördination between the civil service commission and the police department, also discussed in Chapter IV. Such things are characteristic of all American administration and have come down to us from pioneer conditions, where division of power had an important function and operated to meet real needs of society. Mr. Fosdick's recommendation that power be concentrated in a single responsible expert administrative head of the police force is in line with what must be done in every department of the administration of criminal justice if it is to be effective for its purpose.

(6) Police administration suffers especially from what Kipling calls the American idea of versatility—the idea that any man can do anything. A general in the Civil War tells us that for a time the notion prevailed in the North that 1,000 men, plus 1,000 horses, plus 1,000 sabres, would make a cavalry regiment. It was no matter that the men knew nothing about the care of horses. There was a lively faith that they would be able to put up their horses in some sort of peripatetic livery stable at the end of the day's march. In the same way we assume that 100 men, plus 100 uniforms, plus 100 clubs, will make 100 policemen. As Mr. Fosdick points out, most policemen are recruited from occupations whose character is as far removed as can be from the character of the work which they are to do. Naturally, there is a large turnover of police

personnel which is incompatible with effective work. This pioneer idea of succession in public employ, of continual rotation, and that there is no need of careful development of specialists for special tasks stands in the way of effective criminal justice in the modern city in every connection. Examples in police administration in Cleveland are to be seen in the work of the detective bureau, as set forth in Chapter VIII, and the want of adequate provision for prevention of crime, as set forth in Chapter IX. One need not have made a special study of police to perceive the cogency of Mr. Fosdick's argument as to the need of specialization in both connections. His recommendations on these points should be noted particularly.

(7) Finally here, as everywhere else, in our administration of criminal justice, there is no provision and there are no facilities for intelligent study of the functioning of the machinery by those who operate it or are responsible for its operation. There was no need for such study in the rural or small urban community of the nineteenth century. The things that had to be done were simple and were within the comprehension of the average intelligent citizen. It is otherwise with the questions which come up in police administration today. Such matters as those to which Mr. Fosdick calls attention—organization of the patrol service, the use of motors in police work, recruiting and organization of the detective force, organization of the clerical work of the police department, and special service in crime prevention—must be studied constantly in the light of metropolitan conditions exactly as similar problems of organization and management are studied in a modern business establishment. To take one more instance, set forth in Chapter X of the report on police, the detailing of detectives and sergeants of police to do clerical work is an outgrowth of the simpler conditions of the past, when there was little of such work to be done and the policemen could easily do it themselves. Today such a system involves waste of money and waste of administrative power. But there is no one person who is responsible for studying such conditions or has power to deal with them effectively. Hence there is no pressure upon any one comparable to the competition in business which compels the business man to be a vigilant student of the functioning of his plant or to go to the wall.

All the recommendations in the report on police depend upon the one pivotal point of entrusting complete authority to and concentrating full responsibility in a single directing head with permanent tenure, making police service an independent department, as is now done in the majority of the large cities of the United States. The details are in Chapter III of Mr. Fosdick's report, and it would not be useful to repeat them. But the central idea of "a direct line of responsibility running from a single head down through the whole organization," and of avoiding all "short circuits of responsibility," is one which cannot be urged too strongly. Overhauling of the whole administrative machinery of criminal justice with this idea before us is the remedy to which every part of the survey unmistakably points.

CHAPTER VII

PROSECUTION

TWO significant facts are the starting-point from which we must begin in considering the prosecuting system in Cleveland today. The county prosecutor's office was created and its functions were defined more than one hundred years ago, and its traditions and methods had been definitely shaped at the time of the Civil War. The municipal prosecutor's office was created in 1854, and its traditions and methods are still those of the old-time police court prosecutor. It is impressive to compare the one county prosecutor of 1863, when the population of Cleveland was 58,000, when there were 60 indictments and 1,600 arrests in a year, and when the criminal code contained 249 sections, with the eight (one prosecutor and seven assistants) county prosecutors of today, working in a county population of 940,000, with 2,700 indictments and 27,000 arrests each year, and enforcing a criminal code of 1,053 sections. That indictments are 45 times as many, arrests about 17 times as many, and crimes defined by statute four times as many, as in 1863 are impressive facts. But to put it thus is to divert attention from the most significant fact. What we have to deal with is not merely an enormous increase in population, in the number of indictments, in the number of arrests and in the number of legislatively defined crimes. It is a radical change in the conditions and character of crimes and in the environment of prosecutions. The multiplication of the number of prosecutors by eight and of the payroll of the office by 24, which has gone along with the growth in population and in the volume of criminal prosecution, might well have sufficed if there had been a simple question of multiplication. That easy resource has proved unequal to a situation which is not the situation of 1863 multiplied by eight, or by 12, or by 24, but a wholly new one to which the methods and the machinery of 1863 are not adapted.

In connection with the report on Police Administration I suggested seven points of general significance which related the difficulties in police administration in Cleveland today with those found in other departments of criminal justice. It will be worth while to note these identical points as they are brought out no less clearly in the report on prosecution.

(1) Transition from rural to urban and thence to metropolitan conditions has not been met by intelligent reconstruction, but simply by addition of more men and expenditure of more money. Take the municipal prosecutor: the methods of his office are still the methods of the date of its origin—before the Civil War. There is no system or organization whatever, as, indeed, there did not need to be in the simple conditions of that time. Old-time casual methods of indiscriminate lumping of all sorts of cases on one docket, the want of any intelligent segregation of the work, and the consequent disorder and delay which wear out witnesses and lead many lawyers to avoid practice on the criminal side of the municipal court, were proper enough in the police court of a city of 58,000 inhabitants with a municipal code of 100 standing ordinances.[1]

It was well enough then to have no system of segregating cases, to have no system of keeping affidavits,[2] to have no records or file or docket, but rely wholly on the court docket for such information as could not be held in the prosecutor's memory,[3] to have no stenographic record of the testimony on preliminary examinations[4] and to make no systematic preparation of the cases prosecuted.[5] The whole process disclosed is that of the old-time country law office with relatively few cases to be tried at periodical terms with intervals between them where pencil memoranda on the back of a few files will eke out memory and suffice for all purposes. To conduct such an office efficiently under the conditions of today there must be system and organization and intelligent segregation of cases, as well as numerous assistants. So long as the latter is the sole expedient relied upon to cope with the difficulties of the office it is no wonder that complaint is made of insufficient time to handle the great volume of work effectively. Nor is it strange that perjury is rife and prosecution ineffective when there is no stenographic report of the testimony in preliminary examinations. Under such circumstances the testimony at the trial may vary from that at the preliminary examination without any check, and there is not sufficient material available for preparation on the part of the trial prosecutor. Nor is any indubitable proof at hand upon which to prosecute for perjury. If one compares this practice, suitable enough in the Cleveland of fifty years ago, with the English practice,[6] he may perceive another reason for the ineffectiveness

---

[1] The municipal prosecutor's office was created in 1854. The Revised Ordinances of Cleveland of 1855 contained 109 standing ordinances.

[2] Report on Prosecution, p. 35.

[3] Ibid., p. 36.   [4] Ibid., p. 32.   [5] Ibid., pp. 53–54.

[6] Ibid., pp. 117–118.

of the criminal justice here as compared with English cities of greater population.

In the county prosecutor's office, except for a good system of records and provision of a managing clerk in June of the present year, little has been done beyond adding a corps of assistants to differentiate the office from a country prosecutor's office of today or from the office as it was in Cleveland sixty years ago. The result is what Mr. Bettman happily terms "a system of serial unpreparedness,"[1] inevitable when a prosecutor in a city of 800,000 inhabitants and a calendar of over 2,700 indictments each year uses methods coming down from a time when 60 indictments were a year's work and the single prosecutor could rely on his own memory. This seems to have been aggravated by a practice of so arranging the work of the assistants that the trial prosecutor shall not know in advance what case he is to try.[2] This practice, which obviously makes prosecution feeble and inefficient, seems to have been thought necessary to prevent improper influences from being brought to bear upon an assistant who is known to be in charge of a case.[3] Thus the absence of organization and of responsible administrative control compels resort to devices that merely add to the existing ineffectiveness.

(2) Want of continuity in administration is a cause of ineffectiveness in prosecution no less than in the work of the police. Thus, in Mr. Bettman's report[4] we find that in January, 1921, 12 of the first 16 cases tried before one of the judges in the criminal branch of the Court of Common Pleas resulted in acquittals. This is too large a percentage of failure to be accounted for even by the want of systematic preparation for trial which has prevailed in all prosecution in Cleveland and is a legacy of the past. The opinion of the trial judge[5] that the entire change in personnel involved in a change of administration was a considerable factor in this unfortunate result seems entirely warranted. If the reader will note the complete turnover in the personnel of the force on January 1, 1921,[6] he cannot but see that even if there had been proper organization and systematic methods of preparation, it would not have been easy to enter at once upon the trial of 16 cases and to give proper attention immediately to more than 800 indictments. If there are reasons for periodical election of the prosecuting attorney,—which is at least debatable,—some degree of permanent organization in the office is clearly required. When there were but 60 indictments each year, a new prosecutor could come into office on January 1 and pick up in a few days the relatively few

---

[1] Report on Prosecution, p. 86.   [2] *Ibid.*, p. 89.   [3] *Ibid.*, p. 77.
[4] *Ibid.*, p. 88.   [5] *Ibid.*, p. 88.   [6] *Ibid.*, p. 80.

threads that would enable the work of the office to go forward effectively. Under the conditions of today this is impossible.

(3) Rigidity of organization is another factor in the ineffectiveness of prosecution, as in the ineffectiveness of police administration. Both the county prosecutor's office and the municipal prosecutor's office are laid out along hard and fast lines of three grades of assistants at fixed, graded salaries. In practice these assistants are largely independent functionaries, acting on their own responsibility.[1] In the case of the municipal prosecutor, the assistants are appointed by the director of law, the same as their chief. In the case of the county prosecutor, the assistants are appointed by the prosecuting attorney, but there seems to be a tradition or habit of independent action.[2] In effect the positions of assistant prosecutor have been treated as so many political jobs to be handed out, and the assistants have been set up as graded, more or less coördinate prosecutors, instead of an organized staff of subordinates. There is much excuse, therefore, for the incumbents who have not exerted themselves to introduce system and organization and improve methods needed to cope with the business with which the prosecutors' offices are now confronted. Struggling with a huge volume of work, and hampered by rigid lines imposed by law or by traditions of independent action on the part of assistants, who are coördinate rather than subordinate, it is no wonder that prosecutors in Cleveland have shown little initiative in adapting their offices to the work to be done and have not risen to the few opportunities that have been left open to them. The same situation of independent and unsupervised action of assistants is to be seen in many cities. Everywhere it produces the same results. It was much in evidence in the recent proceedings against a prosecuting attorney in metropolitan Boston.

(4) Naturally, as we have seen already in police administration, the conditions just discussed, coupled with division of power and diffused, ill-defined responsibility, have given rise to a tendency to make of prosecution a perfunctory routine—a tendency which is destructive of efficiency. In the municipal prosecutor's office this is strikingly manifest in the purely negative rôle of the prosecutor in trials in the municipal court,[3] in the perfunctory preparation of cases,[4] in the perfunctory drawing of affidavits which often results ultimately in throwing out the case before the grand jury or *nolle prosequi* because the offense charged does not correspond to facts provable,[5] in the perfunctory acquiescence in

---

[1] Report on Prosecution, p. 35.   [2] *Ibid.*, p. 78.   [3] *Ibid.*, p. 30.
[4] *Ibid.*, pp. 54, 55.   [5] *Ibid.*, p. 55.

suspension or mitigation of sentence,[1] in the former laxity as to enforcement of bail bonds,[2] and in the perfunctory attention or lack of attention to the execution of sentences.[3] When we remember that admittedly there is much more than enough work for the whole force of the prosecutor's office to do, the perfunctory presence of an assistant in court in cases in which there is really nothing for him to do[4] is a conspicuous example of how a routine may develop which involves waste of power, precludes efficiency, and prevents realizing of the possibilities which exist even in an outworn system.[5]

In the county prosecutor's office there are many examples of the same tendency, such as perfunctory preparation of cases which, under the circumstances of today, amounts to no preparation,[6] perfunctory observance merging into non-observance of the rule as to reasons for nolles,[7] the former laxity in watching bail proceedings,[8] laxity in the requirements of statute with respect to mitigation of sentence,[9] laxity as to the rule requiring that the court be furnished with a list of known criminals against whom prosecutions are pending,[10] perfunctory examination of trial jurors,[11] and laxity in following cases to the appellate court.[12] This tendency to make important features of prosecution into a mere perfunctorily followed ritual is destructive of efficiency and explains much in the "Mortality Tables" in Mr. Bettman's report.[13]

(5) More fundamental and more serious is the division of power and diffused, ill-defined responsibility which we have seen already in police administration. This is especially clear in the office of the municipal prosecutor, and its results are manifest in Chapter II of the report on Prosecution. In the first place the municipal prosecutor has no real control of his own office. His assistants are appointed by the director of law. But the latter devotes his attention almost exclusively to civil litigation of the city. Hence the assistant prosecutors are substantially without executive control or supervision, and each pursues his own policy or lack of policy, his own interpretation of the law, and his own methods.[14] With no real records to act as a check, in that, in contrast with the practice in civil cases, the records and files do not show who acted in any particular case,[15] responsibility for the wide powers of "no papering" and *nolle prosequi* falls down between the prosecutor, the assistants, and the

---

[1] Report on Prosecution, pp. 56, 57.   [2] *Ibid.*, p. 71.   [3] *Ibid.*, pp. 68–70.

[4] *Ibid.*, p. 113.   [5] *Ibid.*, p. 118.   [6] *Ibid.*, p. 84.

[7] *Ibid.*, p. 95.   [8] *Ibid.*, p. 98.   [9] *Ibid.*, p. 96.

[10] *Ibid.*, p. 89.   [11] *Ibid.*, p. 77.   [12] *Ibid.*, p. 101.   [13] *Ibid.*, pp. 7–11.

[14] *Ibid.*, p. 35.   [15] *Ibid.*, p. 47.

court.[1] The opportunities for sinister influence upon the administration of justice in the lax practice of "no papering" are apparent.[2] No doubt, with the small calendars of sixty years ago, reliance upon memory served well enough. Today, when the number of State cases "no papered" in the municipal court is about one-third of the whole criminal calendar of 1863, it is evident that the proceeding needs a check. But nobody is responsible for providing an effective one. A like situation is disclosed in the matter of accepting pleas of lesser offense,[3] and in the power of so presenting or failing to present a case to the grand jury as to result in the grand jury failing to bring in an indictment.[4] A result is to be seen on pages 11 to 12 of the report on the Criminal Courts. A system under which, in ten years, the same person can be before the courts from 10 to 18 times, largely on charges of robbery, burglary, and larceny, which make it clear that he is a habitual or professional offender, and can escape at least half of the time by discharge on preliminary examination, no bill, nolle, plea to lesser offense, or suspended sentence, with no records showing who is responsible, is nothing short of an inducement to professional crime. Much has been said heretofore about the lack of proper preparation in criminal prosecutions, which is in startling contrast with the careful preparation of civil litigation in the offices of those who practise in civil cases. It is to be noted that some of the most serious features of this habitual unpreparedness on the part of the prosecution flow from divided responsibility.[5] Mr. Bettman's suggestion[6] that all State cases be put in exclusive charge of the county prosecutor from the outset is the beginning of any effective improvement of prosecution in Cleveland.

(6) Another legacy from pioneer or rural conditions which seriously impairs efficacy of prosecution is the assumption of versatility on the part of the prosecutor's assistants, which is involved in a system of choosing them on the basis of politics or of allotment among the different racial groups, and then throwing the work of the municipal prosecutor's office at them as chance dictates, with no distribution or specialization, presuming that they may all rotate from one sort of work to another with satisfactory results. In the old days of small calendars, a small penal code and a small body of standing ordinances, this assumption of versatility on the part of the prosecuting officer was sound enough, for no great versatility was involved. When, instead of one prosecutor to 60 cases, there comes to be one to 318, it is another story.

---

[1] Report on Prosecution, pp. 59–62. [2] Ibid., p. 60. [3] Ibid., p. 65.
[4] Ibid., p. 93. [5] Ibid., p. 122. [6] Ibid., p. 123.

(7) Again, in prosecution, as in police administration, it is no one's business to study the functioning of the system, nor are there adequate facilities open to those who are in some measure definitely responsible for the initiation of better methods, whereby they may be able to rise to that responsibility effectively. Such matters as modernizing the system of beginning every petty prosecution with arrest,[1] or provision of stenographic report of testimony at preliminary examinations,[2] with which all students of English prosecution are familiar, are left in the condition in which they were seventy-five years ago because no one is definitely charged with the responsibility of keeping the methods of prosecution abreast of the requirements of the time and of the best which experience elsewhere has developed, and in large part the crude system of records and the absence of any proper system of statistics of criminal justice do not enable the average prosecutor, however well intentioned, to form any adequate conception of how his office is, in fact, functioning.

Results of the foregoing defects in the prosecuting machinery in promoting perjury and subornation of perjury,[3] in creating suspicion of the whole administration of criminal justice on the part of those who witness its operation,[4] in affording opportunities for favoritism or corruption or abuse or extortion,[5] and especially in affording opportunities to the professional defender of accused persons,[6] are abundantly shown both in Mr. Bettman's report and in Chapter III of the report on the Criminal Courts. One cannot insist too strongly that the remedy is not more prosecutors or more patchwork tinkering along the lines of the past, but rather organization, permanence of tenure, unity and continuity of policy, and concentration of responsibility with commensurate power. Along with these must go a cutting off of the unnecessary steps in prosecution and a pruning away of the excess of mitigating agencies which have accumulated in the course of Anglo-American legal history.[7]

---

[1] Report on Prosecution, p. 116.   [2] *Ibid.*, p. 117.   [3] *Ibid.*, pp. 32, 117.
[4] *Ibid.*, p. 29.   [5] *Ibid.*, pp. 120–122.   [6] *Ibid.*, p. 122.
[7] See report on Criminal Courts, Chapter III.

CHAPTER VIII

CRIMINAL COURTS

C RIMINAL courts in Cleveland show other phases of the picture at which we have been looking in surveying police and prosecution. Here again the pivotal point is that institutions originally devised for rural or small-town conditions are failing to function effectively under metropolitan conditions. Here again a change in the character of the community in which criminal justice has to be administered has been treated as if no more were involved than an increase of population in the same sort of environment. Accordingly, multiplication of judges and patchwork adaptation have been the chief means by which to meet a situation that calls for thorough reorganization. But there is much excuse for the present state of the criminal courts in Cleveland, in that organization of courts is something of State concern, governed largely by constitutional provisions, and it is by no means easy to educate the State at large to the needs of modern cities when existing institutions are working well enough in the average locality, where the conditions for which they were framed still exist. Moreover, when growth takes place so rapidly and the character of a community changes within a generation it is not to be expected that the bar will appreciate at once the significance of growth and change in relation to judicial organization and administration. The natural and desirable conservatism of lawyers will lead them to seek to get along as well as may be with the institutions and legal machinery at hand. It will be convenient to consider certain facts as to the present functioning of the criminal courts in Cleveland under the same heads already made use of in connection with police and prosecution.

(1) On the criminal side there has been little reconstruction since the days when the system of courts was devised for a pioneer community. The Municipal Court on its criminal side is still, in its traditions, its methods, its modes of doing business, its records, and its whole atmosphere, a police court of a small town of the middle of the last century. One notable improvement, namely, the doing away with two trials on the merits in petty prosecutions by reviewing proceedings in the Municipal Court on misdemeanors within its jurisdiction only for

errors of law, stands out conspicuously. For the rest, there are simply more judges and more prosecutors. The Court of Common Pleas still operates on the system, appropriate to the past, of periodical terms of court with intervals between them. It is true that in Cleveland, as in all large cities where the system of terms is kept up, the intervals between the terms tend to disappear and there tends to be, in fact, a continuous sitting, except for a long vacation during the hot weather. But the organization of the business of the court with reference to terms still justifies in appearance the practice of preliminary examination and binding over to another tribunal which grew up to meet the exigencies of a time when the intervals between the terms were longer and the courts were sitting intermittently. Between these terms it was necessary for magistrates to conduct preliminary inquiries, bind over accused persons, and take the other necessary intermediate steps which could not be taken in the court when not in session. Again, the procedure of prosecution, good enough when there were 60 indictments a year, becomes impossible when there are 2,700 a year. The 14 steps in a prosecution set forth in the report on the Criminal Courts[1] have tended to increase rather than diminish in the endeavor to adjust this machinery to the exigencies of criminal justice in a large city.

Tinkering instead of intelligent reconstruction, and addition of new devices instead of simplification, have resulted in a cumbrous process which affords many opportunities to the habitual offender and opposes few checks to his doubtful activities.[2]

On the criminal side of the Municipal Court persistence of police court organization and traditions and methods is particularly unfortunate. The personnel of the bench appears to suffer in particular from that tradition. For if a tribunal is commonly known as a "police court," that fact is bound to affect the action of the public in determining what type of judge should sit therein. But, as is true in so many localities in America today, it suffers especially from the subjection of judges to pressure and the imposition upon them of a need of keeping in the public eye which is involved in the system of primary elections. As is well said in the report on courts,[3] this attempt to "adapt the democracy of the town meeting to a great cosmopolitan population" has disappointed the expectations of its authors. The real significance of this failure is that the primary system attempted to deal with new situations by tinkering old machinery; it took the elective bench, an institution of

---

[1] The Criminal Courts, p. 7.

[2] See Diagram 2, report on the Criminal Courts.   [3] Page 32.

the middle of the nineteenth century, for granted, and proposed to insure that more citizens participated actively in the election. Everyone could and probably did know the character and qualifications of the few conspicuous lawyers who were candidates for judicial office in the judicial district or of the rising young lawyers who sought election as police magistrate of the small town of 1850. Under the circumstances of that time the greater the number of citizens that voted, the more intelligent the choice was likely to be. Today, when the average citizen of Cleveland can know the lawyers and judges only from what he chances to read in the newspapers or as he chances to meet them in the course of litigation or in social activities, it is often true that the greater the number of citizens who vote, the more unintelligent the choice.

Again, the physical conditions and decorum of the tribunal are those of the old-time police court of a small town.[1] There is no segregation of cases, for this was not needed in the old-time police court.[2] The inadequate system of records is inherited from the police court and was good enough for the police court of a small town.[3] The scanty attention to cases which is so unfortunate a feature of the administration of criminal justice in the Municipal Court[4] belongs to the days when the police magistrate knew the town drunkard, as did all his neighbors, and could dispose of the case of Huck Finn's father offhand, with the assurance of one who knew. Today the method persists, but the personal knowledge on the part of the court and of the community which assured that justice would be done is no more. Without this check it results in opportunities for questionable influences in the case of real offenders, danger of irreparable injury to the occasional offender, who is not able to command such influences, and in consequence a general suspicion of the whole process which must affect the attitude of the public toward the administration of justice, no matter how unfounded. Such things as the shifting of cases from one judge to another, with no effective check upon the manner in and the reasons for which it is done, grow naturally out of the multiplication of judges, making the court not an organized entity, with systematized business methods, controlled by a responsible head on an intelligently determined policy, but a congeries of coördinate tribunals, each proceeding as if it had before it its own small volume of business, as if it had the intimate personal knowledge of the men and things before it, and was subject to the check of general knowledge of those men and things by the whole community which obtained in the large town or small city of the middle of the last century.

[1] Report on the Criminal Courts, pp. 50, 51.
[2] *Ibid.*, p. 52.   [3] *Ibid.*, pp. 64, 65.   [4] *Ibid.*, p. 54.

To a less degree the same phenomenon may be noted on the criminal side of the Court of Common Pleas. Increase of work has led to more judges of coördinate authority.[1] There is no executive head. The judges are free to have conflicting policies or to fluctuate in their policies.[2] Judicial approval in the case of *nolle prosequi*, which was effective in the days of 60 indictments in a year, and may well be a real check in a rural community or a small city, decays into an empty form.[3] The supreme court of Massachusetts has recently pointed out that the court must rely on the prosecutor in such matters under the urban conditions of today, and yet the only check on the prosecutor is the scrutiny of the court. The parole system, administered in a large city in courts so organized, leads inevitably "to parolling in the dark."[4] It is assumed, as was true enough in the old days of small calendars in rural communities, that everyone knows or can know all about the offender. When the administration of justice goes on such an assumption in a city of 800,000 persons, the situation discussed on page 97 of the report on Courts is inevitable.

(2) Bad effects of lack of continuity in administration are equally evident. If some rotation of judges is necessary, there is the more reason why the courts should be so organized that the rotation shall not involve fluctuation in policy, divergence in interpretation of the law on matters where such divergence is easily preventable, fumbling methods while the judge for the time being is acquiring experience of a new class of work, and pressure to put off cases or shift them so as to get them before a judge whose policies or methods are believed or suspected to be favorable to or lenient toward the particular accused or one of his type. Such things not only impair efficiency—they weaken respect for courts and for the law. The judicial council, recommended by Mr. Smith,[5] would go far as a remedy. But the ultimate cure is in unification and thorough organization of the court under responsible administrative leadership.

(3) Organization of courts is defective not only in that there are two courts largely dealing with the same cases where one court could deal with all much better, and because those two courts are made up of coördinate judges, with no responsible directing agency, but even more in that the lines are rigidly laid down by law and do not admit of the judges in the large city doing much to meet the special problems that confront city courts, even if they had encouragement to do so. It has been noted that the mode of choice and tenure of judges are the same for rural and for

---

[1] Report on the Criminal Courts, pp. 71, 72.   [2] *Ibid.*, p. 75.   [3] *Ibid.*, p. 100.
[4] *Ibid.*, p. 98.   [5] *Ibid.*, p. 141.

metropolitan courts, although the environment that makes them work well enough in the one case insures that they will work quite differently in the other case. No less serious is the inability to use the personnel of the court to the best advantage under a system constructed for times when one judge in each local district could dispose of the relatively small calendars. When business increased, more judges were added. But when the number increases to a certain point waste of judicial power comes to be likely, and this waste is a serious thing when business has grown so as to tax the energies of the bench. Moreover, provision of a probation department[1] and of a bureau of information,[2] required by urban though not by rural administration of criminal justice, and many things of the sort, ought to be within the powers of the judges when and where they are needed, and ought not to be determined with reference to the whole State by detailed provisions of general laws, as if the conditions of city and country were invariably the same, or as if things not needed in the latter should, therefore, be denied to the former.

(4) Tendency to perfunctory routine appears no less clearly in a judicial administration than in police and in prosecution, and it is the product of the same general causes. In the Municipal Court the casual routine of preliminary examination and perfunctory practice as to binding over,[3] the perfunctory methods whereby a robber (afterward convicted) is released on bail, while his victim is in jail one hundred and six days to insure his attendance as a witness at the trial,[4] the laxity as to postponements and continuances, with its inevitable results in wearing out prosecuting witnesses and enfeebling the administration of criminal justice,[5] and the perversion of the motion in mitigation of sentences[6] are examples of what must happen in a large city until the courts are unified and given a modern organization, and until responsibility and power are definitely located and are concentrated. Similar phenomena are to be seen on the criminal side of the Court of Common Pleas. Laxity in the "passing" of cases, with resulting enfeebling prosecution,[7] the condition of judicial helplessness in the matter of nolles, although 20 per cent. of felony cases are disposed of by *nolle prosequi*,[8] judicial helplessness in the matter of parole,[9] where responsibility falls down between the court and prosecutor, and the "blanket nolle,"[10] with all its possibilities and opportunities for those who habitually represent accused persons,[11] exist be-

---

[1] Report on the Criminal Courts, pp. 101, 102.   [2] *Ibid.*, p. 103.
[3] Report on Prosecution, p. 32.   [4] Report on the Criminal Courts, p. 86.
[5] *Ibid.*, pp. 54–56.   [6] *Ibid.*, pp. 57, 58.   [7] *Ibid.*, p. 76.
[8] *Ibid.*, p. 94.   [9] *Ibid.*, pp. 97–99.   [10] *Ibid.*, p. 101.   [11] *Ibid.*, pp. 94, 100.

cause the attempt to apply the methods and organization of the middle of the last century, with no continuity in administration, with a rigid organization of coördinated judges and no defined and concentrated responsibility, has of necessity made vital steps in the course of criminal justice a mere ritual under the pressure of a great mass of cases to be disposed of without possibility of personal knowledge of the parties or of the circumstances by court or prosecutor.

(5) Some ill effects of division of power and diffused and ill-defined responsibility have been noted already. But this point calls for special emphasis here, no less than in police administration and prosecution. The Raleigh case[1] is not important because it was a farce. When we have said that, we have said no more than is obvious to everyone. The important thing is to know that no one in particular can be held responsible for its being a farce. Again, the situation disclosed in Table 16 of the report on the Criminal Courts, and discussed on the same page of that report, is not merely serious in itself, but quite as much so because no one in particular is responsible. The wide variation in the policies of coördinate judges, shown on pages 77 to 81, is a serious thing. It is quite as serious that it is no one's business to do away with it. Again, the hopelessly defective system of records in criminal cases in the Municipal Court, disclosed in the report on Prosecution,[2] with its result in the absence of any real check on the activities of hangers-on of the police court, is not merely bad in itself, but even worse in disclosing what may happen in the administration of justice in a large city when it is left to direct itself and no one is responsible for making and keeping it what it should be.

(6) Closely connected with the foregoing point is the want of provision for intelligent study of the judicial system in action and want of any system of judicial statistics. There are admirable models here in the English system of judicial statistics and in the statistics published by the Municipal Court of Chicago. But all improvement in this respect depends ultimately on provision of an executive head, with undivided power and undivided responsibility.

When one considers the matters just discussed in connection with what we have seen of the same sort in police administration and in prosecution, it is easy to see why, without anyone in particular being responsible, and even with conscientious, hard-working men in many of the official positions involved, the system is "worked for weak spots" by those who know how;[3] to see why, without anyone in particular being

---

[1] Report on the Criminal Courts, p. 34.   [2] *Ibid.*, Part II, pp. 36–48.   [3] *Ibid.*, pp. 10–14.

to blame, 23 per cent. only of those who are prosecuted are found or plead guilty;[1] to see why it is that the slacker agencies of justice tend to acquire the business at the expense of the stricter[2]—in short, to see how and why the whole system lends itself to manipulation.[3]

It is not necessary to repeat the recommendations in the report on courts, but four of them call for special consideration.

One immediately practicable improvement is to eliminate unnecessary steps in prosecution. In State cases all the steps in the Municipal Court and the grand jury ought to be dispensed with, reserving the grand jury for those occasional situations where a special inquiry is necessary for some particular reason. The grand jury has been done away with in many jurisdictions, and the matter is no longer one of conjecture or experiment. Only good results have followed from eliminating it as an every-day agency. Moreover, the conditions of large cities make such demands in the way of jury service that if the grand jury is done away with as a regular feature of prosecution, pressure upon the petit jury system is to that extent relieved. A practice which operates successfully in 18 States need not be feared by the most conservative, and relief of prosecution from the burden of two preliminary investigations must strengthen the administration of criminal justice.

Another important measure would be to curtail the use of jurors in civil cases. We ask too much of busy citizens in our large cities when under the conditions of business and of employment today we ask them to serve upon juries and use juries habitually for every sort of legal business. If, as in England, the civil jury was reserved for those cases to which civil juries are best adapted—assault and battery, malicious prosecution, slander and libel, breach of promise, and the like, where a certain moral element comes into play—and commercial causes and causes involving property were habitually tried by the court, it might be possible to secure better juries in criminal cases. The situation disclosed in Chapter XI of the report on the Criminal Courts compels us to reflect whether we really achieve anything by our endeavor to preserve the jury system exactly as it was one hundred years ago, and operate it as an every-day agency of justice in a large city.

The civil jury is enormously expensive. Do we succeed in doing enough by means of this time-consuming and expensive agency to make up for the injury that we do to the effectiveness of the criminal jury, which we must preserve? Sooner or later this question must be answered. If we go on as we have been going, we may succeed only in breaking

---

[1] Report on the Criminal Courts, p. 14.   [2] *Ibid.*, p. 14.   [3] *Ibid.*, p. 16.

down the institution of the jury as anything more than a perfunctory adjunct to judicial justice. Something of the sort has actually happened in the case of the grand jury in more than one community.

Mr. Smith recommends the institution of a "public defender,"[1] and his recommendation deserves careful consideration. For myself, I am skeptical. It seems to me that the public defender is called for chiefly because of bad organization of prosecution, bad conditions in the prosecutors' offices, and a tendency to perfunctory routine there and in the courts. In other words, lack of modern organization in prosecution and in courts calls for a remedy, and, as usual, the remedy is sought in adding another functionary instead of in dealing with the difficulty at its source. Unless prosecution and courts are given an organization suitable to the needs of the large city, I suspect that after the novelty wears off the defender's office will begin to show the same phenomena as those shown by the prosecutor's office throughout the country. If prosecution and courts are properly organized, I suspect that no further official need be provided.

Most of all, however, the bar and the public need to reconsider the whole question of mode of choice and tenure of judges. What an independent bench appointed for life can do for a situation not unlike the one we have been studying in Cleveland is shown strikingly in the recent removal of a district attorney in a district including part of metropolitan Boston. Political considerations that would have been a strong deterrent in the courts of most States did not suggest themselves to anyone, and the court proceeded with a thoroughness and decision in marked contrast to the helplessness and indecision and tendency to evade responsibility which are usually manifest in American State courts when habitual or entrenched abuses are to be dealt with. Only one who has practised under an elective short term judiciary and then seen an appointed judiciary with life tenure in action can appreciate the difference. The advertising judge, the spectacular judge, the judicial "good fellow," the judge who caters to groups and organizations and identifies himself with racial and religious or trade organizations, is simply unknown where the common-law tradition of an independent bench still obtains. Nowhere is such a bench so much needed as in the large city of today. The recommendations on page 48 of the report on the Criminal Courts ought to be pondered carefully by all who seek better things in the administration of criminal justice.

---

[1] Report on the Criminal Courts, pp. 82–84, 140.

CHAPTER IX

THE BAR

THREE checks upon those who take part in the administration of justice are relied upon in our polity to insure that the wide powers which the law confines to judges and prosecutors are properly used. These are: (1) Professional training, traditional modes of thought, and habits of decision with reference to principles on the part of the judge; (2) the scrutiny of all proceedings by the bar; and (3) the records which show fully what has been done, by whom and upon what facts. In the case of the judge, his training in law is relied on to impel him to conform his every action to certain known standards. Professional habit leads him in every case to seek such standards before acting and to refer his action thereto. Again, every decision which he renders is, in the theory of our institutions, subject to criticism by a learned profession, to whose opinion the judge, as a member of the profession, should be keenly sensitive. Moreover, every decision and the case on which it is based are supposed to appear in full in public records. In the case of the prosecutor, our polity relies on the scrutiny of his acts by the judge, on criticism of his conduct of his office by the bar, and on the records of the courts which are supposed to set forth all that is done in the course of prosecution and the case in which and papers upon which it was done. No doubt, as in the case of all officials, public opinion informed by the press is also relied upon. But in the nature of things this check can have only a general operation and may not be relied upon with respect to the details of every-day conduct of the administration of justice. So much that goes on in courts is of necessity technical in character and intelligible in its true setting only to experts that the press and public opinion must be ultimate rather than ordinary agencies for holding the administration of justice to the right course.

It has been seen that in the case of the criminal side of the Municipal Court and the office of the municipal prosecutor the records are such as not only to afford no real check, but actually to cover up the facts and to baffle the investigator. When added to this, instead of scrutiny of what goes on by the entire bar, as in the old-time magistrate's court, where law-

[77]

yers were few, were intimately associated, were primarily engaged in trial work, and all knew what was going on in all the tribunals, a group of professional criminal lawyers practise criminal cases and the bulk of the bar know little more of what goes on in criminal justice than the public at large, it is apparent that the checks upon which the theory of our institutions relies are ineffective and it may not be expected that the system will operate as it should. Relying in theory upon the professional feeling of the bar and the scrutiny of official action and criticism thereof by the bar, which were effective regulating agencies under different conditions, we in fact subject prosecution to the sagacious scrutiny of professional defenders of accused persons, who study the weak points in the system and learn how to take advantage of them. In theory the lawyer is an officer of the court, assisting the criminal court to do justice by seeing that the case of the accused is fully and properly presented. Instead, we are not unlikely to find an astute, experienced player of a politico-procedural game, whereby the course of criminal justice is systematically obstructed or perverted. How the numerous steps in a prosecution—the division of responsibility between two prosecutors, the imperfect records of the Municipal Court, and want of continuity or consistent policy in administration—lend themselves to his activities is shown in the report on the Criminal Courts.[1] The disclosures in the recent case in which a district attorney in metropolitan Boston was removed by the supreme court of Massachusetts showed a similar situation there. No projects for improvement will achieve much unless they take account of the relation of the education, organization, and discipline of the bar to the several difficulties with which criminal justice must contend.

Want of education, want of organization, want of discipline of those who are habitually most active in defending accused persons in our large cities, are conspicuous and significant facts. But they are especially significant when looked at in connection with what we have discovered already with regard to police prosecution and courts. So looked at it becomes evident that the present-day condition of that part of the bar which practices in criminal cases in our large cities is only a phase of a general situation, which has grown up in the transition from a pioneer rural society to an industrial urban society.

For one thing, no intelligent reconstruction of the profession has come with the profound change in environment. Two important steps forward have been taken. Bar associations have been organized and admission to the bar has been committed to the supreme court and conditioned upon an

---

[1] Report on the Criminal Courts, pp. 56, 57.

examination conducted under the auspices of that court, instead of being left to the local courts. Each of these steps has great possibilities and each has already achieved something. But neither has done all that might have been done nor may either, as things are, do all that needs to be done. Except for these two steps—chiefly important in their possibilities—education, organization, and discipline of the bar are the same in the metropolitan and cosmopolitan city of today as in the homogeneous small-town or rural community of the past. For example, in 1860 training by way of apprenticeship in a lawyer's office might well have been an ideal mode of preparation. Daily contact with an upright and experienced lawyer introduced the student to the very spirit of Anglo-American law, and the highest professional conceptions as handed down in the common-law traditions. Today lawyers with whom such daily contact would be profitable are too busy to look at students, and their offices are so crowded with business that no effective study of the old type is possible therein. We have the testimony of a committee of the American Bar Association, headed by Elihu Root, in a report approved by that association at its last meeting, that study in the office of a practising lawyer under the conditions that obtain in our cities today can be no real legal education. Mr. Kales' report on Legal Education in Cleveland shows that in this community certificates of study under a practising attorney are used chiefly in order to enable persons who have prepared in some other way and have not qualified in that way to bring themselves within the purview of the rules. In cities this mode of training has ceased to be more than perfunctory, and permission to qualify in this way is an invitation to evade such standards as there are. Again, organization and discipline in a bar of over 1,400 members are very different things from what they were in a bar of some 60 members. Yet the methods are essentially the same for the heterogeneous membership of 1,400 in the metropolitan city as for the homogeneous bar of 50 or 75 in the large town of the past.

Here, also, the tendency to develop a perfunctory routine is evident, and it has operated to deprive the improved method of admission to the bar of much of its potential efficacy. Thus the general attitude of lawyers in the matter of certificates of study under their direction, their willingness to make such certificates, even where there has been no pretense of actual study in their offices or under their supervision and their disposition to treat such certificates as formalities, are in part a survival of ideas from pioneer times and in part a result of lack of any conscious responsibility for the condition of the profession. Likewise the laxity of bar examiners is attributable to the same causes. Both of these phenomena are of general occurrence throughout the country. When everyone at the local bar knew the candidates and knew in whose offices they had been studying, what their antecedents were and what they had been doing, certificates and examinations might well be thought matters of form and disregarded in the same spirit in which the pioneers discarded the pomp and ceremony of court etiquette and even the more important items of dignity and decorum. Survival of that spirit in the bar of a cosmopolitan city serves to recruit the ranks of the police court lawyers, well known in all our large cities. Lack of interest in professional education on the part of the bar is a serious factor in the ineffectiveness of criminal justice. Where large numbers of persons of foreign birth or foreign ancestry come to the bar—as they should do, for every element in our population should bear its part in the administration of our democratic and legal polity—there is peculiar need that they have the best education which we may afford them. Yet, as a rule, those who most need it have the least. Whereas they need to learn the whole spirit of our institutions, they are likely to get no more than a superficial course in the practical details of what goes on in the courts. The need of such persons for general education, for professional education, and for personal contact for a sufficient period with lawyers who know the traditions and spirit of Anglo-American law and of the legal profession as our legal institutions presuppose it, is peculiarly great. Yet none of these things is possible when a person of foreign birth works eight hours a day for an employer and at the same time attends a night high school and a night law school. If we put the period of employment at eight hours and the period required for high school study and study of law at the minimum of six hours each, it means that, if justice is done to all three, the student is putting in twenty hours of work each day for six days in each week. Under the circumstances which obtain in Cleveland, where the night law schools and the night high schools alternate in instruction, each giving three nights a week, if we put the minimum of time spent in recitation and in study at six hours for each during the three days respectively devoted to high school study and to law study, the result is that the student would devote fourteen hours of each twenty-four for six days of each week to his work. One need not say that this is not and cannot be done. When such things are attempted or pretended, we may not expect that the students will understand a system of law and of legal and political institutions wholly different from that in which they or their parents and associates were brought up. Such students need more contact with lawyers of high ideals than the ordinary student for that same reason. But none is possible in any effective way in a three-year night course of three nights a week when the student is at the same time working all day for an employer and pursuing a high school course on alternate nights. More than 40 students are known to have been preparing for the bar in this way in Cleveland last year.

It is not controversial that the standard of the night law schools in Cleveland is in important respects below the standard of such schools in other cities of the size of Cleveland, and very much below what it ought to be. The night schools in Cleveland require of the student six hundred and forty-eight class-room hours as against one thousand and eighty, the minimum in the day schools. Note what this means in the one matter of criminal law and procedure. One of the Cleveland night schools gives twenty-six class-room hours to this subject; the other gives thirty. On the other hand, not to go outside of Ohio, the three admittedly first-class schools, Cincinnati, Ohio State, and Western Reserve, give to that subject seventy-two, seventy-two, and ninety hours respectively. Yet it is more than likely that the student with one-third of the legal training will be the one who will practise in the criminal courts. With one exception the night schools in Cleveland teach only the subjects required for the bar examination. They have inadequate library facilities and their students have no time to use libraries if such facilities were at hand. But this means that they have no time to read the books that every lawyer ought to read if he is to form an adequate conception of his duties and of the system of administering justice of which he is to be a part. For few have time to read such books after admission. These things are not the fault of those in charge of the night schools. They arise from a practical situation in which standards are governed not by what ought to be required, but by low requirements for admission to the bar, loosely administered, and by competition for students.

It is noteworthy that 85 per cent. of those who apply for examination pass the Ohio bar examination, whereas in New York 42 per cent. pass (on an average for the past ten years) and in Illinois 62 per cent. (on an average for the past nine years). The night schools in New York and in Chicago require more hours of attendance and are in no wise inferior to those in Cleveland. There is no reason to suppose that the difference between Ohio and the States named is due to any cause other than a relatively low standard in the examinations. Some philanthropist might endow a night law school which could then run without regard to competition, and could take for its object to give the best possible legal education for students who must attend at night, rather than merely to prepare for bar examinations. Unless this is done, the only practicable remedy is to raise the standards for admission and thus enable the night schools to exact a reasonable education. Mr. Kales' recommendations as to improved standards for admission are conservative and immediately practicable, and even this minimum ought to result in marked improvement in the quality of those who are admitted to the bar. Special attention should be called to Mr. Kales' recommendation of exercise of visitorial powers by the bar examiners or a committee of lawyers under their direction. If the work of visiting the law schools is done thoroughly and intelligently, the resulting understanding of each other's aims and methods by law schools and bar examiners will produce good results.

Education must be followed by organization and discipline. The subject of organization is complicated by the difference in conditions between city and country, and the notion that one hard and fast scheme must be made to serve both. The possibilities of corporate organization have been shown abundantly in the experience of incorporation of the lower branch of the profession in England. Bar associations may do much. Yet membership in them is voluntary, and the officers and committees of these associations are busy men, whose primary responsibilities are to their clients and who can give but a residue of their energies to professional discipline. What they can do after the event is shown by the vigorous action of the Boston Bar Association in presenting charges against a district attorney and seeking his removal, and in proceeding for disbarment of practitioners in the criminal courts whose activities have become notorious. But there ought to be professional agencies for dealing with such things before they become notorious, and before their notoriety breeds disrespect for law and for the courts. The plan of the American Judicature Society for corporate organization of the bar deserves to be studied and pondered by all lawyers who have the good of the profession and the improvement of the administration of justice at heart.

It is easy to say that the bar has a large responsibility, both to improve itself and to improve the whole administration of criminal justice. When one looks beneath the surface, however, he soon sees that there is no bar to hold responsible in any real sense. There are 1,400 lawyers. But 1,400 lawyers of all sorts, of the most diverse antecedents and the most divergent interests, practising in a city of 800,000 inhabitants drawn from every part of the earth, do not constitute a bar except in name. Nor can those lawyers who, by their standing in the profession are in a position to lead, be held responsible. The legislature has control of standards of education and admission. The courts have control of discipline. In each case, as things are, political considerations and the timidity that goes with short tenure and choice by primary election preclude decisive action and result in occasional spasmodic efforts, with long intervals of apathy. The real responsibility upon the leaders of the profession is one of perceiving the situation, of studying what has been done elsewhere to meet like situations, and of intelligently considering the projects which have been proposed in order to make the bar an organized, self-governing, responsible entity, instead of a mere collective name for 1,400 money-getters, each following his own interests. When it is deemed a sufficient answer to a proposal for incorporation of the bar to say that "lawyers are as honest as other people," the lawyer is inviting the unintelligent and destructive application of the legislative steam roller by the layman, which always comes eventually when he refuses to put his house in order intelligently on his own motion.

CHAPTER X

PENAL TREATMENT AND CORRECTIONAL INSTITUTIONS

MANY aspects of correctional institutions in Cleveland make a bad impression on one who has studied the subject of penal treatment and has formed some scientific conception of what such institutions should be in order to achieve what is demanded of them in the sight of today. But here again one cannot but see that rapid growth and persistence of ideas and methods appropriate to conditions only outgrown yesterday, as it were, are chiefly responsible. As one reads Mr. Lewis' report he soon recognizes certain common points that run through the conduct of all the institutions examined.

(1) There is no proper segregation of the inmates. At the city jail there is no grading or segregation except according to sex, and with respect to whether or not the case of the accused has been disposed of judicially. At the Warrensville workhouse the prisoners are habitually thrown together, more or less indiscriminately. At the county jail prisoners "mingle indiscriminately" during the exercise periods. At the Detention Home there are no adequate means of segregation. In other words, nothing adequate is done in these institutions to prevent them from operating as seminaries or breeding-places of more crime. All this belongs to the old-time town lock-up and old-time county jail, and is a survival from the conditions of the past. As is true in most localities, the city jail shows this most noticeably. The careless and indifferent handling of prisoners in that institution is something with which the student of our penal methods becomes but too familiar. What can happen in such institutions to innocent persons is unhappily illustrated by the two extreme cases in Chapter I of Mr. Lewis' report. It is humiliating to think that such things are far too common in cities of twentieth-century America, and nothing could point more eloquently to the need of responsible and effective administrative supervision and of unified administrative organization, which alone can assure such supervision—a need which is apparent on every hand in the administration of criminal justice in large cities.

(2) Again, records are almost invariably inadequate for the requirements of today. In the city jail the only record is a jailer's docket,

containing the name of the prisoner and the charge. The Warrensville workhouse has no proper records, and reliance is had on memory rather than on records, with unfortunate results for the system of parole. The records of the county jail are inadequate. There are no proper records in the Girls' Home at Warrensville. The same reliance on memory is to be seen in connection with parole, and probation work also is handicapped by crude and unsatisfactory records. Here again we have a survival from the time when no records were needed such as we must have in order to deal effectively with the crowd of delinquents who pass in and out of the correctional institutions of today.

(3) Lack of administrative system is general. It begins at the top, in the failure to develop any machinery to permit the Director of Public Welfare to exercise adequate control over the different divisions which are supposed to be subject to his authority. A mere paper federation of divisions and bureaus with no administrative cohesion and functioning only as an agency of suggestion to the chiefs of divisions and superintendents cannot be expected to accomplish results of moment. Examples of this lack of administrative organization and system in particular institutions are to be seen in the Warrensville workhouse, where each officer is a power unto himself, and in the Girls' Home at Warrensville. They are to be seen especially in the crude and undeveloped system of parole, where the results are serious. Results of lack of organized administrative control and definitely located responsibility may be seen in the absence of any modern system of receiving prisoners and eliminating vermin at the Warrensville workhouse, in the lack of a modern system of identification at that institution, and in the idleness and demoralization there. They are to be seen also in the inadequate training of guards at the county jail and in the lack of suitable employment or directed recreation at the Detention Home. Most of all, and most unfortunate in its consequences, want of organization of administrative agencies is making nugatory and injuring public confidence in the most promising of American discoveries in penal treatment. There has been much just complaint as to parole and probation in Cleveland. But who is to be held responsible for the utterly inadequate staff of parole officers, overwhelmed with work and unable to give proper time to probation? Who are responsible for the utterly inadequate clerical facilities for this work? Instead of dealing with this matter at the root by modern administrative organization, the legislature enacts a statute which is a distinct step backward, with the result that what ought to be done by modern methods by a thoroughly organized and responsibly supervised system of probation, is left to executive clemency, which

ought to be reserved for occasional and exceptional cases. The discussion in Chapter IV of Mr. Lewis' report should be read and pondered. But here, as elsewhere, the pivotal point is thorough organization of the administrative agencies of criminal justice, so that such matters may be studied intelligently before mischief occurs, and someone may be held distinctly responsible if mischief is not prevented.

How completely the administrative and the judicial are interlocked in criminal justice is illustrated in the case of probation. The judges, finding that they cannot rely on the inadequate staff of State parole officers to make the painstaking investigations which the probation system demands, attempt to do the work of individualization themselves. But they have no means of doing it intelligently, and the consequent fluctuation and vacillation in the disposition of cases injure respect for the courts. The courts are forced to attempt work that belongs to a correctional system after the tribunal is through with the accused; but they have more than enough to do in their own province, and the results are necessarily unfortunate. Organization of all the administrative agencies of justice is imperatively required in order to make this essential part of criminal justice function as it should. While this organization of administrative agencies is coming, Mr. Lewis' recommendations will do much to improve correctional measures and to pave the way for better things.

A much brighter picture is presented by the Juvenile Court. Here again the court is handicapped by too small a staff for a tribunal handling over 4,200 cases a year. Here also legacies of the past are to be seen in a tendency to trust too much to memory of details, in inadequate records, in some waste of administrative power, and in some lack of coördination with other agencies. But these are of minor importance. It is evident that the central difficulty is that, because of rapid growth of population and of special conditions making for juvenile delinquency, the volume of work has increased far beyond existing facilities for dealing with it properly. The court itself, with an ampler budget and a larger staff, is equal to making the needed improvements on its own initiative.

CHAPTER XI

THE UTILIZING OF MEDICAL SCIENCE

THERE is much reason for the backwardness of criminal justice in taking advantage of the enormous strides made by medical science in the last generation. Things have moved so rapidly that, even if the courts had not been struggling with a steadily increasing volume of business and the continual need of new adaptations to conditions of transition from a rural to an urban society, it would not have been easy to keep up with the march of knowledge and the rise of new methods in medicine, in psychology, and in psychopathology. But the judicial system has not been so organized as to be able to take advantage of these things in any systematic or effective way in any event. All the phenomena that we have observed in connection with police and prosecution and courts and penal treatment stand out in this connection also.

(1) There has been no intelligent reconstruction of the medical side of criminal justice, but only patching and tinkering and addition of more officials, without giving them organization or responsible supervision or coördinating their activities. Each court and each administrative agency which has seen the need of better expert medical assistance has gone about the matter in its own way to do what it could with the means at hand. Thus all that has been done has been done in an unrelated fashion, with resultant overlapping, with important gaps unattended to, and consequent ineffectiveness. In some part this is due to a survival of the old-time notion of punishing the vicious willed. Practically no use is made of medical, and especially of mental, treatment in dealing with adult offenders, except in the occasional obvious case. The old attitude of faith in the efficacy of strict discipline and rigorous punitive methods makes us slow to realize the need of individualization, the need of intelligent study of the person we are dealing with, in all cases of correctional treatment under the circumstances of today. This has come to be recognized in connection with juvenile courts. But it is needed in all cases in order to make the work of the courts and of administrative officials after conviction intelligent and effective. It cannot be said too emphatically that this is not a matter of sentimentality or of mushy humanitarianism. It is a practical matter of saving the expense in-

volved in bungling efforts to deal with pathological cases by methods devised for the wilful wrongdoer and of insuring effective handling of criminals instead of futile attempts to deal with crime. Experience where courts and psychopathic hospitals have worked together intelligently has demonstrated that an actual saving of expense is possible if such agencies are properly organized in relation to court and the prosecution, are used in the initial stages of a prosecution, and are employed systematically and as a settled policy. Prevention is especially a matter for medical science, and preventive justice is the weakest side of our system. Examination of children before delinquency develops, instead of afterward, intelligent disposition of socially incompetent and delinquent types when they first appear in petty cases in the Municipal Court, before they commit major crimes, and investigation of the mental condition of all those prosecuted in the Court of Common Pleas before indictment, or, at least, before sentence, are things for which adequate provision ought to be made and might be made almost immediately. Nor is addition of an expert here and one there, the setting up of a bureau or laboratory here and another there, the real remedy. Proper utilization of medical science in the administration of criminal justice is a part of the whole problem of organization of courts and organization of the administrative agencies of justice.

(2) Lack of continuity in administration operates also to prevent thoroughgoing employment of the results of modern medical science anywhere in the course of criminal justice. In general, Dr. Adler's study shows that officials to whom these things are committed are ill equipped for constructive work, and the occasional exception makes the rule more marked. Cleveland is fortunate at present in a coroner who is doing well under antiquated conditions, and gives an example of the best that we may expect from conscientious officers under a bad system. But he is elected for a two-year term, and the public cares little about who is chosen or how he conducts his office. A change might occur at any time which would alter the whole character of the office. Moreover, even when administered as well as it can be, and, indeed, better than the people have reason to expect, it falls far short of what ought to be and could be done with a proper administrative organization. Dr. Adler's recommendation that the office of coroner be abolished and an office of medical examiner created, as in New York and in Massachusetts, is justified by the experience of those two States, and should be followed. In a city as large as Cleveland it is unsafe to entrust the work that now devolves upon the coroner in connection with criminal investigation in homicide cases to anyone but a highly trained and exceptionally compe-

tent pathologist and medicolegal expert. In the general run of things no such person will be secured for an elective short-term office, open to anyone who happens to be a physician.

(3) Rigidity of organization is noticeable here as elsewhere. The police, the coroner, the prosecutors, the Probate Court, the Juvenile Court, and the criminal side of the Court of Common Pleas have each their own way of securing and using medical expert assistance.

(4) Also a consequence is seen in a tendency to perfunctory routine. This is illustrated strikingly in the coroner's records. Perfunctory entries taken from the records and set forth in Dr. Adler's report show that the existence of records is wasteful, and, indeed, investigation by the coroner is wasteful if the records are so kept and if the records truly reflect the actual investigations had.

(5) Division of power and authority and consequent diffused, ill-defined responsibility, both for effective work and for utilizing the results of medical science, are in evidence everywhere. The police department has a police surgeon, but his position is inadequately provided for. He has too many men to examine and his equipment is insufficient. The staff of the coroner is appointed by the county commissioners, and their tenure is subject to the pleasure of those officials. The coroner has no power over them. He is responsible to the people at the next election. His assistants are responsible to the county commissioners. It is no wonder that the work of the office, even under a good incumbent, is often perfunctory. Again, a special constable is attached to the coroner's office who has large discretion as to what witnesses to subpoena at an inquest. It appears that selection of witnesses usually depends on his judgment. These are large powers in cases where homicide is suspected, and go with little responsibility. Jurisdiction over lunacy and feeble-mindedness is in the Probate Court, which has no special experts, no equipment for such cases, and is in no position to make any selection of cases or to coördinate its work in such matters in any way with the administration of criminal justice. The defective delinquent may come before the Municipal Court for violation of a city ordinance or before the Court of Common Pleas for a felony, or before the Probate Court to be adjudged a lunatic, and each tribunal will look at his case from its own special angle. This is wasteful as well as ineffective. In the end a system of examination and observation of all cases at the outset would save money as well as insure intelligent handling of the case, as has been demonstrated wherever it has been tried.

(6) Nowhere is the pioneer assumption of versatility so out of place as in the relation of medical science to the administration of criminal

justice. The days have gone by when one physician is like another in such matters. Physicians no longer take all medical knowledge for their province. Only responsible and systematic organization of the administrative agencies of justice, with secure tenure for the expert subordinates, can insure the sort of medical assistance which the administration of justice in criminal cases now calls for at every step. To merely prescribe that this or that independent elective functionary or assistant appointed for a term be a physician assures nothing.

(7) Nowhere, also, is provision for constant intelligent study of the system of criminal justice and the possibilities of making it effective more called for than in the present connection. The importance of prevention of crime, rather than of punitive methods afterward, the whole problem of dealing with criminal behavior at its source, the importance of mental hygiene, the question of mental-health stations for juvenile cases—these things and many others will press for consideration by a responsible administrative head of a properly organized system of criminal justice in the modern city. They will be urged in medical associations and discussed in scientific periodicals. But the discussions will bear no fruit until it becomes someone's business to be vigilant in seeing to it that the best means that are at hand are intelligently sought for and intelligently made use of in the administration of public business, even as in the conduct of private business.

CHAPTER XII

GENERAL CONCLUSIONS

CERTAIN immediate improvements are practicable. The details will be found in the several reports, where they are discussed at length and reasons are given. I shall do no more than sum up what seem to me the salient points.

(1) Mr. Fosdick's recommendations for separation of the police from the department of public safety; for a director of police, a single, civilian, administrative head with undivided authority and responsibility, charged with laying down policies and devising programs of police work and with seeing to it that his policies and programs are carried out by his subordinates; for committing the subject of promotions and discipline to the director of police, making use of the civil service tests as minimum qualification standards; for a board of promotion; for the use of motor equipment in regular patrol work, the establishment of patrol booths, consolidation of police precincts, and reorganization of patrol beats; for giving the director of police power to recruit detectives from outside the police force by original appointments where it seems advisable; for a special service division and for a secretarial division, show the way to put this part of the legal treatment of crime upon a modern and effective basis by means which are no longer experimental, but have proved their efficacy in the experience of other cities.

(2) In the municipal prosecutor's office, provision of a managing clerk, systematic organization of the work and coördination with the other agencies of criminal justice in Cleveland, and, above all, control of the assistants and subordinates, and consequent responsibility for what they do and what they fail to do; in the county prosecutor's office, control of the assistants, firmer and more intelligent organization of the business, systematic modern methods of criminal investigation and preparation of cases, and, above all, continuous and systematic coördination of the work of that office with that of the police, municipal prosecutor, the administrative agencies of the courts and the courts themselves, together with the laying out of policies and organized supervision to see that they are carried out—all these things are immediately feasible improvements which will accomplish much. The further step of turning

over the whole course of a State prosecution from the beginning to the county prosecutor should come next.

(3) In the Municipal Court systematic, intelligent segregation of business upon the trial calendars, orderly handling of the cause list, with an established policy as to transferring cases from one session to another, a proper system of records, better methods with respect to order and decorum, stenographic records of testimony in binding over cases and in misdemeanors in which habitual, professional crime or commercial vice is involved, and better methods in the despatch of trial business, insuring sufficient attention to each case to assure a just and intelligent disposition of it; on the criminal side of the Court of Common Pleas, abolition of terms of court, provision of a permanent executive head to guide the administrative work, give continuity and uniformity to policies, and insure more intelligent and systematic use of the personnel of the court in the disposition of its business and provision of an adequate probation department, with modern facilities—these are measures of immediate improvement which are not in any wise speculative, for which we may vouch experience in other jurisdictions. The next step should be a unified court, to be secured by transferring of criminal business to one court.

(4) In criminal procedure, beginning of prosecutions by summons rather than arrest in case of minor offenses, abolition of the grand jury, simplification of the bail system,[1] regulation, if not abolition, of the "no-papers" practice,—which is not known to common law nor to legislation,—provision for requiring written statement of reasons for "no papers," nolles, and acceptance of pleas of lesser offense, participation of the prosecutor in proceedings in mitigation of sentence, and a clear policy with respect to new trials, are feasible improvements about which, in the light of experience elsewhere, there can be no real controversy.

(5) With respect to the bar, abolition of admission to take bar examinations on certificate of study under a practising attorney, requirement of at least a four-year high school course, to be completed before beginning the study of law, as a necessary preliminary education; requirement of a minimum of class-room hours per week in all law schools, day or night, so as to insure that the time devoted to study in night law schools is at least approximately that required in standard day schools, and visitorial supervision of law schools and of private schools giving preliminary education to law students by the bar examiners or

---

[1] Report on Prosecution, p. 126.

[92]

under their auspices—this is a minimum program, less than that adopted by a six to one vote at the last meeting of the American Bar Association, and one to which the present proprietors of night law schools in Cleveland entirely agree. Ultimately, the bar should urge the standards recommended by the American Bar Association. For the rest, the Bar Association may and should bestir itself to rid the profession of an element active in criminal cases which brings the profession and the law into disrespect. This is a difficult and thankless task, and demands much sacrifice on the part of the busy, high-minded, public-spirited leaders of the bar. But it is the only resource until corporate organization of the profession provides a continuous agency for enforcing discipline and insuring adherence to proper standards, acting on its own motion, and responsible for maintaining the conduct of the profession at a high level.

(6) More adequate facilities should be provided for the juvenile court.

(7) The opportunities of the office of Director of Public Welfare should be emphasized, facilities should be given that officer for rising to those opportunities, and the public should then demand that he do so.

(8) A statute on the lines of the New York Indeterminate Sentence and Parole Law should replace the present statute in Ohio, which is a typical product of hasty legislative striking in the dark at evils that are attracting public notice for the moment.

(9) The office of coroner should be abolished and a medical examiner provided, following experience of the wisdom of this change in New York and Massachusetts.

But these immediate measures of relief will not insure a continuously efficient functioning of criminal justice as something permanent, going on automatically after the excitement of the moment has gone down. Perhaps nothing will do so entirely. So far as these things can be insured, we must look to unification of police administration, with undivided authority and responsibility under a director with permanent tenure, dependent only on results; to unification of the prosecuting agencies, with permanent tenure and undivided authority and responsibility; to unification of the courts and organization of judicial business under a responsible administrative head; to unification and organization of the administrative agencies of criminal justice under a responsible administrative head with secure tenure; to the incorporation of the bar, with provision for responsible disciplinary agencies; to adequate provision for legal education, and, above all, to the taking of the bench out of politics and restoring the common-law independence of the judiciary, preferably by returning to the system of judges appointed for life or good behavior, or, at least, by some of the alternative plans proposed in the report on courts. These things must come slowly. The bar should be thinking of them and studying them, for in the end the convictions of the bar in these matters will be decisive. In the formative period of our institutions faith in the efficacy of intelligent effort enabled Americans to make over the institutions of mediæval England, as they came to us in the Colonial period, into a modern, workable system for pioneer rural communities in a new world and in a wholly changed environment. Relatively, our task today is the easier. Our judicial organization is much better as a foundation on which to build than that which was left to us by the Colonies, or than the eighteenth-century English organization which was the only other model. Our law is better organized, more accessible, and much more complete than that on which Marshall and Kent and Story labored. The bar is better taught and in far better public esteem than it was at the close of the eighteenth century. If American lawyers of today have to face public suspicion, legislative indifference to the demands of legal justice because of the more pressing exigencies of politics, and the constant pressure of the advocates of specious nostrums for the cure of all ills of the body-politic, the lawyers of the end of the eighteenth century and beginning of the nineteenth century had to face these same obstacles, and to face them with much less effective weapons than those available to the lawyer of today. The advantage which they had was a juristic optimism involved in their faith that law was reason, and hence reason law, and their belief that by sheer efforts of reason they could achieve a perfect system. A like faith in the efficacy of effort, and a like 'determination on the part of the present generation of lawyers to devote their energy and ingenuity to making over the institutions of rural America for the predominantly urban America of today, will achieve no less and will make the first half of the twentieth century a classic period in American law no less truly than was the first half of the nineteenth century.

Lightning Source UK Ltd.
Milton Keynes UK
UKHW012246140219
337323UK00011B/724/P